Early Acclaim for *Along*

"More than the mere adventure of two brave men, it is a grand and noble quest for peace, as well as a spiritual voyage that will leave readers emotionally and intellectually replenished...I immensely enjoyed reading this book. His writing combines a marvelous sense of Zen with good humor, and his personal style makes you feel as if you were there taking part in it all."
~ Mayra Calvani, *Midwest Book Review*

"Written from the soul and salted in wisdom, Brandon Wilson's third adventure takes him and his companion along a centuries-old road haunted by the specter of war. Rich with descriptive detail, replete with humor and never lacking in the life-altering experiences of his previous journeys, this is arguably Wilson's most personal, passionate book yet – a resolute plea for compassion in an often intolerant world..."   ~ C.W. Gortner, author of *The Last Queen*

"...A rhapsody on the theme of pilgrimage. May Brandon Wilson's goal of fostering peace along the glory roads of the world inspire a trail of pilgrims to create their own sacred journeys in the interest of world peace."
~ Phil Cousineau, author of *The Art of Pilgrimage* and *The Book of Roads*

"*Along the Templar Trail* writes the message in brilliant, even blazing letters: Peace and shared prosperity are undeniably possible, and they can come in our time for all time. If only a few more ordinary mortals had the will and fortitude of this author, we would live in a very different world..."
~ Joseph W. Bean, book reviewer, *Maui Weekly*

"The vivid prose and passion for adventure make this book an exciting read....Through reading his books you can live vicariously, although I must say I am more inspired than ever to walk each day." (5 stars)
~ *The Rebecca Review*, Amazon Top 10 Reviewer

"A vivid and eye-opening blend of history, adventure, religion, mysticism and modern conflict...We cannot resist being swept along with the fervor of this quest."   ~ Richard Bangs, author of *Richard Bangs' Adventures With Purpose*

"A book destined to inspire others...Readers of Brandon's other books will be snapping this up. Great, touching and hugely interesting."
~ Jessica Roberts, *BookPleasures.com*

"...A journey that sparks the imagination and inevitably inspires the desire to take your own long walk." ~ Dan Austin, author of *The Road Trip Pilgrim's Guide* and director of *True Fans*

Along the

TEMPLAR

TRAIL

Seven Million Steps for Peace

Also by Brandon Wilson:

Books:

Yak Butter Blues: A Tibetan Trek of Faith

Dead Men Don't Leave Tips: Adventures X Africa

Anthology Contributions:

"Life When Hell Freezes Over"
They Lived to Tell the Tale:
True Stories of Adventure from the Legendary Explorers Club
The Lyons Press/The Globe Pequot

"Thoughts from Along Life's Trail:
War and the Environment Within"
Wounds of War: Poets for Peace

Along the

TEMPLAR

TRAIL

Seven Million Steps for Peace

by
Brandon Wilson
award-winning author of
Yak Butter Blues: A Tibetan Trek of Faith

PILGRIM'S TALES

Along the Templar Trail

Copyright © 2008 by Brandon Wilson

PUBLISHED BY PILGRIM'S TALES, INC.

Cover: Nexus Design + Marketing; original cover photo by Émile
All interior drawings/photos by the author, unless otherwise noted.

Pilgrim's Tales books are available from Ingram and Baker & Taylor, or from Gardners and Bertrams in the U.K.

Publisher's Cataloging in Publication Data
Wilson, Brandon.
Along the templar trail: seven million steps for peace / Brandon Wilson
LCCN: 2007930562
ISBN-13: 978-0-9770536-8-1 (perfect paperback)
ISBN-13: 978-0-9770536-9-8 (hardcover)

1. Travel   2. Pilgrims and pilgrimages   3. Templars
4. Adventure and adventurers–United States Biography
5. Europe description and travel   6. Wilson, Brandon–Travel

Printed in the United States of America

Dedication

To all those people
of the world who keep peace in their hearts.
You are not alone.

This story is true.
However, some names have been changed
to protect the innocent.

CONTENTS

ATLANTIC
OCEAN

GERMANY

DIJON
FRANCE

VIEN
AUSTR

PLANNED ROUTE MAP
DIJON, FRANCE
TO JERUSALEM

The Pilgrimage

by Sir Walter Raleigh (1604)

Give me my scallop-shell of quiet,
My staff of faith to walk upon,
My scrip of joy, immortal diet,
My bottle of salvation,
My gown of glory, hope's true gage;
And thus I'll take my pilgrimage.

Blood must be my body's balmer;
No other balm will there be given:
Whilst my soul, like quiet palmer,
Travelleth towards the land of heaven;
Over the silver mountains,
Where spring the nectar fountains;

There will I kiss
The bowl of bliss;
And drink mine everlasting fill
Upon every milken hill.
My soul will be a-dry before;
But, after, it will thirst no more.

CHAPTER ONE

Heeding the Call

"For in their hearts doth Nature stir them so,
Then people long on pilgrimage to go,
And palmers to be seeking foreign strands,
To distant shrines renowned in sundry lands."
~ Chaucer, The Canterbury Tales

The apparition stood by Samir's bedside. In his other life, Samir, a muscular fellow in his forties with short-cropped hair, was a Druze policeman in northern Israel. Active in the international peace movement, he was also a father, husband and an otherwise sensible man not prone to hallucinations. Still, he could hardly ignore the gaunt man with flowing long hair and holes in the palms of his hands who appeared before him crying, "There is a river of blood running through Jerusalem."

Samir tried to move, but was paralyzed. He tried to speak, but was mute.

Meanwhile, the apparition insisted the policeman draw a picture of him. He wasn't an artist, and eventually was able to move his lips enough to mutter the excuse, "I have nothing with which to draw." However, the visitor persevered with his demands. An hour later, when Samir was finally able to stir again, he discovered paper and drawing supplies had mysteriously appeared in his room. So he had no choice, but to follow the stranger's instructions.

The next morning, clearly still distressed, Samir presented a striking portrait he had drawn to the priest at the rectory where he was staying during the peace conference in Norway. Then he guardedly told the Father about the strange specter who had appeared with his warning. Hearing this

1

story, the priest became equally fearful and gave Samir a large cross to wear during his stay, as well as holy vestments.

A few years later when I met him, Samir was still shaken by the events of that day. He struggled to understand the stranger's visit and its meaning. Were his words prophetic? Or simply a reminder of the seriousness of the task at hand?

As the world's "Doomsday Clock" approached two minutes to midnight, the specter's appearance and its implications could no longer be ignored.

Flying at thirty thousand feet, head above the clouds, always had a way of putting life into perspective. Still, it was a helluva notion, even from a heavenly height. It was a new adventure, and as usual I had little idea where the road ahead might lead. Yet sitting on the long, cramped flight to Zurich, I had plenty of time to retrace the steps that had brought me to what some might consider the threshold of madness.

My odyssey into the unknown had its genesis in 1999 when I was a simple, hobbling "pilgrim" or traveler on an inward journey along the Camino de Santiago in Spain. Although I'd rigorously trained in advance of my five hundred-mile pilgrimage walk across Spain, it only took one day on the trail to reduce my well-laid plans—and me—to a stumbling, bumbling, festering mass of blisters. My air-supported shoes had "popped" as I slid down a heap of slag from Roncesvalles to Zubiri, and before long I sported four oozing blisters on each foot.

Oddly enough, the simple act of slowing down forced me to quiet my mind and body, as each step had to be carefully placed, so as not to bruise a blister or cause another one. The Zen-like method of "deliberate walking" also unveiled a beautifully complex and tranquil world with every step.

The sunshine on the surrounding vineyards was radiant. At times, the heady aroma of fresh thyme flooded my senses. I wallowed in nature's abundance. It was a chance to rediscover my place in the natural world. Slowing down also allowed me the luxury of companionship, as I learned that walking a pilgrimage was a journey outside—while traveling within.

Each day, after walking twenty-five to thirty kilometers, I'd arrive at an albergue or hostel where fellow pilgrims or *peregrinos* from around the world spent the night together. We'd suffer through cold showers, aches and blisters, and then savor a bottle of local Rioja wine. As difficult as it was, there were no sweeter times.

We'd all voluntarily left homes, families, jobs and outside life on an incredible journey of simplicity to the supposed burial place of St. James the Apostle. It was a 21st century act reminiscent of days a thousand years earlier. However, we weren't alone. Many faiths had similar traditional journeys to their centers of devotion or sites of miracles throughout the ages, whether it was Muslims traveling on *hajj* to Mecca, the Hindus wandering to Varanasi on the holy Ganges River, the Buddhists crossing the Tibetan plains from Lhasa to Kathmandu, such as my wife Cheryl and I had done with our horse Sadhu in 1992, the Jews on their way to the Western Wall in Jerusalem, or Christians on their journey of penance, faith or in search of miracles to Rome, Lourdes, Jerusalem, or Santiago de Compostela, among others. A pilgrimage was a physical link to the spiritual plane; to one's cultural traditions, to kindred spirits, to God.

As much as it immersed us in culture and cuisine, it also forced us to confront our lives head-on: our hopes, our fears, our relationships, our life's work and choices. It was a month to "unplug" and remove ourselves from the din and distraction of the outside world. For once, there was no noise reverberating in our heads—no music, no commercials, no late-breaking news, and no cell phones or pressing emails. We were alone with our thoughts, a surprisingly rare occurrence these days. How often in our lives do we have the time to slow down and examine our life's path? How often do we have the time to commune with a force greater than ourselves?

Along the way, there was a gentle unraveling of life as we peeled away the onion-like layers of our "walls" and insecurities. We learned to trust our intuition again, to trust others and celebrate the small victories: the simple act of making it another thirty kilometers along the trail, finding water when it was so blistering hot you swore you couldn't walk another step, or having an "angel" on the trail surprise you with a welcome cup of coffee, a "Buen Camino," or "thumbs-up" sign of encouragement. It was those small "miracles" that made us appreciate the larger ones along the path—and in life.

It was along the same trail that I first met Émile, an amiable Frenchman in his sixties. It was early morning atop a rise ringed by a field of herbs. At first, he looked eccentric with his leather cowboy hat and full bushy white beard. We briefly exchanged greetings, him in his gentle, self-effacing tone that instantly transformed my opinion of him from a salty seadog to Père Noël; me in my rusty, Inspector Clouseau-accented high school French. ("Do you 'ave a lissansse pour zis minkee?") Our first meeting was brief. We talked in simple sentences, because his English was even worse than my French. Despite his age, having already walked from his home in Dijon, France, his feet were in far better shape at that moment than mine. He sped ahead and we soon parted ways on that hillside.

It's odd. Life has its own plan that may or may not coincide with our own. That night, I met the French wanderer again at the albergue, along with four others who just happened to be on the same path, at the same time, and at the same pace. We six found our lives thrown together—as well as our future fates. Eventually, after the others left the trail to return to their "normal" lives, Émile and I continued alone. Although communication should have been difficult, our friendship grew because our words were few and spoken more from the heart. Perhaps we were long lost "brothers," if not in a familial way, then one far stronger.

Oftentimes, Émile spoke of walking from his home to Jerusalem with his wife Sophie after she retired. I marveled at the idea and was intrigued by the prospect, but at 2,700 to 3,500 miles (4,000 to 5,000 kilometers) it seemed too formidable. Nevertheless, I'd chased a few outrageous dreams myself and it held great appeal. If we don't have our dreams, what do we have? Besides, if the "mere" five hundred mile Camino de Santiago (or Chemin de St. Jacques, as Émile called it) was so rewarding, just imagine the challenge, adventure and possible enlightenment of walking to Jerusalem? Yet even then, he made it clear it was something he and Sophie would walk together as a couple. So I'd just have to look on in envy.

Our parting that chilly morning in October 1999 was unexpectedly sad, as sharing a month-long pilgrimage forges an unforgettable bond among *peregrinos*. Still, I couldn't shake the feeling that our paths were destined to cross again.

In the ensuing years, I continued following simple pilgrim's paths on a continuing inward journey of "walking meditations." These historical treks became my passion, my reason for living. When I wasn't walking, my mind was on the trail, immersed in introspection. As I trod these paths, mostly alone, they confirmed the simplistic beauty of walking in quiet contemplation, peace, and inner tranquility. Over the following six years, I followed my sweet obsession. Over two autumns, I walked the historic 1,150 mile Via Francigena from Canterbury, England to Rome. Another summer, I trekked the path of Norwegian *pilgrins* from Oslo to Trondheim on St. Olav's Way. Then finally, since I'd regaled Cheryl with my own tales of El

Camino, we walked it together in 2005. Although the trail had changed little, I'd grown and now felt like I was there to lend support to others.

After reaching Finisterre, once the edge of the early European's known world, I returned home to the edge of my Hawaiian volcano expecting to return to an all too normal existence. Life, once again, had other plans. One day, out of the blue, a simple email, a short correspondence from long-lost Émile set my mind reeling.

> "Sophie is unable to make our long-planned walk to
> Jerusalem. Would you be interested in joining me?"

The possibility was both exhilarating and incredible, but what about logistics? Could I simply close-up my quiet upcountry life, cancel engagements and find the gear? Could I afford to go? Could I leave home without feeling like the husband who ducked out for a quart of milk never to return? Then again, was I willing to brave a spiritual marathon across two continents and a distance greater than the width of the continental U.S.?

If our experience in Tibet had taught me one thing, it was that I was the type of person who was unwilling to give up once I focused on a goal—even when saner minds cried "Enough." I could be tenacious, which was both a blessing and a curse. I knew I could handle one month—but seven? Could my body survive what could amount to a 3,500-mile trek at my age?

Then, there was the routing and security. After planning for six years, Émile suggested we follow the Danube Valley through Germany's Black Forest, then to Vienna, Austria and Bratislava, Slovakia to Budapest, Hungary, then south through Serbia, Bulgaria, and across the vast plains of Turkey's Anatolia.

It was a path steeped in history. The route roughly coincided with the one followed by Godfrey de Bouillon, the Lord of Bouillon and Duke of Lower Lorraine, and his forty thousand troops during the First Crusades in 1096, as well as some early pilgrims. After fierce battles, Godfrey and his men reclaimed the Holy City in 1099 and he was named King of Jerusalem. Nine of those knights who served with him became the first Poor Knights of Christ of the Temple of Solomon, or Knights Templar, created in 1118. An order founded on poverty, chastity and obedience, they pledged to protect pilgrims on passage through the Holy Land and to protect Jerusalem from all aggressors. Other sections of our proposed route existed as far back as Roman times when the Danube River marked the northern border of their empire and remote outposts protected its frontier. Beyond there lay "barbarians." Then the route's southern portion, built in the 1st century A.D., was once known as the Roman *Via Militaris* or *Via Diagonalis*, stretching 1,054 kilometers from Belgrade all the way to Constantinople (now called Istanbul).

Assuming we'd make it that far, then came the tricky part. Eventually, the route would lead us through Turkey to Syria into Jordan. Thanks to recent disastrous policies in Iraq and the Middle East, I could imagine our presence would be about as welcome as a pork barbecue at a mosque.

Still, I jumped at the chance. There was no use waiting for all those problems to be fully resolved—or doubts to be set in stone.

It was our destiny and an opportunity that fate had placed on my doorstep, a chance that would never present itself again. Besides, I saw it as more than just a personal pilgrimage in the traditional sense. I viewed my journey as having a greater purpose: a trek for peace, which was especially ironic since our path was to follow a route used over a thousand years for war.

I've always been a firm believer that events in our lives happen for a reason, some inexplicable at first. Each person can effect change by their actions, however small. I had long admired the dedication of an older, simple American woman called Peace Pilgrim, who'd walked across the country with only the clothes on her back for twenty-eight years and over 25,000 miles with a simple message of peace. How many lives had she touched? How many still remembered her message today?

If, to paraphrase Mark Twain, "Everybody talks about peace, but no one does anything about it," possibly now was my chance for action, if only to remind people of our similarities as citizens of this fragile planet and the necessity of considering other paths for resolving our differences. With courage, faith and resolve, maybe we could accomplish something greater than ourselves. How could I not heed the call?

Once I'd committed to the adventure, the nagging details surfaced and were surprisingly quickly resolved. Traveling light was especially important since the distance was so great and the terrain especially challenging in Asia. Luckily, I found sponsors for high-tech marathon shoes to replace my heavier boots, and Nordic walking sticks to decrease the stress on my knees, one of which had undergone arthroscopic surgery to remove cartilage years before.

Then I took care to prepare my family to the idea of my long absence. Although Cheryl wouldn't be able to join us for the entire trip, she looked forward to meeting us in Budapest for ten days on the trail. The rest, well, I'd work out along the way.

After two full days in the air, the seatbelt sign finally illuminated and we prepared to land in Zurich, the polar opposite of my pineapple isle. It was too late for last-minute doubts. Bracing for impact once again with the earth, I prayed that with a pure heart and courage God would provide the rest.

CZECH
REPUBLIC

DEGGENDORF REGENSBURG
BOGEN
MATTING HOFKIRCHEN
VOHBURG WORTH
EN WELTENBURG
WEICHERING
DONAUWORTH PASSAU
JNZBURG LINZ
N
N AUSTRIA

CHAPTER TWO
France/Switzerland

The Agony of De Feet

"It's not the road that wears you out—
it's the grain of sand in your shoe."
~ Old Arabic saying

Weary, carbed-out on bad airline food, and plane grotty, I arrived at my friend Peter's place where we toasted my arrival with Poire Williams, my favorite Swiss pear schnapps, and I caught up on sleep, food and more sleep. Little did Pete realize how much his hospitality meant to me, plus the chance to land in something other than a hotel "sanitized for my protection" was certainly welcome. Then again, it was always refreshing to be back in a well-organized city where the trains actually meet the planes, and where there is an air of contentment and prosperity.

All too soon, it was time to head off to meet my train to Lausanne, which arrived exactly on time. Gotta love those Swiss. Before long, we were speeding through a countryside dotted with tidy villages, rolling emerald hills, and terraced vineyards hugging shimmering Lake Geneva.

Arriving at the station, I had just seven minutes to spare before connecting with the fast TGV train to Dijon, home of famous mustard, memorable wine, and my awaiting friend. Within hours, he was greeting me on the train platform with a warm French embrace. Smiling widely, Émile looked exactly the same as when I'd last seen him. All dressed up and rarin' to go, he sported a jaunty green fedora and khaki shorts exposing lily-white, slightly bowed legs. His familiar traveler's pouch already encircled his neck.

'Glad to see he's ditched the leather cowboy hat,' I chuckled to myself, remembering his caricature-like resemblance to St. James, the patron saint of pilgrims, complete with his huge walking stick.

Rushing out of the train station, we narrowly missed being hit by an oncoming Citroën. Then piling into his late-model Peugeot, we threw caution (and traffic signs) to the wind as we ducked and wove through traffic on Monsieur Toad's Wild Ride. At last, pulling up to chez Émile, his wife Sophie, a petite dove of a woman, welcomed us, cooing an enthusiastic "Bonjour!" from an open window. Before long we were comparing boots, walking sticks, gear and dreams for our long walk ahead.

Émile had decided to wear heavy hiking boots, a type best suited to tough, backcountry hiking, while I chose waterproof, lightweight adventure racers for the first few months. I'd switch to lighter, mesh-top marathon racers for the steamy summer months and the Middle East. My friend would carry a twenty-seven pound backpack, while I'd pared down my gear to fit into one weighing just seventeen pounds filled. If all went according to plan, I'd switch out to an even lighter, smaller backpack once we cleared the snow and rain, and send my heavier clothes home with Cheryl in Budapest.

Although Émile had supplied me with a detailed itinerary in advance, showing each daily "stage" and distance, he'd kept all the actual maps to himself. I'd offered to pick up others, but he assured me it wasn't necessary.

Then with our quick gear review completed, my friend's focus turned to more important matters—like eating. Although I'd once briefly lived on the French Riviera, I'd forgotten how important food was to the French. It was more than mere sustenance. It was a reason, not a means, to exist. With pride, Émile introduced me to a plate of *prosciutto crudo*, a delicious Bourgogne wine and three types of savory cheese. After a bit of sleep, we began gorging again on tomato tarts, quiche, more wine, coffee liquor and schnapps. There was little rest before continuing our movable feast the next morning in Dijon *ville*, then returning to his home where his family had already prepared a huge going-away *fête* with a seafood salad and local wine, sausage, cheeses, olives and pistachios followed by grilled meat, baked eggplant with tomato sauce and apple or cherry tarts. Of course, bitters, whiskey, cassis, wine and more wine accompanied all this.

Throughout it all, there was also a bountiful outpouring of love and support from his wife and two sons, his sisters, an ex-wife and her boyfriend, in-laws and assorted kids. I was a little envious of their unbridled affection. My own departure was certainly understated, with just Cheryl and me hugging a lingering embrace at the airport, as if we'd never see each other again.

Émile's young niece had drawn a clever picture of him walking to Jerusalem, which he emotionally pasted into his journal to carry along on the journey. Meanwhile, another one, twelve-year-old Chloe, asked him one question I'd often asked myself.

"Why are you going on this journey?"

"It is for the four Cs," he explained. "Culture, contemplation…" then his voice trailed off as he struggled to remember the others.

Afterward, all eyes turned to me. Since my feelings seemed too complex to explain in my elementary French, I asked Émile's son, who spoke English, to translate.

"Of course, I agree with my friend," I began, "but it's also about peace. I believe the world is in an ever-more precarious position these days. It's all too easy to declare war and to try to settle our differences from thirty thousand feet. It's time for people to be reminded there are better ways to solve our problems than by killing…before it's too late. Maybe in some small way I can help spread this message to countries that have suffered so much from war for so many centuries."

At first, there was silence around our table, and then warm approval as the translation was completed—and our feasting continued. It was late by the time our party wound down and I was finally able to waddle off to bed.

At best, I grabbed a couple of hours of sugar-plummed sleep before waking like a kid on Christmas morning. The day we'd dreamt about for years had finally arrived and I couldn't wait to get started.

After a soup-bowl sized cup of strong coffee and baguette with cherry preserves, *confiture*, we made our final preparations. Émile loaded his immense backpack, while I made a quick check to make sure I had everything, including extra room for hope. Before we knew it, there was a gentle knock at the kitchen door and we were soon surrounded by most of the family members from the party, along with an assortment of nearly twenty others. The number of people who'd pulled themselves out of bed at that un-godly hour spoke well of my friend. Of course, there was much kissing and hugging all around until we couldn't postpone the inevitable a moment longer.

We formed a curious procession, two *peregrinos* followed by an entourage of well-wishers outfitted in shiny new hiking boots and daypacks, as we wended our way through silent Sunday streets. It only took us forty-five minutes to reach the park where another ten or more friends joined in, and then we continued our impromptu promenade onto the well-groomed path bordering Canal Bourgogne.

It couldn't have been better hiking weather, as sunlight filtered through rows of linden standing like *gendarmes* at attention. Everyone was exceedingly polite, even to the point of not looking aghast at my awkward French. A few even tried their hand at speaking English, which was appreciated, but reassuringly just as bad.

As the day grew warmer, we ran into local families trying their luck at catching dinner in the canals, using awkward-looking fifteen-foot wooden poles to catch foot-long carp or trout; either a case of over-kill—or under-fish. Shortly after noon, Sophie arrived by car with pâté, prosciutto, baguette, cheese, apples and beautiful small tomatoes, and we savored a picnic lunch by the river, before saying a final "*au revoir*" punctuated by tender embraces. Half our group solemnly waved a tearful goodbye until we were finally out of sight.

Almost immediately our pace slowed down. Was it the pâté? Bad goose karma? I could already sense that Émile was struggling with the weight of his pack. Although it seemed far too heavy for his size, age, and especially the distance, Émile had certainly "walked the walk" so he knew what he was doing. It was his burden to bear.

There was nothing like a pilgrimage to persuade you to travel light. In fact, I'd once heard that murderers in early Spain were sometimes sentenced to carry their victims on the Camino for five hundred miles. Now that was a lesson bound to linger a lifetime (and a hard aroma to wash out of your clothes). After my walk to Santiago, I'd considered the pilgrimage trail to be a metaphor for life, so I tried to never carry more on either than I absolutely needed.

It was nearly 5:00 p.m. by the time we reached St. Jean de Losne, and we made a beeline on tender feet to Émile's friend's gracious old manor that'd provide us beds for the night. He'd arranged for a number of his friends to host our short French portion of the journey and in a few capital cities throughout Eastern Europe. I was surprised to learn that his "friends," in actuality, were members of his club. He'd never met most of them before, except by phone. So I was especially appreciative of their hospitality. It was much easier to arrive in a strange city and already have a place to stay.

They—not to mention their cheese—would be missed all too soon once we departed France and were left to our own strange devices.

After wobbling up two sets of creaking wooden stairs to our cozy rooms on the top floor, we wasted no time hopping around in freezing showers, and then joined our hosts, Annie and her husband, fifteen walkers and others in the yard below for more food and conversation, those most cherished of the French arts.

Everyone was politely curious about our journey, as the garden party flowed from one delicious course to the next. I didn't know if it was a side effect of cheese-inebriation, but there was an abundance of kissing all evening. Take thirty people, multiply it by two kisses rotating cheeks, one set for the introduction and another for our departure, and I couldn't remember when I'd had so many kisses all at once in my entire life. In America, it might be a setting for a *"Seniors Gone Wild,"* but in eastern France it was all part of life, the *joie de la vie*.

Between bites, Émile circulated his diary and guests scribbled warm sentiments with thoughtful deliberation. There was such an outpouring of love and interest even for me, as they asked about Hawaii, my work and travels. Until eventually, after several hours, as if on silent cue, people began approaching us with ample hugs, kisses and more than a few wishes of *"Bon courage!"*

At long last, shuffling upstairs to bed, I slid open the window to my third floor room that doubled as an art studio. The cool air refreshed and I snuggled deep beneath a handmade quilt. In the tranquility of a food-induced coma, I gave thanks for my new friends and the opportunity looming ahead.

At sunrise, after the usual *pain, beurre, confiture* and *café du lait* provided by our kind hosts (all guardedly watched by their dog, a hefty Doberman on steroids), we said our *"adieus"* and were out the door by eight o'clock. It was certainly a more relaxed pace than I was used to, but I figured all that would change soon enough.

All morning, we traced the Canal Saone, once part of an elaborate system to barge goods from village to town. It had since become home to pleasure craft and barges converted to houseboats. A lock or *écluse* was planted about every half-mile, so it took a boat forever to go a very short distance. If no other vessel was already in the lock, it might take fifteen minutes to clear it, fill it with water and allow the boat to chug out the other side. Then again, most people who floated along the canal were in no real rush.

Before long, our tiny canal merged with the larger Canal Rhône-Saone and I noticed my friend was breathing heavier than normal and falling behind. That surprised me, especially since I knew he'd been training regularly for months by trekking two forest trails near his home. In fact, he'd named them Little Jerusalem and Big Jerusalem because they extended fifteen and thirty kilometers. So to accommodate him, we often grabbed short breathers throughout the morning, then at noon took another long pâté, bread and cheese break. Afterward, as I looked on in amazement, Émile nonchalantly tugged a full-sized blanket and poncho from his backpack, unrolled them, and stretched out for his afternoon *siesta*. Speechless, I nervously glanced at my watch, as ominous rain clouds rolled in from the west.

'It's not practical to do this every day,' I thought to myself. 'It'll make for very long days and put us into villages too late to find a place to stay.'

Not a moment too soon we began moving again. However, it was two hours before we reached Dole, a thousand year old town perched on the banks of the canal. Émile's friends Jean-Claude and his wife met us, and he, of course, insisted on (what else?) walking us around his village—before our compulsory nightly feast.

In the morning after breakfast, Jean-Claude led us along the canal, passing fields of corn and potatoes, along with the usual barns and bucolic pastures. We hardly encountered another soul. The *écluses* were eerily empty. The rain stayed away and we enjoyed a cool morning walk, interrupted only by more food. Jean-Claude proudly explained the uniqueness of Jura wine and cheese and how that part of the Republic had once been a separate country—and they still relished *la différence*. Already I couldn't remember when I'd eaten so much while hiking. If those banquets continued, it would be the first trek where I actually gained weight—quite the opposite of when I'd lost thirty percent of my body weight in forty days while crossing Tibet. Ah, nothing beat that ol' Himalayan Weight Loss Plan.

By noon, after our first bitter taste of road hiking, we reached another hamlet along the canal. Over the past thousand years, villages along the Templar trail had sprouted into towns, cities and metropolises and we'd be forced to contend with growth, traffic and pollution. Sure, I knew we'd soon link onto bicycle paths following the Danube River from Germany to Budapest, but not much of Eastern Europe or the Middle East would have dedicated bike or walking trails. So, street walking was bound to become a way of life for us.

After saying goodbye to our friend, Émile and I hobbled over to the local truck stop for a *plat du jour*. It could have been any Midwest truck stop, just exchange the *cassoulet* for meatloaf and lima beans. Likewise, the entire restaurant grew silent as soon as we entered, as they weren't used to seeing backpackers. After spotting Émile's scallop shell hanging from a string around his neck, one beefy fellow asked, "You on your way to Santiago?"

It was a sensible question, since the shell was the symbol of the Camino.

"No, Jerusalem," my friend replied with a twinkle in his eye.

Everyone in the room was stunned, and exchanged those facial "shrugs" that only the French have mastered. They can mean, "Imagine that," "Who'd have thought," or perhaps more cynically, "Who are they kidding?" But we assured them it was true, and after a quick meal they made it a point to wish us a hearty "*Bon courage.*"

Back on the canal trail, the sun was high and our progress was only slowed by yet another rest stop for Émile—and more food. I had to chuckle as I remembered my silent promise to Cheryl after our seven month overland safari across Africa with a British company a few years earlier. I vowed back then, after having lived on crust-less cucumber sandwiches and a "proper" cup of tea, to make my next long journey with the French. At least, they knew how to eat well.

'Have to be careful of what I wish for in the future,' I thought to myself.

Surprised to find ourselves already in lower Dampierre, Émile quickly called his friend Denis and we were shuttled off to his cozy home. Along the way, for the first time, Émile introduced me as "My American friend," and I quickly pointed out, "Well, actually I live in Hawaii." Already I'd discovered an ill-disguised European prejudice toward Americans, especially our politicians and foreign policy. Our latest war in Iraq was on everyone's mind and left many scratching their heads. Many wondered, "Why isn't there more protest in your country?" or more emphatically they asked, "How could you elect your president for a second term?"

Personally, I didn't want to spend our entire journey discussing politics, and I preferred that people judge me by my actions instead of by my nationality. So I quietly suggested to Émile that he introduce me as Hawaiian in the future and let me take it from there. Besides, I feared that wearing my flag on my sleeve could have more dire consequences once we reached the Middle East. Three peace workers had recently been kidnapped. The Swede and Canadian were released. The American, a pacifist doing humanitarian work, was murdered.

Still, over dinner that night, Denis, his wife and I quickly found a common ground in our interest in peace. In the process, maybe I'd convinced two Europeans that we weren't all cut from the same right-winged cloth. With only another 728 million to go, much more pâté diplomacy remained to be done.

The next morning, although we left shortly after 8:00 a.m., it turned out to be a very long day. We anticipated walking an easy twenty-five kilometers, but life had other plans. In all our last minute Dijon partying, Émile, who'd organized our journey for the last six years, had left home without our canal maps. Normally, that wouldn't be insurmountable, except for the fact the canal merged with the river and then the signage presented three options. After doing an "eeny-meeny-miney-mo," we hoped for the best. Unfortunately, we chose the wrong "mo". Meanwhile, it started to rain. Then Émile wanted to eat at 10, 12 and 2 o'clock, followed by his *siesta*. As I grew increasingly frustrated by his delays, two sweet grannies from Grandfontaine batted their eyes at us and insisted we follow them home. After plying us with hot coffee and cookies for nearly an hour, they gave us much-needed maps and even walked us a few kilometers back to the path.

Apart from our hosts, they were the first "angels" of our journey, folks who helped us by providing food, water, friendship or maybe even a place to stay without asking—and usually without expecting or accepting compensation. Random acts of kindness sprouted from their hearts, and from my other pilgrimage walks I knew to leave myself open and remain grateful for those magical encounters. We'd often met folks like them while trekking across Tibet: families who gave my wife and me a place to sleep, or shared a roasted yak leg over their family's fire, or sewed a new pillow for our horse's saddle. I'd met others on the Via Francigena and St. Olav's Way. They'd given me fruit, a place to spend the night, or a glass of wine to toast their fallen American comrades from WWII. You can't imagine how reassuring it was to know that they'd continue with us along the lonely trail to Jerusalem.

By the time we finally reached the old walled city of Besançon, my water bottle was empty. My feet felt as though they'd been beaten on the bottoms by ball-peen hammers, and I'd managed to earn my first major blister of the journey. On the plus side, however, another of Émile's friends, Jean-Jacques, royally wined and dined us yet another night.

Before turning in, Émile smugly shared the French canal maps he'd received via email from Sophie. He'd redeemed himself. Still, my huge blister had a longer memory when it came to a mistake that turned a twenty-five kilometer day into forty—far too long for only day four of our journey.

Blustery weather greeted us in the morning. After Jean-Jacques led us to the canal, we set off at a brisk pace with our maps that made finding the right trail so much easier. All was going well, too well, until an hour outside of town Émile discovered he'd left his hearing aid back at the apartment, so he called his friend to ask him to deliver it. Sure, I'd noticed his small earpiece the first day in Dijon but said nothing, as I didn't want to embarrass him. Although it was an addition since our earlier trek together, it was just one of those things about growing older. As long as he wore it, I figured his hearing shouldn't affect the safety of our trek—or so I hoped.

Afterward, we resumed walking amid the chirping of songbirds and wind whistling past our faces, until the barometric pressure dropped and the skies let loose their fury. Figuring it would only be a short cloudburst, we continued along the Doubs River whose pathway was completely washed out at points. Then, just when I began to think it couldn't get any worse—it did. It was a tough trudge all afternoon in the pouring rain, as our itinerary's estimated twenty-five kilometers grew to thirty-four. In the back of my mind, I hoped Émile had estimated the distances better on the rest of our trip—especially when a nine kilometer difference each day over that many months could add another two thousand kilometers to our odyssey—far from a walk in the park.

It was nearly sunset by the time we reached Baume les Dames, and I was unprepared for an unpleasant surprise. The camera I'd kept so carefully sealed in my raincoat was damp. It was just the second time I'd carried a digital camera on a long trek and I should have known better. Usually I brought my steel-bodied Nikon, a reliable workhorse that had been around the world several times. Now, after only a week, my digital was ruined.

After meeting our contact at the local library, we hopped into her car for a quick ride to the home of local artists, Jacques and Ghislaine, our hosts for the evening. Before the appetizers were even finished, of course, our conversation once again turned to American politicians, but I skillfully managed to segue from stinky politics to ripe cheese, as I complimented our hostess on her outrageous handmade *Cancoillotte*, a Jura specialty with the consistency of honey; nirvana when spread on home-baked bread. World affairs could wait until tomorrow.

Early the next day, I was reminded why I enjoyed long-distance trekking so much—the "angels." They always brought out the best in people and restored my faith in humanity. For example, our host took us to the trail-head where we hugged and were on our way. Our path followed the Doubs River through Franche-Comté on an overcast day, close to fifty degrees. Drizzling, it was one of those bone-numbing mornings where all you wanted to do was curl up in front of a raging fire and sip hot soup. Although no one else was on the trail, we quickly lost our steam. By 10:00 a.m., we'd already stopped for what Émile liked to call a "Napoleon" break, because apparently the general gave his men a ten-minute pause every hour while marching. I wasn't so sure it was the wisest thing to do in Russia's (or France's) climate. However, we ducked inside a barn for a few minutes to warm ourselves, then continued following the frigid riverbank. Before long, I spotted a tiny cottage with a barbecue and a picnic table just inside its fence.

"Maybe it's a café and we can duck in for a quick cup of coffee?" I suggested, half kidding.

Émile nodded and we gingerly approached, until a man suddenly popped his head out the front door, asking, "Would you like coffee? Wine?"

Well, we were shocked by his offer, but didn't hesitate to reply, "Wine, please" in unison, as he led us inside his cozy bungalow. After shedding our wet clothes and hanging them onto wooden pegs on the white plaster wall, we huddled around his kitchen table not far from a wood stove radiating welcome warmth. Then, as if it was an everyday occurrence, Yvon, our host, pulled a bottle of rosé from his cupboard and kept our glasses filled for half an hour until we reluctantly rose to head back into the frigid rain.

"You must stay for lunch," he insisted, with a look of disappointment.

As you might imagine, he didn't have to invite us twice. Yvon brought a pot of lentils and sausages from a side room into his kitchen, while his wife Jacqueline herded two adorable and well-behaved children into the room. His son, just nine, was already learning English in school, and his daughter, perhaps five, with tussled blonde hair, stared at the bearded strangers in wide-eyed fascination. Finally, his youngest son, just three with rosy cheeks, joined us, and then proudly presented Mom with a dandelion, as if it were the most precious gift in the world—and I figure it was to her.

The kind family of "angels" shared their hearty stew, as we finished their wine, and then they brought us fruit and more local cheese. Their generosity quickly warmed our spirits, and I assured our host, "The rosé is bound to make sunshine for us. Thank you, Yvon and Jacqueline, for all your kindness. You've made this day very special."

"No" he insisted, shaking our hands, "We thank you for yours."

I was humbled by their kindness. They'd never know how much it warmed us to our cores, but finally satiated, we had to press on. They never asked us for a "*sous*," as Émile might say, and wouldn't accept one. Reluctantly, they helped us on with our backpacks, and handed us another small bag of fruit for our journey. Then leading us outside, they all stood in the icy drizzle and waved goodbye until we were out of sight.

Now, some might say, "How can you accept charity? Aren't you just taking advantage of people?"

No, quite the contrary. I believe it's man's more natural state to be kind and giving. In fact, maybe our own culture had misplaced something very valuable along life's fast track.

The rest of our day was brightened by their bigheartedness. We bathed in the stillness of the dark river. Emerald garbed Mallards dove from shore as we approached. Small villages appeared and just as quickly vanished. There was the perpetual realization that our destination was always straight ahead—usually farther than we preferred. "*Sempre diretto*," ("Always ahead"), one of my favorite sayings, was a phrase Italians used along the Via Francigena when they wanted to say, "It's down the road. Who knows how far?" Only now it was replaced by the French equivalent, "*Tout droit, tout droit.*" Then again, "Only two more kilometers" usually turned into five or more. Did it all really matter when your destination was thousands of kilometers ahead? Not really. With families like Yvon and Jacqueline's, we looked forward to whatever waited around each bend.

Arriving in Isle sur le Doubs, we stayed in another room arranged by a friend of a friend. Although exhausted from walking in foul weather all day, we were invited to a local doctor's house and made the short stagger up the street to the stranger's front door. There, an immaculately dressed, handsome older couple greeted us like long-lost relatives and invited us inside.

Our evening began with lively conversation. I practiced my French and was convinced it was becoming better—until I learned that our host's wife was actually English from Kent. Although my ego was deflated, I was still fully capable of enjoying her Bœuf Bourguignon and roasted potatoes "Just like home" she promised. (I hated to tell her my "Just like home" was fish and rice.) Then we played a unique game with four different bottles of wine. Jean Marc, our host, hid each inside a sock and we had to try to guess their type and vintage before they were ceremoniously unmasked and uncorked.

Lately, Émile had been overly concerned with my pet blister or *"ampoule"* as he called it. For some odd reason, he enjoyed bringing it up in polite dinner conversation each night like an aperitif. True, the day's rain and wet shoes had made it more painful and larger, already covering nearly half the ball of my right foot. Still, I'd come to expect its resurgence on each major trek as a welcome sign that I was truly on the road. Funny, I always got one in exactly the same spot, no matter what preparation I made. I'd changed shoes (light, medium, heavy), tried different types of socks (two pairs and one), bandages and assorted creams. Out of curiosity, I eventually checked with an orthopedist and found that a slight bone deformity caused me to have less support in the center of the ball of my right foot. So, I'd even worn a boot insert with marginal success. Surprisingly, the best solution I'd found was to follow the advice of a wise older Spaniard on the Camino de Santiago. He recommended applying a small amount of petroleum jelly to the bottoms of my feet each morning and night until I built up muscle mass around the center. That always seemed to work, although I had to deal with the initial pain of the first blister—and smelly, well-lubricated socks.

After dessert, the kind doctor took a quick glimpse at my tender foot in his office, and then gave me a tube of medicating cream and an enormous pack of gauze. As a final parting gift, Jean Marc generously gave us a demi-bottle of Jura wine for a picnic the following day. That, his sweet wife explained, was a uniquely French custom. Given the Jura's fine reputation, it was worth carrying the elixir in my pack for just the right moment—though I sensed it wouldn't take long.

In the morning, we began trekking first on a national highway and then onto a GR (*Grande Randonnée*) Trail, a long-distance European footpath that carried us to the *chemin de canal* and through a huge park. By then, Émile and I had found our rhythm and I had to keep reminding myself of the five to seven months we'd be trekking. That made a huge difference from the usual one-month hikes I made every fall. Although excited, I was intimidated by the distance and wary of expending one hundred percent every day when there was so far to walk. To help our morale, we'd planned the journey so we could take a day off every ten days, or whenever we reached a town of some significance. That week, it would come just in time. My feet were swollen from the long, soggy days and my huge exposed blister was on fire. So I hoped it would heal after resting in Hegenheim.

By 3:00 p.m. we reached the village of Exincourt where Émile telephoned his friend Michel, who lived with his family quite some distance out of town, but they were particularly welcoming. Before dinner, he gave me a week's supply of a wound wrap made of foam. The thin first layer covered your blister while the outer thicker layer stuck to your feet like contact paper.

Later, of course, came the traditional wining and dining portion of our day. Three of our hosts' friends joined them, although no one spoke much English. As you might imagine, I found it impossible to follow five people speaking rapid French at the same time, so I was sadly relegated to sitting there like the family dog, smiling and nodding my head, barking, "*Oui, oui*" at all the appropriate times, or so I hoped.

Frost etched a winter's mosaic on the gable windows when I awoke. It was hard to believe tomorrow would mark the start of May. All I could do was wrap my *ampoule* with the new material and hope for the best.

After breakfast, Michel and his wife led us to the trailhead and we set a fast pace beside the canal, soon encountering something I've never seen before. The canal traffic was cleverly designed so the channel actually flowed beneath the river instead of intersecting with it. Shortly after, we began trudging through several inches of water on the *chemin de canal*, until reaching our first *écluse* where our hosts departed and we were on our own again. We followed the tranquility of the passage at a leisurely four kilometers per hour pace, until it officially became the Rhône-Rhine Canal. At that point, we faced about a dozen locks in quick succession as we dropped to the valley below.

"Welcome to Alsace," Émile chirped. In a particularly chipper mood, he bellowed a silly song (a French version of "Ninety-nine bottles of wine on the wall") at the top of his lungs. His voice echoed through the valley below.

That evening, we were left to our own ingenuity, as we had no "friends" in town. But it took us no time to find a *zimmer frei* or available room in a private house, since many had signs in German announcing their availability. I was half-expecting "quaint" after passing several rooms on our way up the creaking stairs. Yet after seeing our disheveled look and muddy shoes, they obviously gave what was best described as "Anne Frank's room" in the attic of the hundred-year-old house. Since it was a Sunday evening and finding a place to eat in any small village in Europe was easier said than done, our innkeeper agreed to guide us to a local restaurant. It was hilarious, with him leading our way on a small Vespa, not wanting to walk the three blocks. We were dogs chasing the hare. He'd speed ahead for a block, wait for us to almost catch up, then zoom off again.

Afterward, hobbling back to our attic "penthouse," to compensate for our evening of overpriced local fare, we were eager to follow the doctor's orders—and crack open his bottle of Jura wine. Sublime.

In the morning, we sensed it was bound to be a long day, as we left the canal, cutting across the countryside. First, we trekked through quaint Alsatian villages past homes with rugged timber and white plaster façades. The people seemed less cordial and more suspicious, as if they'd never seen strangers like us before.

"Must be our hats," I joked. However, Émile's leather cowboy hat and my green felt Austrian Trachten weren't all that unusual.

"No, this is Alsace," my friend whispered ominously. "They *are* different here."

Spotting a man walking his dogs, we asked for directions, hoping to find the remains of the ancient Roman road that once ran all the way to Constantinople and beyond. Well, his instructions sent us into a dense forest where we encountered probably half a dozen unmarked trails. Unfortunately, there was no one to ask except for two pretty girls, who quickly galloped past on their horses, so we were forced to backtrack to the junction.

Eventually, after nine long hours, I stopped to change the dressing on my blistered foot and slip into my sandals, hoping to take some of the pressure off my swollen feet. Just as I plopped down onto a curb, a cheery fellow approached us riding a bicycle and stopped to take our photo. That wasn't odd, as we'd already attracted a lot of attention along the path. However, that fellow turned out to be Luc, Émile's ex-wife's brother. Of course, he offered to give us a ride in his Renault the rest of the way, but we refused and walked another hour or so, as he pushed his bicycle alongside.

Claudette, his charming wife, awaited our arrival and did our laundry while we cleaned up and then relaxed over beers mixed with bitters. Switzerland was virtually just over the hill and Germany was a mere six kilometers away, so our hosts and their meals were an interesting *mélange* of three cultures.

Finally, after more hours of feasting, I was able to retire for the evening and put my feet up. The shin above my blistered foot was nearly the size of my thigh and my blister was so tender I had trouble standing. But I refused to pamper it, figuring a day off my feet would do it a world of good.

Unfortunately, the next day, my "best laid plans" gave in to running around. Since my camera was destroyed, I spent too much time shopping for a replacement. Afterward, we all piled into Luc's car to drive across the border to Schopfheim, Germany, our destination the following day. With a little searching, we eventually found a *gasthaus*, or inn-like guesthouse, made a reservation, and then drove back to his home for more culinary treats. All in all, I was amazed at how much effort it had taken. No, it wasn't a simple matter of calling the tourism office or pulling out a phone book.

Alsace *was* another world.

CHAPTER THREE
Germany

Sun in the Eyes

"The body walks while the mind wanders." ~ Matsuo Basho

O ur day back on the well-marked Weise River trail was glorious. We finally ran into others enjoying the sunshine. Although they initially seemed less outgoing than their French neighbors, it didn't take long before one corpulent fellow asked about our journey. Unfortunately, he only spoke German and mine was limited. Despite the fact Émile had studied German in school for six years, he remembered less than his nearly non-existent English. So, we were reduced to imbecilic nodding and silly smiling.

"I'm a little worried that I can't speak German," Émile confided after he left.

"Haven't you ever traveled here before? We're not far from Dijon."

"Never," he admitted, with a shake of his white head.

"I figured you've traveled all around Europe."

"No. I have been through England, and of course walked across Spain. Then Sophie and I flew to Los Angeles once, but that's the extent of our traveling. I guess I don't get out too much. I am a cee-tee mouse," he added with a shy grin.

I was shocked. I'd assumed my friend was an avid traveler since he lived in the center of Europe. Now I understood why he introduced *me* as the "globe-trotter." If he thought learning German was difficult, Hungary, Serbia and Bulgaria would be like visiting another planet. When we traveled there several months before the Berlin Wall came down, few people spoke

English. I don't remember anyone knowing French, but maybe things had changed with its Westernization.

As the day grew warmer, the Weise River tempted us to stop for a swim, as we passed swans and ducks doing the same. But we were on a "mission," and stopping at midday just made it harder to begin again. However, we did set an easier pace since my blister was no better and ankle on the same foot remained twice its normal size. As near as I could guess, the foam bandage had limited my foot's movement and made me strain it even more. Still, I pushed myself as much as I dared, until a sharp shin pain sent me limping onto a nearby bench. Sympathetically, Émile shared his analgesic cream to relieve my pain long enough for us to reach the Schopfheim *gasthaus* where we'd reserved a room the day before.

Pain aside, it was good to be back in Germany. I was surprised there was no border control, maybe because we entered from a tiny corner of Switzerland near Basel. There wasn't even as much as a *Willkommen* sign to announce we were in Deutschland—let alone a wall. Now, that was civilized.

A legendary German breakfast buffet of meats and cheeses, breads, cereals, fruits, coffee and juice greeted us in the morning. It was consistent with the old European saying, "In the morning eat like a king, at noon like a prince, and at dinner like a pauper." Even Émile was impressed—except he missed his usual basin-sized cup of café au lait.

After our feast, we set a reasonable pace and caught the yellow-diamond-marked trail wending through the Black Forest above the river. Everyone was in a good mood as they jogged or walked their dogs on that sunny day after a long winter and five meters of snow. People passed with a subtle nod of the head or *"Morgen!"* Some looked startled to see us, me in my green Tyrolean mountain hat and Émile in his leather cowboy *chapeau*. With our beards and outfits, we looked like giant garden gnomes. Plus, my friend carried his menacing walking stick or traditional pilgrim's *bourdon*, as he called it, standing seven feet tall and as big around as a baseball bat with a knob on one end and metal tip on the other. Intricately carved, it was decorated with a long winding vine and the symbolic Camino scallop shell. Émile had lovingly crafted it himself before walking the Camino and intended to carry the ten-pound staff all the way to Jerusalem. More power to him.

We followed a long valley along the Weise River from one tiny hamlet to the next, unremarkable except for the peace they radiated. Even at their

limited size, they were well designed with green space and a refreshing lack
of graffiti and billboards. The scenery reminded me of Colorado with its
lush hillsides of conifers and deciduous trees, although I was also surprised
to spot magnolia trees so far north. The slopes, nowhere near as steep as
the Rockies, were draped with a soft velvety curtain that when pulled aside
revealed one bucolic town after another.

That afternoon, rounding one last bend in the forest, we entered Totnau
and headed to the tourist information office where a helpful woman called
several *privat zimmers*, rooms in private houses for us. Unfortunately, either
no one was at home—or they weren't answering their phones. With perseverance, she was finally able to reach Frau Fridl in nearby Brandenburg,
who didn't hesitate to cart us back to her place up the valley. After washing
some clothes, I hung them on her balcony and then relaxed on the terrace.
As the hills lowered their smoky veil, I stretched out, calmed by the river
drifting below.

One dependable tenet of long-distance walking was that you could only
depend on the unpredictable. Our next day began with a strenuous climb
beside the highway from Brandenburg toward The Feldberg, Europe's
highest point in the Black Forest at 1,493 meters. We set a quick and determined pace as we strained four kilometers up the mountainside from our
pensionen. The trail must have continued off to the side of the road, since
we soon lost sight of any markings. After an hour's climb, we looked forward to nursing a hot bowl of soup upon reaching the top—yet everything
was closed. Soup was "out of season," I guess.

Since we'd been forced to keep an eye out for cars careening down the
mountainside toward us over the past hour, I suggested, "Let's catch the
actual trail at the first chance we get." It wasn't long before we veered off to
our right and promptly ran into a little leftover snow.

'After all, it's May,' I thought. 'There can't be much. These must be the
last dregs of winter.'

How could I have been so wrong? At first, the surface was perfect, hard
on top and it crunched with each step, so we continued. Yet sooner than
expected, it turned into deep powder under the trees and at one point I
sank into a snow bank up to my knee. My Nordic poles shone under those
conditions, but my lightweight shoes were never designed for snow
hiking—not to mention my shorts. It made for slow going, since neither of
us wanted to risk breaking a limb, and it was anyone's guess just how far it
was to the next village. Still, we'd already gone too far to consider turning

around, so we proceeded through the pristine forest hoping each bend would bring an end to the snow. Eventually, we reached a clearing and quickly descended on a steep dirt path into Titisee–Neustadt, a health resort.

That explained the throngs of visitors. Once again, we had no trouble finding a room in a private house, and then wasted no time in heading next door to the lakeside *biergarten* for a bite to eat. Sitting under an umbrella, we watched as pregnant black clouds rolled across the lake, until we were suddenly jarred out of our seats by a crack of thunder.

"I hope it gets this out of its system tonight," I said, as we exchanged worried glances. "Tomorrow, we have a difficult climb of thirty-five or forty kilometers to Donaueschingen and the source of the Danube."

To save us one more worry, I decided to phone ahead and reserve a room at the *Naturfreundhaus*. I'd stayed at a few of those hostels before and they were generally well kept. A good value, they were frequently in the midst of "naychaw," as my Brooklyn friends might say.

As the rains let loose their torrent, Émile scoured the gewgaw shops for a small German flag. He planned on buying one in each country we traversed, tying them onto his baton along with his French pendant. Personally, I preferred to travel without a flag. After all, why give someone you don't know the opportunity to automatically place you in a box? I'd seen it happen all too often on the road. "Oh, they're so French. Or, you're Ameri-can!" someone would moan with a sneer. Sure, I might fly a pilgrim flag if one was available. Otherwise, why feed the flames of nationalism when tensions were already so high throughout the world?

Then again, there was always the chance his flags would bring us some positive attention—so we could talk to more folks about peace. After all, it *was* a little subtler than wearing a sandwich board.

Our morning began with a strenuous climb on a national autoroute, taking us hours to reach Neustadt, just the next village where the snow had recently melted. Cold and hungry as always, we were relieved to drop into a bakery for warm croissants and espressos, and even more so to discover a coffee barista who spoke English. After hearing the purpose for our trek, the young girl with a gentle smile went out of her way to direct us to the nearby mountain trail.

The peaceful Kirsch Way was Ronald Reagan-straight and we followed it until we reached Lager Allee. Conifers lined both sides of the dirt trail and only two cyclists passed in as many hours. Isolated, I wore the solitude like a comfortable cloak. It was a primeval sanctuary, the most holy of cathedrals. I embraced its cool darkness and wrapped its filtered light around me like a shroud. It was perfection. Allowing introspection and quiet contemplation, it reminded me of an omnipresent magic in the world, a force of never-ending birth and death, creation and destruction.

All too soon, we left the forest refuge and were relegated to road walking again into Donaueschingen. The home to the source of the famous Danube River was spread-out. By that time of day, sightseeing was the last thing on our minds.

'Just where is the *Naturfreundhaus?*' I wondered.

Fortunately our "angels" were already watching over us. The first fellow we asked for directions insisted on taking us right to its front door, and then stayed long enough to make sure we had no problem in communicating with the lady who ran the cozy forest inn. Although our room was smaller than usual, the restaurant's *dunkel hefeweizens* (dark wheat beers) were cold, the *gemütlichkeit* (Bavarian for a comfortable feeling) was warm, and its steaming *schnitzels* were colossal.

"What's a *schnitzel?*" Émile asked.

"You've never had one? They're de-boned pork or veal cutlets, pounded thin, breaded and then deep-fried. They're the national dish here and in Austria and Hungary. We'll be living on them for the next few months. In Vienna, I once ate one the size of your head. Like this!"

His eyes lit up in wonder.

'He is an innocent,' I thought. 'Hard to believe we're only 450 kilometers from Dijon.'

When our waitress appeared, Émile didn't say a word. He simply waited for me to order—then held up two fingers with a grin. Secretly, I winced at his reluctance to even try to say "*Schnitzel.*" It was going to be a difficult journey if he expected me to do all the talking. Although surprised, I began to assume that *everything* was new to my old friend. I was dismayed by how little he'd planned for such an odyssey; the fact he'd brought no walking maps for the nearly 1,400 kilometers to Budapest, even though I'd asked him well in advance. What was he thinking? Sure, we hadn't trekked too far off course—so far. But I couldn't help but remember that famous American frontiersman Daniel Boone who once replied to someone who asked if he was ever lost, "I have never been lost, but I will admit to being confused for several weeks."

Fortunately, I'd brought a bicyclists' guidebook to the Danube Way bike path or Donau Radweg from home. We'd meet it following day. Well marked, it would lead us past mountains of *schnitzel* all the way to Budapest. After that, we were on our own.

We left at sunrise and headed down the hill to the town center, still asleep on Sunday. Following the cool Brigach River, we soon passed the Grecian-looking Temple of Donau, the spot where the Breg River joined the Brigach to become the Donau or Danube. Before long, our quiet river path diverted into the flat countryside, and then morphed into an asphalt bicycle path. It was ideal for cyclists, but hardly my choice as a walker who had to pound it for eight to ten hours every day with a backpack. However, I remained impressed with the simple beauty of the countryside and community planning. Although major highways ran nearby to Baden and the Black Forest, they were hidden from the serene pastures below, all without the use of those ugly concrete freeway barriers that had become the scourge of suburban America.

Although we were alone at first, the valley soon swarmed with cyclists, inline skaters and joggers out in the long-awaited sunshine. Each offered a Bavarian *"Grus Gott"* as they zoomed past. Many looked surprised to find wayward backpackers on their trail. A few tittered and others outright laughed, but most were respectful of the extra effort it took to trek at our slower, more deliberate pace.

Frankly, I found myself questioning our decision to walk the *radweg* and spent all afternoon lost in thought—and doubt. The trail was hardly contemplative at that point with nearly a hundred bikes whooshing past all day. Still, part of my rationale in following that particular path was the possibility that others might one day follow in our footsteps. The trail could become another Camino de Santiago where people from around the world could walk all or a part of it in peace and fellowship. Just as importantly, it had to be a route that others could trek in safety with food and accommodations along the way, rather than a "life on the edge" path strictly for my own adventure—seeing how many months I could tough it out with the worst possible food, weather and sleeping conditions. Been there, done that.

Still, the duration of our journey would provide the ultimate test. Whether it took five months or eight, we faced mental and physical challenges. How long would our attitudes sustain us to get up early each morning for months on end to walk another thirty or forty kilometers in all kinds of weather? Blisters aside, so much could go wrong at any age. Could we sustain our caloric intake to keep up our energy? Or find enough water across the deserts of the Middle East? Could we stay healthy enough to fend off illnesses?

Then, there were the political unknowns. Would we be allowed to cross Syria? I'd been unable to get a visa from their embassy before I left, as they were only valid for six months and we'd enter after that. Nowadays, there was nowhere to pick one up along the way. At best, I might cross their border with a tour, then disappear and continue on my own. Émile might not have that problem, as the requirements were different for the French. Then again, would conditions in Iraq worsen and its civil war spread to neighboring countries? Would the US attack Iran in a preemptive strike, since they were allegedly producing nuclear weapons? And Israel was always the wild card. As former Israeli Prime Minister Eshkol once said: "When America sneezes, Israel catches cold."

All that traipsed through my mind as I ambled through the valley. No one knew the answers. There was little I could do except have faith that we were meant to be there. Perhaps, it was simply as Émile would say in the only Arabic phrase he'd mastered. "*Inshallah*"—if God wished it.

Arriving in Möhringen, we easily found the village hotel where they wanted sixty euros for a room. By many travelers' standards that wasn't excessive, but it was far outside the budget of two *peregrinos* traveling for months. In fact, we'd each agreed to spend just thirty-three dollars per day for everything, since we were on the same pilgrimage, staying and eating in the same places. Sure, it would have been easier to have deeper pockets, but our finances were more in line with what pilgrims typically spend on the Camino de Santiago and affordability was key.

Eventually, we enlisted the aid of a friendly bartender who made a call to the *Naturfreundhaus*. It was set on a picturesque hillside overlooking the valley, and for just fifteen euros it offered a large room with private bath. As I arranged all the details in my shattered German, and then translated it all back into French, Émile remained detached, relaxing over a cold lager. Afterward, I made it a point to explain the process to him with the hope he'd catch on and soon start pitching in. After all, any successful expedition was always a joint effort.

The next morning was calamitous from the start. After leaving the hostel, we headed across town and attempted to find the trailhead. Following close behind, Émile sprained his leg as he climbed a steep embankment and doubled over in severe pain. However, once his legs warmed up, he was able to limp into Tuttlingen six kilometers away. I ducked into a phar-

macy for muscle relaxant that seemed to do the trick, and then we traced
the trail a few more hours, until we made a straight descent through dense
forest to the Benedictine Monastery at Beuron.

Now, as a veteran of the Via Francigena, I knew a thing or two about
asking for a place to stay in an abbey or convent, having been through the
routine more than a dozen times throughout France and Italy. Plus, traveling with Buddhist monks in Tibet had taught me the nuances of begging
for a room. But this time was different. An ancient monk, stooped with a
cane and hearing aid, met us in the foyer. He only spoke German. I presented our official looking letter of introduction (complete with impressive
looking stamp) that I'd obtained from a Monsignor at the Vatican. He studied it with a confused look. We got the same reaction when I offered a
second letter of introduction from the *Priore* of St. Trinità Monastery in
northern Italy. It was going to be harder than I thought. Eventually, the
monk pulled his own monastery stamp out of its drawer and reached over
to stamp our letters.

"No, no, that's all right," I assured him, since he'd completely misunderstood. I pantomimed that maybe he should call a monk who spoke
English or French.

Eventually, Brother Thomas, a gaunt, robed Benedictine brother
appeared. Quickly assuring us, "Of course, it is possible to stay," he shep-
herded us to tidy, private rooms overlooking a central courtyard.

After cleaning up, we attended vespers in their lavish Baroque chapel
and marveled as the monks and a few locals sang the thirty-minute service
in Gregorian chant, a song transporting us through the ages to far simpler
times.

Afterward, we retired down silent hallways to the cloisters for a dinner
shared with lay people visiting for a few days or a week. It wasn't unusual
for lone professionals or groups of weary friends to spend their holiday in
reflection at German or Austrian monasteries, removed from the demands
of the outside world. What a sane alternative it was to a hectic week spent
at a luxury resort with wall-to-wall activities, umbrella drinks, and surly
staff—surrounded by all those characters that make your life more stress-
ful at home.

Still, tranquility is fleeting. With the windows wide open, I woke nearly
every hour to the tolling of church bells. Then, at 4:30 a.m., they clanged for
five minutes straight, loud enough to wake even the drowsiest monks for 5:00
a.m. services.

It was nearly eight o'clock when we finally set off at a fast pace, partly because of our renewed resolve and partly to keep warm in the rainy forty-degree weather. The trail was as well marked as always, but meandering turns nearly had us going in circles. Growing weary of the path looping back and forth, I finally suggested we take to the road for a while. Sure, it was a little dicier with all the rain and passing trucks, but I was convinced it would save us hours.

All the same, it was late afternoon by the time we arrived in Sigmaringen and located the tourist information office (via the big "I" sign) near the main church in the *zentrum*. The *ratskeller* or town hall was almost always in the center square. It became a silly game as we stood dripping at the counter while an earnest twenty-something phoned several *privat zimmers*, but no one answered. To her credit though, she persevered and eventually found us a private room on the outskirts of town. The only downside was that it was another forty-minute slog, but we couldn't get much wetter.

Once we settled into our room, Émile comically suited up like Jacques Cousteau to prepare for his nightly quest to find sparkling mineral water, or *agua con gaz*, as he called it on the Camino. My friend was so convinced the carbonated version had added medicinal benefits, he'd spend added time and effort to find his magical elixir—even if it meant trudging back out into the deluge.

As for me, I was more concerned about the *agua* falling in buckets from the sky. I still had a hard time wrapping my mind around the seven-month duration of our pilgrimage. For a while, I said to myself each morning, 'Well, we've walked one percent, two percent, or three percent of the way to Jerusalem. Only ninety-nine, ninety-eight, ninety-seven percent to go.' But that just became too depressing. Finally, I convinced myself I couldn't look at the journey in one exhausting half-year chunk. I'd just have to face the challenges one step, one day at a time. Let the *agua* fall where it may.

It was cool and misty when we awoke, but it had finally stopped raining. It was an easy backtrack onto the Donau Radweg headed east. We made good time as we crossed valley floors and forests, through deserted villages, and across vast fields of sunflowers or *tournesol* used for cooking oil. While we walked, I noticed a wistful glance from the utility workers when we passed, much like an indoor dog enviously watching another running outdoors. Then, a few elderly faces lit up when they spotted us through discerning eyes. Each real mutt we passed, from the smallest dachshund to Alsatian, sensed adventure. We passed pastures of curious horses that approached, poking their heads over the fence to allow us to scratch soft, fuzzy noses. They'd trot right up to the edge of their pastures, as if to say, "Take me with you."

"You really want to walk all the way to Jerusalem?"

In a melancholy way, they reminded me of Sadhu, our stout Tibetan horse, our ol' wander-buddy, that'd walked with us across the wild Himalayan plains.

I suspected there was a special place in the German heart for wanderers. In their language, "wander" originally meant, "to experience." Maybe it was part of their national character, a call to earlier times. Or better still, it was part of all of us deep down—a call of the open road and wild, unfamiliar places. Each time, their reactions made me smile in gratitude, knowing we were able and lucky enough to realize our innate desire to live life fully, to look forward to each day and discover what waited around life's next bend. And not to become, as Henry David Thoreau once called them, "men who live lives of quiet desperation." If only everyone was so fortunate.

For lunch, we discovered a *gasthaus brauerei* or brewery, the local hangout. At first, we felt a little "shock and awe" when we entered. There was a drop-dead silence. Apparently, they seldom saw grotty hikers. On the other hand, once they heard about our journey, the waitress, owner and customers grew helpful. Someone even fetched a map to show us a more direct route to Riedlingen, far better than our asphalt-covered roundabout. We enjoyed their warm attention if only for an hour, and then were eager to resume our solitary trek.

In many ways, as I explained to his family before we left, Émile and I were, "*Ensemble, mais seul.* Together, yet alone." If I carried a flag, that's what I'd inscribe on it, a simple pilgrim's motto. For each of us, it was a personal quest faced alone each day. No matter how much we supported each other on the trail, it was up to us individually to confront our own insecurities, pain, limitations and fears. In that sense, the trail once again was a metaphor for life.

Still, along the path each day, it amazed me that everyone, young, old, sophisticated or down-to-earth greeted us without reserve; from the little girl riding her shiny new bike in the village to the simple workmen digging ditches; from the pretty teenaged girls with flushed cherry cheeks whizzing by on their way to school to the elderly hanging clothes on a line. Many offered greetings, while a few commented on Émile's baton or scallop shell, thinking we were returning from *Jakobsweg*, their name for the Camino. A few even shouted, "*Hola!*" in true Spanish *peregrino* spirit.

Would we be so welcoming to a couple of bizarre looking characters like us back home? With our post 9/11 fears and paranoia after New York's World Trade Center was tragically destroyed, I doubted it.

Another lasting impression was the look of prosperity in the country-side. The houses were large by our standards and meticulously kept and painted. Barns were equally well-tended and appeared modern and water-proof. Lawns were small, but planted with a mosaic of brilliant flowers and flowering apple and cherry trees. Of course, none was complete without an abundant sprinkling of garden gnomes and lawn ornaments. Even the smallest villages boasted well-maintained parks and green spaces, walking malls for shoppers, and public meeting areas that would be the envy of many a small town U.S.A.

I spotted a huge number of Mercedes, Audis and BMWs that seemed unusual for the rural setting. The stereotypical rusting pick-ups, trailers, rundown farms or shanties covering some of our own farmland were absent, nor did I see much trash along the highways. That's not to say it didn't exist, just I didn't see much with my own eyes those weeks roaming the countryside. Ironically, whatever I did see came from one source—the local American fast-food chain. However, I did see a fellow out in a small truck along the trail that stopped to pick up each little scrap of litter, and then drove his truck until spotting another.

Finally, there was the vast trail itself, stretching across three countries. It was well kept, paved or graveled and marked every couple of kilometers. I'm sure the path was a great boon to eco-tourism, as well as promoting local healthy lifestyles. Was it so incomprehensible for us to create the same?

Arriving in Riedlingen ahead of schedule, we proudly wandered its cozy streets trimmed by half-timber fronted houses. I felt like we'd turned a corner. We could walk without a limp after thirty-five kilometers, still had an appetite—along with the energy and willpower to do it all again the next day.

However, people are strange and there's nothing like a long trek to bring out folk's eccentricities. The next morning while walking a "road less taken," Émile inexplicably began waving like some visiting French monarch at each passing truck, as they blew their horns or waved in response. I was close to tears in laughter.

We eventually reconnected with the Donau Radweg; a first-class route for bicycles, but hard on the feet and never the shortest path from Point A to B. Invariably we'd walk fifty percent more than necessary. Given the choice, we soon opted to head back onto the road. It would save us an entire day that we might need later, and it sounded like a fair trade-off. Unfortunately, it also meant we were back on the national highway. It was horrible. There was no room to walk on the shoulder and traffic was heavier than ever. Finally, out of concern for our lives, I suggested catching the nearest country path headed in the right direction. Although some purists might disagree, if I saw a better route, I never hesitated to risk "coloring outside the lines," since many times they paid off in time and energy.

Émile looked a little dubious at my decision, as if it was outside his narrow comfort zone, but nevertheless tagged along as we wended our way down tractor tracks through fields of maize until Ehingen sprawled before us on the horizon like the Emerald City of Oz.

The following morning, after yesterday's cross-country foray, Émile insisted on sticking to the trail. In contrast, it was dependable and predictable—perhaps too predictable. Following the Donau Radweg, we sluggishly wound round and round the city of Ülm like a pinball moving in slow motion until we finally caught a riverside trail. Just offshore, muscular blonde fräuleins effortlessly sculled sleek boats down the Danube. However, for us, it took an hour to reach Neu-Ülm, climb the old city walls, hike down the other side, cross the river beside the "Crocked" House and search for the *rathaus*. Not surprisingly, it sat across from the Cathedral Ülminster, featuring the world's highest spire. Its construction began in 1377 and wasn't completed until 1890. Talk about cost overruns.

For a city of 165,000, I was quickly impressed by how livable Ülm appeared. The birthplace of famed physicist Albert Einstein boasted an eclectic collection of inner city architecture from timber framed plaster houses to the fascinating chrome and glass pyramidal library. It was refreshing to visit beautifully kept city parks with inspiring public art and culture. They didn't insist on starving public arts, or removing art programs from schools in the interest of cost cutting.

Their *rathaus* directed us to the nearby hotel where we rented huge rooms under the eaves for two nights, since we'd take our first well-deserved day off since beginning. We could shed sweaty clothes and hot shoes, plus allow our breathing and heartbeats to return to normal. Finally, it was a chance to do laundry, sightsee and catch up on correspondence.

Unlike Émile, who chatted with Sophie twice a day on his cell phone, I walked without mine since it operated on a different system than Europe's.

It had been too long since I'd had contact with the outside world, so I was relieved to find an Internet café.

After dinner, on our way back to our rooms, we were wrapped in a relaxing calm. In the heart of the city at 9:00 p.m., there was no traffic or loud music to bombard our senses—only birds singing sweetly and the occasional church bells' chime. Padding down silent cobblestone streets, I paid particular attention to my friend. I'd become a little worried about his health. By late afternoon each day, Émile grew flushed, breathed heavily, stumbled and acted erratically, like walking into traffic without looking. I tried to keep a closer eye on him without being too obvious or obnoxious. Although I wanted him to succeed in reaching Jerusalem—I also wanted him to live to tell the tale.

By morning it was raining again. We slogged across the busy market square already awash with food booths and busy shoppers to the pyramidal library to hunt for Hungarian trail maps. Unfortunately, we didn't have any luck. Although Émile remained stoic about our lack of information, I grew more concerned that bicycle or hiking trails even existed past Budapest where the Donau Radweg ended. I'd even written to Cheryl asking her to scour the Internet, hoping if all else failed we could find a national hiking or biking association once we reached Budapest. As it was, our itinerary and the distance covered each day were far from cast in stone, varying with the weather, our health, opportunities and commitments along the way. We'd already re-arranged our stops for the following ten days to synchronize our rendezvous in Regensburg with Sophie and their friends Henri and his wife Lydie, who planned on walking with us for a few days. Personally, I looked forward to having fresh company, especially since Henri spoke English.

More importantly, Émile assured me he'd bring maps for Hungary, Serbia and Bulgaria. I trusted that they were better than his useless auto maps. If only I'd known, I would've carried real hiking or topo charts. But that possibility fell into the category of "woulda-coulda-shoulda." At least, we had the *Cicerone Danube Cycleway Guide*. It would have to do—until something better came along.

All night, lightning etched crooked scars across the skylight of my room. The rain subsided a little by sunrise, but still fell lightly on my windowpane. After breakfast, we set off through a still sleeping town on a snoozing Sunday morning. After making our way through old city walls, we turned back onto the path tracing the Danube. Rested, we set a faster pace down deserted trails and I relished the cool mist against my cheeks as we passed a circus encampment and locals walking their dogs. Otherwise, in welcome contrast to last weekend's parade, we were alone. The "fair-weather" cyclists and roller-bladers had slept in.

We made good time and reached Leipheim by noon. Not wanting to needlessly wander into the maze of the town, and remembering the difficulty of finding an open restaurant on Sundays, I spotted a sports center just off our trail. Figuring "where there's soccer there must be food," we followed the aroma of grilled *wurst* over to their restaurant and were soon greeted by a bemused group of locals. Roland, a roly-poly fellow, could speak a little English and he motioned for us to join him and his friends around their table. He had vacationed in the States and was eager to tell us about his time there and how everyone was so friendly. Then he apologized for his countrymen who were standoffish, like the ones who'd left his table the instant we sat down.

Between his broken English and my sauerkraut-chopped Deutsch, we managed to communicate pretty well over the *hefeweizens* or wheat beers he ordered.

"I've come to believe that people are the same everywhere," I explained in simple words that he might understand. "That's one reason we're walking. For me, this is a trek for peace. If our governments can just get out of the way, I think people can learn to get along with each other."

He smiled and nodded in agreement as our massive plates of *schnitzel* arrived. Our generous friend attempted to pay for those as well, but we wouldn't hear of it.

"I know you are good people, I can see that in your eyes—I'm a good person, too," Roland said. "I will be sitting in this same spot when you return to Leipheim. It is my town. I only ask," he added, with a quiver to his voice, "that you send me a postcard from Jerusalem. I will treasure it."

"We promise," I assured him, while Émile solemnly nodded.

When we eventually turned to leave, he again refused payment for the food and drinks, gently patting his chest, as if to say, "This is a small gift from the heart."

"We will remember you and your kindness," I pledged. "Keep peace in your head and heart. One world. *Eine Welt.*"

"*Ja. Eine Welt,*" he said forming a small, round globe with his hands and then cradling it in his palm.

It was a short trek to Günzburg. Still, it took us another hour before we could begin our search for the elusive *Naturfreundhaus* outside (always outside) of town. By then, thunderclouds blanketed the sky and we saw the first bolt of lightning. No one we asked seemed to know exactly where the hostel was located. Once we reached a petrol station, Émile with his limited German (and best "hang-dog" routine) began approaching drivers to ask for a quick lift to the inn. Finally, a sweet local lady who spoke no English or French adopted us. After stuffing us with all our gear into her tiny Volkswagen, we sped off in search of our lodging. By then it was pouring *"Katzen und Hunde."* She had no idea where the place was either, but after a few mis-turns we eventually found the cozy country hostel. Then, even with the rain, she insisted on serving us fresh-baked apple strudel right from a dish in her trunk, before ducking inside with us to make sure they had room.

As darkness fell, I thought about all those folks we were fortunate to meet. Maybe you only had to leave yourself open and expect the best from people. The Universe would provide the rest.

As though to prove yesterday was no once-in-a-lifetime fluke, the following day turned into another one touched by kindness. We encountered little bicycle traffic all day as the trail wound along the river and across fields of lettuce and sunflowers, then past a nuclear power plant that towered over the bucolic countryside. Only once did we temporarily "misplace" the trail, finding ourselves in someone's backyard. After lunch, it was a short trek to Dillingen's peaceful center.

"Maybe we should try to stay at the Franciscan convent," I suggested, since our last experience at the monastery was such a memorable one.

Émile heartily agreed. It surprised me when he took the initiative again to approach elderly nuns walking past and asked in German for directions to their convent. He had such a way with the older women and I congratulated him on his efforts.

Once inside their office, I pulled our letters of introduction from my pack and we were quickly shown to a comfortable room, and then invited downstairs for coffee and a snack. Heading into their gift shop, we asked, "Is there an Internet café in town for us to check our email?"

Overhearing our request, a customer standing at the counter volunteered to escort us to the library down the street, then to the nearby college. They were both closed. Equally frustrated, in fractured-English, the well-dressed woman suggested, "You wait here at convent. I send husband with car to pick you up. We have Internet at house."

Well, her husband who spoke a little more English soon arrived and drove us to their beautiful home nearby. After checking my email, Émile updated his blog, while I told our hosts, Bàrbel and Werner, all about our journey as together we traced the route on their maps. When my friend returned, our hosts instantly starting speaking German to him as he told them he'd studied it for years. Unfortunately, as I already knew, it was like talking with the family goldfish.

"That's okay," she assured him. "I'm embarrassed when I go to visit my daughter's family in Cal-i-fornia," she admitted, pronouncing the name of the state like Governor Schwarzenegger. "My grandkids introduce me as the 'Grandma who doesn't speak English too well!' But I hope to change all that soon."

The kind couple certainly went out of their way to make us feel welcome and share their *gemütlichkeit*. Learning it was Émile's birthday the next day, they presented us with two small flasks of fine local wine to celebrate. At first, I thought they were hospitable because of their California kinship, but then I realized, 'It's more than that. It's a fellowship shared between pilgrims—those who travel with their feet—and those who join us with their hearts.' When we finally said our goodbyes, I was shocked when Werner gave us both a huge hug for the road.

'So much for the stereotypical stern German,' I chuckled to myself.

Energized after a good night's sleep, we set off at a brisk clip and were feeling mighty pleased about our good fortune and progress—until we realized we'd been walking in the wrong direction. I know what some might think, but it was an innocent mistake. We had an expression, "Sun in the eyes," or "*Le soleil dans les yeux*." It was an easy reminder to always head east in the morning toward the sun. Unfortunately, for us that didn't help much on cloudy days and the roundabout *radweg* had my usually dependable internal gyroscope in a tizzy. It took us forty minutes to realize our mistake and another twenty to arrive back in town. We no sooner left the other side of Dillingen than heavy rain clouds barreled across the sky and all hell broke loose.

After it passed, we spent the next few hours traversing farmland bordering the highway, and walked nearly forty kilometers before we eventually reached Donauwörth. I finally felt like my feet were in pretty good shape (right on schedule). Émile still fought shin pains, although he made a good effort to match my pace. As we searched for the Franciscan cloister, the skies let loose again in a torrential downpour. Reaching the refuge, we were disappointed to find the Sister's reception just as sunny.

She spoke no French or English, but went into a rambling explanation in German about why there was "no room at the inn." Even our letter from the Vatican and the name of the Sister where we'd stayed the night before cut no proverbial ice. In due course, she tried in vain to telephone the local monastery, but was unable to get through—even though I later learned they were just three blocks apart. Still, the weather turned worse and three blocks might as well have been three miles in that deluge.

Finally, with Émile fading fast and me all out of patience, we made a mad dash for the doorway of Heilig Kreuz, a serene Baroque church containing a relic of the Holy Cross. Once inside, we shuffled up the stairway like a pair of salmon at the end of their exhausting climb upstream. The Father welcomed us in French, much to Émile's unabashed delight. Obviously sympathetic to our quest, he offered us simple rooms along with an invitation to join him and his other guests down a maze of halls, stairs and rooms through two buildings to the dining hall.

"And I forgot my breadcrumbs," I muttered, as we stumbled in confusion.

We easily found common ground around the simple table. Since one of the fellows at dinner spoke English, I shared my thoughts about the beneficial aspects of being alone, contemplation, and the experience of trekking every day on the trail.

"I believe that walking in nature can be a transcendent experience," I began, "a Zen-like meditation where inner peace is achieved slowly, step by step. If you walk without fixing your mind on any one thing, anchored only to the soil, memories, emotions, thoughts and messages pass through, as waves entering an empty grotto. Inner peace is achieved as the cave is filled, emptied, filled and emptied again. Waves leave only a glistening rock when they depart, before the next cascades in."

Philosophy aside, by the time dinner was completed, my feet were so badly swollen it was hard to become too enthused about another day of slogging through more rain. Still, we were thankful for what we did have. Our beds were comfortable at the boarding school, the sheets were clean, we were well fed, and eager for a good night's sleep. What more could we hope for? A fine wine? *Mais oui.*

It was May 16th, Émile's birthday. He was a young sixty-eight. So we enthusiastically shared the two small flasks of wine Werner had given us the night before, toasting my friend's good health and our fortune to be on the pilgrimage trail.

Well, the next morning it happened again. We asked directions when we left Heilig Kreuz—and were sent in the wrong direction. It took us eighty minutes to discover our mistake and return. By then, I was more than a little peeved it had occurred two days in a row. We must have asked four people along the way and they'd all sent us in the wrong direction. Still, I had to laugh. Whenever I asked directions in English or German, Émile, having no idea what they were saying, impatiently nodded, "*Oui, oui*" and then set off at a rapid pace as if he actually understood. If it wasn't so tiring, I had half a mind to let him run for a few hours, just to let him get it out of his system.

The rolling countryside continued, but we dodged the rain. After lunch, the trail became unmarked, so we followed the road to Rennertshofen where we quickly found a room in the Di-Da Hotel.

Later that evening, we dropped into their restaurant/bar and found ourselves in an animated discussion with two fellows who'd known each other all but three of their forty years. They spent every night together in that same bar. On that occasion, they invited themselves over to join us while our hostess prepared a *leberwurst* salad for us to try. It was a lot like something a five-year-old might concoct if set loose in the kitchen: chopped bologna in a mound, smothered with dressing. Émile was interested in ordering the *schinken* until he discovered it had nothing to do with chicken, but was pork, the mainstay of our diet since entering Germany.

Meanwhile, I was amused to hear those locals going back and forth like an old married couple, a Bavarian Chip and Dale, the Disney chipmunks. Hans, the chunkier one, explained that although Germany was one country since the reunion with East Germany, there were still regional differences, especially when it came to dialects. Their Bavarian version was a separate *patois*.

"It's only understood by other Bavarians," he bragged with undisguised glee. "We each have our own unique dialects, as well as regional food and beer."

"And the Austrians?" I asked, knowing they spoke German too.

"I can't understand them at all sometimes. Everything they say sounds like, "Shee, shee, shee," he chirped with a chuckle.

When I eventually told the couple about our journey to Jerusalem, their eyes lit up with excitement as they imagined themselves on the trail.

"You *could* always walk the Camino through Spain," I suggested. "It's well marked and a good place to just get away and think."

"Oh, yes, that's good for you," Hans said, "but I could never leave my home for that long."

"You could probably walk it in a month."

"No, I am a father and I have responsibilities," he pointed out, belly to the bar.

"Well, I guess it all depends on your priorities," I pointed out, as his harried East German wife arrived with their babies in tow.

Personally, I always chuckled when folks pointed out how relaxing it must be to travel "without any responsibilities." No, on second thought, I wanted to roll on the ground in sidesplitting hysterics every time I heard that comment. Travel, for me, was the polar opposite. Every day was rife with decisions and tasks: Where do you sleep? How do you get from here to there? Where do you eat without getting food poisoning? How do you travel safely down busy foreign streets without getting mugged? Where do you change and then hide your money? Plus, you couldn't help but worry occasionally about how life was progressing at home without you. Everything was an uncertainty for the modern nomad, even though you did your best at planning and making the smartest choices along the way. In the end, so much was left to a roll of the dice, just plain luck and divine providence. You just had to have faith that everything happened for a reason—and hope for the best. So, if you truly wanted less responsibility, perhaps it was best to take a cruise, where your biggest decision was whether to choose the "surf" or the "turf."

Still, for me, I wouldn't have had it any other way. I'd always yearned to learn what's over the next hill. Travel's constant surprises and improvisation has a way of keeping your mind fresh, while the exercise and clean air keep your body in better shape than most people your age.

Morning came all too quickly. I tossed and turned all night as my friend snored a death rattle. After breakfast, it was easy to find the trail (headed in the right direction) and we made good time to Neuberg crossing. The path divided just before town and we decided to take the right fork in order to check our email, and then walk the most direct route to Regensburg, since we needed to arrive the following week to meet Sophie and the gang.

Unfortunately, by the time we left the Internet café, the streets were pummeled again with rain and we ducked back inside to suit up in our ponchos or rain jackets and pants, plus cover our backpacks with rain covers.

Then reluctantly, we headed back into the storm, eager to make up for lost time. Imagine our frustration when the trail suddenly ended in a cornfield and we couldn't find a marked path. It was ridiculous walking without a good map and I vowed to resolve the problem in the next big city—once and for all. Meanwhile, we tried to ask directions to Weichering, but even that became complicated.

Émile in his wind-whipped poncho and flag-draped stick approached several cars as they headed toward us on the road. Yet as each grew near, they swerved and sped off—as if afraid of the friendly sheepdog of a Frenchman. Eventually though, with perseverance we managed to find a tiny path to the quiet farming hamlet and providence led us to the first *zimmer* we spotted.

"Look," I reminded my friend, "I'm usually the one asking for rooms. It's time for you to give it a go."

He frowned pitifully, but I insisted until he gingerly knocked on the farmhouse's front door. A robust, rosy-cheeked Frau soon opened it.

"You 'ave…rrroom?"

"Yes," she replied, wiping her hands on her apron.

"How much?" That was always an important question.

She looked us up and down from our wet hats to muddy boots. Then her eyes settled on Émile's scallop shell.

"You are pilgrims?"

"Yes, we're walking to Jerusalem," I explained.

Well, that was the magic word, the "Abracadabra."

"There is no charge for you to sleep here," the big-hearted "angel" announced leading us inside. "No charge for pilgrims!"

I couldn't believe it. We'd had an especially tough day, we still had no good map, and a guidebook showing a route that had changed. Then Dorothea was sent to us. Or were we sent to her? What force had led us to her house where we had a large room, clothes drying downstairs, a kitchen with cold drinks, an easy chair, plus a real bathtub for a long, hot soak?

Our next day was a vast improvement both in weather and mood. It was amazing what a good night's sleep could do. Then again, it certainly helped that we could find our way out of town without getting lost. We followed train tracks for as long as we could and reached Ingolstadt before noon. After a quick lunch in a café set inside the old city walls, we followed the trail along the Danube until it diverted through a field and we suddenly found ourselves in the midst of a herd of sheep.

I talked briefly with the unassuming stranger who just happened to speak very good English—better than Émile. I couldn't imagine a shepherd in our own country speaking German. Did we still even have shepherds? Or were they "outsourced" long ago to make room for another strip mall?

It wasn't long before my friend and I passed an electrical generator along the river, and I kept scanning the murky water to see if I could spot an American girl who was reportedly swimming the length of the frigid Donau from Donaueschingen to the Black Sea. Earlier that morning, we'd passed a fellow who'd had a chance to speak with her. It was certainly a difficult adventure—and far from traditional, but she had my admiration. I half-expected to see her head bobbing up and down, but he assured me that she was headed to Regensburg more than sixty kilometers away. The Danube must have had one heckuva current.

As for us, we approached the first *zimmer* we found in Vohburg and were led to a rustic cabin in the fellow's backyard. When I asked the price, the owner paused before saying, "Well, I guess being pilgrims, you can't spend too much. So is ten euros okay?"

Okay? It was *wundervoll*.

We wasted no time in returning to town to find an ATM. That was the easiest way to handle money on a long journey. With a debit card, I could access my bank account and never had to carry large wads of cash, as we'd done in the past when we traveled for months. Plus, I never had to find a moneychanger and pay extra commission. Unfortunately, Émile had brought traveler's checks and banks were less willing to accept them. If you were out of cash and they were closed for one of their frequent holidays, you had a real problem. Nowadays, you could definitely leave home without them.

Still, when the bank machine didn't issue a receipt, I had to traipse inside and convince the young teller to write one by hand, just in case there was any problem once I reconciled my statement. After telling her about our long walk, she handed me the paper, then spotted Émile hovering nearby in his weathered hat.

"Well your friend over there *does* look a little like Forest Gump," she gushed. "Run, Forest, run!'"

At first, I was offended by her condescending tone, and ready to fire back a snide comment, but then I remembered the old classic film and thought, 'Well, maybe she's right in one sense. Maybe we're all Forest Gumps in life, running away from demons in our past that are chasing us until we rid ourselves of our braces or chains that bind us. Only then can we sail on down the road.'

'Still,' I thought, 'if "Life is like a box of chocolates," it's stocked with more nuts than chews.'

The next morning over breakfast, our hosts proudly introduced us to fatty smoked pork, a local delicacy, showing us how to chop it finely before eating it with toast. Afterward, they pulled out maps, suggesting we follow the Donauweg instead of the *radweg*. It was the same path we'd found the day before atop a high levee-type barrier designed to hold back Donau floodwaters. Hopefully, it was more effective than those in New Orleans had been during Hurricane Katrina.

Our gravel path was nearly deserted, and we encountered just a dozen cyclists all day. Thank goodness for clouds, as we'd been told a thousand bicyclists might hit the Donau Radweg on a warm summer's day. We set a fast pace as we attempted to reach the world-famous Benedictine Abbey at Weltenburg before the rains began again.

It had a rich history. The original monastery was started back in 600 A.D. until St. Boniface converted it to an abbey in the 8th century. Plus, it happened to have the oldest monastic brewery in the world, founded in 1058. So, of course, we felt obliged to sample the dark chocolate ambrosia called *Klosterdunkle* at its source, along with a simple Bavarian fare of *wurst*, kraut and dark bread.

As usual, Émile's broken teakettle wheezing helped spur me forward. It wasn't a hum or a whistle per se, but an annoying buzz. He kept repeating some military march over and over. Although I figured it created a rhythm for him, to me it was an itch I just couldn't scratch. So I either sped ahead to get out of its range—until Émile jogged to catch up—or I slowed down and let him pass. Unfortunately, that would instantly cut our pace by twenty-five percent and I found myself nipping at his heels.

In his defense, he probably didn't know I could hear him, since I always walked ahead. Then again, his hearing had seemed to grow worse since his hearing aid batteries were *kaput*. He'd already had one near miss with a passing cyclist, and then he missed my warnings about an oncoming car.

By lunchtime, the river widened as we reached Essing where we stopped into the local riverside *biergarten*. With its casual picnic atmosphere, large striped umbrellas and friendly staff, it was exactly what we needed. As my friend enjoyed a fried trout and I sampled a traditional *currywurst*, it began to rain again, but that didn't discourage the Bavarian rock band that appeared aboard a river barge for an impromptu concert.

We followed the *radweg* close to the river's edge for the next two hours. A new Bikeline bicycle map we'd finally found made life on the trail much easier. We could now actually tell where we were—and where we were going. Imagine that.

By late afternoon, we sensed we were near the abbey, as the river widened and grew faster beneath the limestone cliffs that cropped up along its edge. I spotted a ferryman aboard his vessel, tied off and waiting to take passengers to the opposite shore. Then suddenly, the abbey's side entrance appeared—along with a flood of visitors attending a wedding. Seeing them, we could only hope they'd still have room for two waterlogged *peregrinos*.

Concerned about our chances, we checked inside several doorways surrounding the square with its *biergarten*, gift shop, museum and brewery until we found the Secretariat office. However, no one answered the buzzer. Finally, we located a phone and called Father Leopold, who spoke excellent English and invited us up to his office. For once, we were happy to play along as he grilled us about our purpose for the journey and then asked for our letters of introduction and identity cards, all before confirming he had space. Once satisfied, the tall man in the black robe became more hospitable, shepherding us to two single rooms.

After a relaxing bath and quick *siesta*, I met Émile downstairs in their beautiful Baroque church. I felt sorry for the ten Brothers who sang the entire service. Out of the hundred visitors in the *biergarten* and restaurant, we were the only ones attending Mass. Still, swept up in its simple melodies, I marveled at the extraordinary surroundings. The opulent setting boasted a gold-gilded interior, a magnificent fresco of Columbus arriving in the New World, celestial paintings atop the rotunda, twisted marble pillars, and a huge pipe organ. The ornate chapel dedicated to St. George featured a larger-than-life silver statue of the saint on horseback killing the serpent, right on the altar. Best of all, light filtered down from a mysterious source (as there were few windows), illuminating the face and heart of the saint.

In the morning, we celebrated an early Mass where Pater Leopold welcomed us as pilgrims to Jerusalem. Then, after a private blessing, he sent us on our way. Nonetheless, our trek was far from "on the wings of angels." It took us two days to finally arrive in Regensburg, a regal old city astride the banks of the Donau.

Craving a cup of coffee, we ducked up some stairs to an historic museum that was unfortunately closed. However, we did run into a group of American/Canadian seniors on tour. Since they were curious about our outfits, we were pleased to share the story of our pilgrimage and answer questions, especially since it allowed us a few extra minutes to warm up in the foyer. Crowding around, they snapped photos and one lady even shot a video, I guess to show the two mad pilgrims to the folks back home.

Yet they were polite, asking us questions like, "Is it just the two of you?"

"Yes," I laughed, looking around for our imaginary retinue.

"Aren't you worried about your safety?" another wondered.

"Not at all. I've found people are hospitable to travelers wherever I've traveled."

"Well," one beefy woman demanded, "who is supporting all this?"

"Supporting?" I had to laugh. "Other than sponsors for my shoes and sticks, we're supporting ourselves. Besides, it doesn't cost too much when you travel like this." That seemed to either impress or confuse them, considering how much they must have paid for their organized tour.

Their question & answer session might have lasted an hour, if their tour guide didn't finally interrupt, suggesting, "Well, I guess we should be moving along."

Before leaving, one jovial fellow sporting a crew cut stepped forward and presented us both with Canadian flag lapel pins, whispering, "In case you need a disguise."

"Thanks," I chuckled. "Is this all we need to confuse the 'terrorists?'"

Then another small, well-dressed lady pulled me aside and slipped me a euro coin.

"Oh, that's not necessary."

"No, no," she insisted.

"We *really* don't need this."

She refused to take it back, saying, "No, use it to buy..." and she made a hand gesture as if tipping a bottle.

I didn't know whether to be thankful or offended? Did she think we were two vagabonds wandering to Jerusalem?'

Her donation did buy me half a cup of tea at a sidewalk café across the river, however, we didn't linger long, as we'd be back in a few days with Sophie and their friends for more serious sightseeing.

It was dark by the time we reached the hamlet of Worth on der Donau and settled into the first *gasthaus* we found, the Butz, which lived up to its name.

Early the next morning, we left in the fog, attempting to follow small surface roads in the right direction. However, it was another case where the Donau Radweg went meandering far out of the way. That was no big deal if you were on a bicycle traveling 80-120 kilometers a day, but for walkers, those leisurely diversions were a waste of our limited energy. No one could imagine what it took physically, mentally and emotionally to get up every morning (in mostly rain) and set off for another thirty kilometer slog.

For lunch, we were relieved to find a Bosnian café. It was far from fancy with aged, yellow antlers decking the walls, smoke seeping out of every crevice, and plum brandy that ran like water. Still, we were thankful to just find a warm cup of soup and omelet out of the cold. Just as we finished eating, a sixty-year-old woman decked out in a skin-tight sweater and garish make-up sashayed past. All was fine until we rose to leave and reached across to gather our hats, backpacks and walking sticks. She had the audacity to chortle at us, right in our faces. Were we that ridiculous? As much as I would have liked to ignore it, her laughter cut to the bone.

That night in Bogen, however, there was an even odder incident. As usual, Émile and I turned out the lights at nine o'clock to allow us to get up at five-thirty or six the next morning. All was fine, until I woke to the sound of a rustling plastic bag, the frantic gulping of water and what sounded like candy wrappers.

"Hey. What's going on?" I blurted out in the darkness.

There was no answer, not a word. Something strange was definitely happening, but what? Was Émile sleepwalking? Did he need medication? He'd recently admitted he was a diabetic—something that would have been great to know in advance.

Émile sat in the dark on the floor, quietly munching for what seemed like an eternity. Then he hobbled back to his bed.

"Everything okay?"

"*Oui. Ça va bien,*" he mumbled.

Struggling to get back to sleep, I worked to connect all the dots about my friend's health and grew more worried for him. What if he had a diabetic seizure? What could I do out on the trail? More importantly, what else hadn't he told me?'

In the morning, nothing was said by either of us about the incident the night before. We left at daybreak and made good time along the trail, only encountering a few bicyclists. The terrain was dotted with gently rolling hills, trellises of hops and tidy villages of perhaps a hundred people each. By early afternoon, we rolled into Deggendorf where Émile had told Sophie to meet us at the *bahnhof* (train station), while he'd told his friend Henri to meet us at the *rathaus*, same village—two completely different directions. All morning he'd tried to call them on his cell phone, and when Émile was finally able to reach him, we discovered he wouldn't arrive until seven that evening. We'd rushed all day for nothing.

By then, we'd already spent an hour in an Internet café, toured both St. Peter and St. Paul churches, and moseyed up and down Main Street several times. Next, we milked one drink for two hours in another café, until eventually, Sophie, Henri and pixyish Lydie showed up in the square. There were hugs and kisses all around, although no apologies were offered for the six-hour delay.

Afterward, we and our gear were crammed into Henri's already bursting Peugeot, then he sped like a groundhog avoiding his shadow all the way back to Regensburg. It felt bizarre to cover the same ground in forty-five minutes that it had taken us two days to walk, but we soon arrived on the outskirts of Regensburg at the French-run Etap Hotel, with its tiny, exceptionally sterile rooms reminiscent of Japan's capsule hotels.

Honestly, I was not looking forward to the next few days. Although I enjoyed the company, I imagined they'd consist of eating, walking, eating, walking…and then eating some more.

The next morning, with life reduced to group consensus, decisions took longer than normal—but that only gave Henri and Sophie time to chain-smoke a few more Gitannes before we all loaded back into the Peugeot for another Grand Prix drive into Regensburg for a little sightseeing—on a major national holiday to boot. Funny, their rendezvous had been planned for at least a month, yet no one realized it was Assumption Day. During that major national holiday, everything was closed—except for the churches and restaurants.

After finding a parking lot still open and smoking a few more cigarettes, we began our church tour with nearby St. Jacob's, founded by Irish-Scots monks in the 12th century. Since a service was in progress, we stayed outdoors to marvel at the intricate carvings on the facade, especially the unusual lions and lionesses surrounding the doorway—not creatures found in the usual Irish or German forest. Scholars still tried to unravel its mystery. Then we visited the twin-spired Dom St. Peter and had the rare opportunity to hear the "Cathedral Sparrows," their version of the Vienna Boys Choir. It was spectacular to listen, especially in such a regal setting. Unfortunately, the others became bored after ten minutes and began to leave. To where? Another church, of course. We browsed the Karmelitan, then the Alte Kapelle with its royal booths, paintings and rich Baroque designs—many constructed of wood painted to resemble marble.

Finally, in search of food, (what else?), we headed back across the same stone bridge we'd crossed earlier with my one-euro coin, and ducked into a cozy, wood-paneled *biergarten* just as it began to rain again. Now, I couldn't say if it was our particular group, but it took my four companions fifteen minutes to hang up their coats and settle into their chairs. Our waitress already hovered, demanding our order. After all, it was Germany and efficiency was king. I could only give her a sympathetic shrug, as if to say, "My hands are tied."

Since the menu was in German and none of them could read it, I did my best to translate, and then explain it back to them in French. Basically, it was pub food and you just needed to decide whether you wanted thick or thin sausages, and beef or pork. Meanwhile, our statuesque server returned two more times, while my friends launched into a long discussion weighing the desirability of each item, as if it was a major life decision—and not just lunch. Eventually, noticeably exasperated, the waitress took our small, simple brat orders and then impatiently stood tapping her foot, as if to say, "That's it? After all this time?"

"*Oui.*"

Afterward, on the wild drive back to our hotel, we stopped at Walhalla, a "Parthenon" of Europe's historical luminaries set upon an imposing mountaintop. We climbed through woods, then up its steep stairs to admire the breathtaking view of the Danube and open plains below. However, its museum paled in comparison. In reality, Walhalla was part of King Ludwig I's national "feel-good" campaign dating back to 1842. The impressive Greek Revival-style building with Doric columns contained nearly 126 busts and memorials to Europe's *Who's Who*, although the majority was from Germany, Austria and Switzerland. England had maybe three members and about the same for France and the Netherlands. I don't know if Spain or Italy even made the cut. All in all, most of their inspiration went into the exterior—ironically, a copy of a Greek design.

Following another long-drawn-out discussion, it was decided that Henri, nursing a bad foot, and Sophie would drive ahead to Hofkirchen with everyone's bags, find a privat zimmer, and then walk the short distance back to meet us on the trail. Perfect.

In the morning, after a day off, I was energized and eager to leave. With our bags in the car, we only had to carry raingear, water and cameras, so it was much easier. Cloudy and cool, it was the perfect walking weather. We heard the distant cry of cuckoos and spotted our fair share of ducks, swans, and even a giant hare, but rarely encountered anyone else, not even the lone swimmer that I half-expected to see bobbing like a red, white and blue ice cube in the Danube.

For us, it was a straightforward hike beside the canal and I set the pace, pausing occasionally and turning like a dog on a family outing to make sure chatty Émile and Lydie followed. We covered twenty kilometers by noon and arrived in Markt Winzer, a hamlet not far from Hofkirchen where we'd spend the night. Given our past success at planning, I was relieved when Henri and Sophie arrived on schedule and we could shuffle over to the local gasthaus for lunch. Fortunately, it was easier to order since they only offered their *plat du jour*: *sauerbraten* with dark gravy, salad and *knödel*, a baseball-sized dumpling. After the heavy lunch, before we had a chance to curl up and go to sleep, all four of us waddled off together to Hofkirchen in the rain.

'This must be a gorgeous area in good weather,' I kept reminding myself, but after weeks of drizzle and fog, I remained unconvinced.

Still, even with less than perfect conditions, we soon arrived to our *gasthaus*, not a *privat zimmer* as planned. That might have given us more privacy. As it was, Henri, Lydie and I settled into our triple room with its psychedelic carpet, baggy wallpaper, and shower in a closet with a reluctant showerhead dribbling an unimpressive trickle. Then we headed down to their bar for dinner. It was welcoming—in a communist-era, Eastern European sort of way. Eight locals in the smoke-filled room feverishly slapped cards onto their table, while we gorged on colossal *schnitzels*, goulash, rotellini pasta, and drinks that Henri topped off with a humongous chocolate sundae.

Lydie and Émile had both warned me that Henri was a snorer, but that was an understatement, like saying the pyramids were "kinda big for their age." That night, over-sized Henri began grunting even before the lights were out. In fact, he was still awake and reading—and snoring at the same time.

"How do you do it?" I asked sweet, patient Lydie.

She just shrugged and sighed, "Oh, you get used to it."

However, that was little consolation, since it was just his warm-up overture. After the lights dimmed, the symphony really began. Henri's racket was like having a woodpecker nested inside your head—and not the cute, rascally Woody. It was a constant staccato of five or six thunderous blasts every ten seconds…for hours. During one brief intermission, I finally reached into my kit and pulled out earplugs, a pilgrim's best friend and worth their weight in zzs.

Sometime during the night a circuit blew, so there was no heat in our room when we woke. Yes, it got that cold in Bavaria in late May. Then the light in the bathroom didn't work, so we showered and shaved in the dark.

Over our high-fat cold cuts breakfast, the group agreed that Henri and petite Sophie would drive ahead to Passau to locate a *privat zimmer*, and then drive back to Worth where they'd leave the car and walk six kilometers to meet us.

Émile, Lydie and I made good time again, arriving at our rendezvous shortly after the others who'd driven most of the way. After lunch, while they walked back to their car, Émile and I continued on into Passau where Henri had already selected another wacky hotel. The Rotel, set on the banks of the Danube, had rooms about six by fifteen feet. Baths were down the hallway, which incidentally was where you also had to go to change your mind.

Still, its privacy was treasured, and I took time to visit a few Passau gems on my own: St. Paul Church with its unique ebony, ivory and gold Baroque architecture, the Cathedral of St. Stephan with the world's largest church organ, and the Monastery of Niedernburg with St. Gisela's tomb. Then I just lost myself in the old part of the beautiful city dating back nearly seven thousand years.

The following day, "rain" was again the operative word. It began even before I made it out of bed. After meeting for the skimpiest of breakfasts, it was time for us to say our *"adieus."* It was especially sad for Émile and Sophie, but if all went according to plan they'd meet again in Istanbul. As for me, I was relieved to be back on our own again; ready to re-don the cloak of the *peregrino* and leave the "tourist" behind.

My friend and I followed the Donau Radweg along the river in relentless rain, dodging puddles, the spray from passing trucks, and squadrons of bicyclists that chose that particular day to hit the trail. By noon, we arrived on the main Hauptstrasse of Obernzell, just in time to join a parade. We tagged alongside a brass band dressed in traditional Bavarian attire: starched white shirts, *lederhosen* and embroidered suspenders. They were followed by a bevy of maidens in *dirndls* of wide skirts, colored aprons, poofy shirts and pointy shoes, then a cadre of fifty firefighters, married matrons, and a legion of men in military uniforms. Townspeople waved from windowsills; others applauded from doorways. A few, like us, were simply swept up in the festivity. When they eventually veered off into a park with its tents and another brass band, I was sad to leave. No matter what the weather, it was impossible to be melancholy when surrounded by brass bands and oompah music.

Soon afterward, we entered Jochenstein and crossed the Donaukraftwerk, an enormous hydroelectric power station spanning the Donau River. It was also the border between Germany and Austria. I was excited to be back in Österreich, one of my favorite countries and a benchmark of how far we'd trekked—more than one thousand kilometers already. By the time we reached Vienna, we'd be ahead of schedule, so we'd be able to slow down to meet Cheryl in Budapest. That took a little of the pressure off.

Besides, with our extra days, I was eager to find a good route through Bulgaria and Turkey, especially since Henri had only brought more auto maps—and I didn't look forward to dodging Skodas, Ladas and Trabants all the way to Istanbul.

CHAPTER FOUR
Austria & Slovakia

The Kindness of Strangers

"You cannot travel the path until you have become the path."
~ Buddha

When we said goodbye to our hosts, they predicted we could look forward to at least four more days of rain. Although the forecast was distressing since the weather made our journey more physically difficult, worse still was the way it wore away at our psyches, one drop at a time.

As luck would have it, it was only misty when we left, following a country road along the Danube. The northern Donau Radweg continued back into Germany, while our southern branch had its own quiet charm and challenges. The villages were even farther apart and that posed a problem. All day long we aimed for the village of Kaiser, since there were no towns before it and afterward it was another two hours to Aschach. When it eventually began to rain again, we poured on steam to reach Kaiser before its only hotel became full. Imagine our surprise when we walked into the large, eerily quiet *gasthaus* in mid-afternoon—only to be told they were already booked solid.

"Full?" I asked the brooding desk clerk in astonishment. Now, I could handle rejection. But when I saw no other guests, no cars, bicycles or other signs of life except for the five local fellows in the bar, I had to wonder. So after checking my breath and body odor, I tried again, going into my whole spiel.

"Look, we're pilgrims walking to Jerusalem. It's raining. We've already walked nearly thirty-five kilometers. My friend is sixty-eight years old and he's very tired."

The receptionist took a deep drag on her cigarette, then gave me an indifferent "So what?" shrug.

So I tried a different tack, asking, "Where is the church?" We could always try staying there.

She glared like a hound hearing a far-off, high-pitched sound.

"The church, the "*Kirche*," I repeated. Still, all I got in response was her blank look. I repeated the German word for "church" with six slightly different intonations while she vacantly stared as if I was speaking Mongolian.

Finally, her friend standing nearby chuckled, "Aschach." It was the same place as the other "available" rooms. All my cards had been played. We had no choice other than to continue in the rain another hour or two.

"Bless you," I sarcastically mumbled, as I trudged back outside to Émile who lay crumpled under the awning. I still didn't know what game the woman was playing, but she even ducked her head outside to make sure we'd left the premises. How odd.

Bone-tired, waterlogged, and sore we trudged those last six kilometers into Aschach and easily found the Radweg Information Center where the volunteer confided she'd had five other similar complaints about the Kaiser Hotel in the past week.

'So it's not just us," I joked, only partly relieved.

To make up for it, she wasted no time in finding us a *privat zimmer* on a farm on the far side of town. The host actually came to pick us up, and then later took us back into town to his friend's restaurant. They were so genuinely kind that I was struck by what a remarkable day of contrasts it had been.

"Never does one door close, but another opens."

Our hosts extended their hospitality the following morning. They served us a huge Austrian *frühstück*, just as large as the German version, pulled out brochures of Linz's famous cathedrals, and even presented us with a postcard as a memento.

On a less welcome note, however, it was already raining when we first poked our heads outside and it continued all day, as we followed a *radweg* so straight that the blind could have found their way without getting lost. After passing another hydroelectric dam, the trail evaporated on our side, so we hopped a five-minute ferry across the Donau to Offensheim. Ever since leaving Dijon, we'd made an intentional effort to reach Jerusalem by traditional means on foot—without accepting the many rides we were offered. Yet taking a ferry in that instance was not only practical but also time-honored. Ferrymen had always played an important role in lives and trade along the vast river, the lifeblood connecting much of Europe. Then again, once we arrived in a village, if our *pensionen* was far off our route, we had accepted a ride on occasion if it was late or the weather was threatening.

As Émile's leg had given him problems again all afternoon, it was late by the time we hobbled into the Tourist Office on Hauptplatz in the historic town of Linz. Their receptionist spoke French, as well as English and German, so I was a little annoyed when my friend dramatically announced to everyone he was going to "take a pee-pee" and wandered off, assuming I'd again handle all the little details.

Taking pity on me, the pretty brunette directed us to the Goldener Anker Hotel. Off their main square lined with stately Baroque style buildings, it was a convenient, affordable, no-frills piece of local history, as it had once been a watering hole for Anton Bruckner, famous composer and nearby native son. She was also kind to contact the international freight office in Graz for me, who confirmed that my second pair of Montrail shoes was waiting at their Linz office. The only problem was getting there, since they were on the far side of town and couldn't deliver until the next day.

As I'd feared, fetching them turned into another two-hour adventure. After checking into our hotel, I set off alone and caught one of Linz's efficient trams all the way to the end. However, en route, I discovered I'd bought the wrong ticket. Luckily, there were no self-important officials like the one I'd once met in Budapest to check for tram deviants.

It was during our younger, crazier days in the old communist Hungarian capital. Subways were inexpensive, probably all of ten cents, and Cheryl and I hopped them everywhere for weeks. Each day, we'd buy another ten tickets before starting out and we'd ride from one museum to a sauna to a concert or pub until they ran out. After weeks of doing this and never seeing locals buy them, or anyone check for tickets on board, we got lazy. We left our apartment and walked to the metro in the early morning fog. The ticket booth was still closed and we just hopped on board heading into *centrum*. Before long, a gruff and shaggy train conductor approached, demanding something in Hungarian.

"Tickets?"

"Yes, tickets!" he snarled.

Well, I'd been saving stubs and stuffing them into my pockets for a week, so I reached into my jacket and produced several dozen punched ticket stubs.

He was not amused. "No, for this ride. Now!" he commanded in Hungarian.

"Sorry. We don't speak Hungarian."

"*Fahrkarte!*" he thundered.

"Sorry, no German either. Only English."

By then, the subway was slowing down at our stop and we began to slide past him to get off the train.

"You wait, you just wait," he insisted, grabbing my arm. "You come to station with me."

"Sorry, but we have to go," I answered in English, still pretending we didn't understand the gist of what he was saying. We weren't about to go to their police station. Who knew if we'd ever surface again?

"No, you come!" he screamed, tugging my arm.

"No, no, thanks," I answered with an embarrassed smile. "Sorry, we have to go," and I broke free of his grasp.

As we scampered off, we left the frustrated conductor spouting and spewing, "Phooey, phooey on you. Phooey!"

Now, at the end of my Linz tram ride, I still had to ask a few people, locate the *radweg* under the autobahn, and then make my way through an industrial area. When I finally arrived, their clueless staff informed me that my shoes were already delivered—to Vienna.

"Vienna? That can't be. We phoned Graz a few hours ago and were informed the box is sitting somewhere here in your office."

It took three very bored people gazing into their computer screens a very long time and then one more call to Graz to confirm that, yes, the shoes were in their office right there.

By the time I returned to the hotel, Émile was rested and eager to find an Internet café, but I passed. With my two-hour misadventure, I still hadn't had a minute to shower or even change out of my sweaty hiking clothes. So he set off alone.

After cleaning up, I was content to roam Linz's exquisite plazas and cobblestone streets, past the Trinity Column and neo-Gothic New Cathedral with seating for twenty thousand. Then suddenly, hearing street protests, I rushed in the direction of the screaming. Rounding a corner, I was surprised to almost run right onto a movie set. A Nazi-era film was being shot and a seething crowd of movie extras waved anti-Jewish signs and shouted slogans. It was all exciting for a few moments until the director screamed, "Cut!" and they broke for the night. However, after the

actors moved off the set, they were willing to pose for a few final shots of
my own in the fading evening light.

We awoke to rain again. The weather was taking its toll on our attitudes,
as if walking thirty kilometers a day wasn't hard enough. As we left Linz,
the showers tagged along past vast industrial areas, ports, gravel pits and
factories for hours. We traced the Donau all morning until we reached
Langenstein, site of Gusen, a former World War II concentration camp. It
was a sub-camp of the infamous Mauthausen. For six years, Jews and
"incorrigibles" from twenty-seven countries were interned there as slave
labor in granite quarries operated by the SS-owned Deutsch Erd-und
Steinwerke GmbH. Beginning in 1943, the prisoners became forced-labor
for the armaments industries. Then in 1944, Gusen II opened for the production of Messerschmitt fighter aircraft.

Nowadays, all that remained was a haunting memorial consisting of the
crematorium ovens surrounded by memorial plaques, photographs and
wreaths dedicated to those who'd died at the hands of the Nazis. In all,
nearly 70,000 innocent civilians were imprisoned there with more than
35,000 starved and literally worked to death. Few survived longer than
eight months.

Émile and I stopped into the new visitors' center and spent a long,
silent hour studying its exhibit of horrifying photographs and correspondence collected as testimony to an era when the world had gone mad. The
more I saw, the more I had to wonder, 'How could all this have been going
on in this village without everyone knowing? In a small town anywhere,
there are no secrets. It's inconceivable you could dispose of 35,000 bodies
over five years without anyone noticing.'

As we exited, I couldn't resist asking the same question of the motherly
older woman tending the center. "How could this ever happen here?" I
asked, not really expecting an answer.

She sighed heavily. Gazing with tender eyes, she struggled to hold back
tears.

After visiting the crematorium, I felt uneasy about staying in its neighboring village, so we continued to Au on der Donau, a hamlet of six hundred or so. Along the way, I reflected on the other Nazi death camps I'd
visited in Europe over the years: Dachau outside Münich, Auschwitz outside Krakow, Poland, and others. It was valuable to visit them firsthand
and learn history—so it should never have a chance to repeat. Their horror
was not so long ago and unfortunately people seldom change. One of the

greatest nations in Europe was held hostage by a radical faction who usurped control of the government, military, media, education and business—while blaming minorities for all their economic problems: Jews, radicals, leftists, liberals, communists, gypsies, homosexuals, foreigners and others. I was also reminded of the Jewish families who were rounded up and transported to camps by railroad car, after being promised they would be "safer" there.

"Well," as many must have said, "if we will be safer, then we must go along." And we all know what happened next.

More than repeating a simplistic, "Never again," I realized each person has a duty to remain constantly vigilant against extremists who create a false atmosphere of fear, a sense of imminent danger to confiscate freedoms. Resist those who insist on draconian plans "if we want to remain safe," while they dismantle rights and liberties. Perhaps Benjamin Franklin said it best when he admonished, "Those who would give up essential liberty to purchase a little temporary safety deserve neither liberty nor safety."

Although Au on der Donau's Pühringer Gasthaus was in repair and its restaurant was closed to prepare for the summer season, its owners, Ervin and Claudia, more than made up for the inconvenience.

"As soon as you're dried off," the friendly fellow chuckled, "why don't you join our family and warm up around the fire?"

He didn't have to invite us twice. After showers, we walked down the freezing hallway to their large apartment where they'd already set out a feast with ham, cheese spread, olive-sized capers, pistachios, pickles and beer. As we warmed ourselves, their children provided entertainment as only kids can do, bouncing all over the room, wrestling with their father, then racing across the room in a plastic car. Then, as we sipped a local pear schnapps, Hanna, aged seven, soulfully played a solo for us on her flute, followed by Eric, two and a half, who pounded out a "concerto" on the family piano. We could have been in a family's home anywhere. It was all a welcome contrast to what we'd seen earlier that day.

Later, as we watched the news on his big-screen television, I was shocked to hear U.S. Secretary of State Condoleezza Rice sounding as if an American invasion of Iran was imminent. I could only wonder if all our posturing really made us feel safer?

It was frigid in our room when we awoke—so cold we could see our breaths, plus it was already raining on the street below. How many weeks had it been since we'd had a day of sun? I'd lost count. Despondent, we shuffled downstairs to a breakfast of the same cold cuts, cheese and bread, but when we attempted to pay Ervin for our room and meals, he refused, insisting, "No, you are our guests!"

We were both astounded by his generosity. All we could do in return was to share photos of our lives back home with him and his children, and then promise to send them a postcard from Jerusalem once we arrived.

Our walk was brisk along the river all morning. The unseasonably cold, rainy weather dramatically reduced the number of people riding or walking the popular trail, much to the chagrin of local restaurant and *gasthaus* owners. As we slogged along the frigid Donau on the first day of June, I flashed back to a woman who'd once called my wife and me "Ugly Americans" simply because we didn't shower dollars onto the Tibetans who'd shared with us, as we walked across their country. She just didn't understand. In some ways, it was like receiving a valuable gift and then saying, "Thank you. How much can I pay you for this?" No, I was convinced people shared their homes, lives and dreams out of a greater purpose than money. It was called compassion and charity, whether to friends, travelers or innocents passing through; a simple human kindness that we'd lost in our busy, materialistic culture. Our ancestors would have known it, especially those living through the Great Depression. Nowadays, when no one has time anymore in their lives and fear cautions us against contact with strangers, our charitable acts are limited to writing a check or calling in to the telethon. To open our homes and hearts to a "pilgrim," a seeker passing through, is sadly against our more practical nature, and contrary to our supposed survival.

If it was in my power, I'd grant a special pilgrim's blessing to all those who extended kindness along that trail, as I did for those in Tibet. I'd pray their kindnesses would be returned a hundred fold.

That afternoon, the final six kilometers into Grein flew past and we avoided rain for the rest of the day. It was a pleasant village set along the Donau with a picturesque countenance. Using the *zimmer*-listing sheet we'd picked up the day before, we easily found a place to stay where our hostess even offered to do our soggy laundry. It had been far too long since our clothes had had a "proper" machine washing—and we could only get them so clean in the sink. With all the rain, we smelled like wet dogs. (No offense meant to my canine buddies.)

In the morning, it was cloudy when we stepped outside in the bone-chilling air, which left my legs feeling like lead. The wind whipped our faces and we were forced to "streetwalk" through a few villages before catching the *radweg* once again. Émile was especially dragging. By mid-morning he announced, "I have to get some rest today—if I'm going to be able to continue."

Personally, I was also worried about his hearing, as it grew worse. Only the day before, I had to pull him out of the way of another oncoming car. He heard maybe half of what I said, and at times I swore he read my lips.

What's more, I was convinced that his heavy boots made his trek harder. So I gave him a pair of my Montrail inserts. My sponsor could only ship them in quantities of three, so I didn't think they'd mind. All he'd had in his leather boots were the paper-thin, factory issue.

However, more than rest—since we already had nearly ten hours of sleep each night—I was convinced the weather was eroding our energy. For that very reason, I'd planned a sauna stop in Ybbs. There was nothing like a eucalyptus steam to take the chill out of your bones and put a bounce back in your step.

It was a short trek across another massive hydroelectric dam to Ybbs on der Donau. It took us no time at all to find a *privat zimmer* just off the river, as well as a sympathetic hostess. Someone in her family had recently walked the *Jakobsweg*, as we spotted the familiar blue and gold scallop shell tile proudly displayed just inside her doorway.

After a quick shower, we wandered past the remains of an ancient tower and moat, the serene St. Lawrence Church, and crude lines on a riverside wall marking a history of disastrous Danube River flood levels. Many communities along the waterway were still recovering from a horrendous year.

Before long, we reached the community sports center. That tiny village boasted a huge, heated, indoor swimming pool, a wet and dry sauna, steam room with eucalyptus or chamomile vapors, and a new Japanese infra-red therapy chamber that was said to be good for weather-caused depression (SAD or "seasonal affective disorder") among other things. Seeing all that, I was personally a little "sad" that for puritanical reasons saunas and steam baths throughout the U.S. were still relegated to exclusive heath spas, and out of the reach of everyday Americans (who I'd figure get just as cold in winter as Germans).

It was different in Ybbs. Nudity was common in the mixed-sex, five-euro sauna; however, sexuality was checked at the door in the land of *schnitzel, schnitzel und mehr schnitzel*. In the steam room, I sat across a man who must have weighed three hundred pounds, stewing in his own sweat.

Although my stomach was a little queasy, I enjoyed the steam too much to pay attention. That was, until he pulled out a razor and began shaving his face, knocking whiskers to the floor.

Europe's spas were anything but exclusive.

That was enough steam for me, so I took a cold dip and then headed into the dry sauna. As I practiced deep breathing among the vapors, Émile was in seventh heaven in their dining room, savoring a *cordon bleu* and catching up on his email. As the Donau slowly surfaced and bubbled out of my own system, I reflected on the past forty days and 1,200 kilometers along the famous river.

'Johann Strauss must have been high on Austria's famous Linzer torte when he composed the *Blue Danube*. Most days, this river's a brown or gray or green, at best. But I guess the *Muddy Brown Danube Waltz* doesn't have the same pizzazz, now does it?'

"Da da dee da da. Gurgle burp. Gurgle burp."

We woke to another Pacific Northwest winter's day. I'd heard on the news the night before that it was snowing again in Germany (in June) and found that easy to believe. At least we were able to set a faster pace, since the sauna had worked its wonders and sweated the lead out of my legs.

The river glided like a giant brown serpent through the grass. The valley was narrow and dotted with small hills, a patchwork of green. In many ways, it reminded me of my native Ohio River Valley, yet those early German-Austrian settlers must have thought they were in Paradise in Pennsylvania with the warmer weather, sunshine and cheap land.

Within a few hours we reached Melk, home to one of the world's most famous monastic sites and one of Austria's spiritual centers. By then, Émile's "meal alarm" was loudly clanging and I knew we only had a short time to reach the famous abbey before he started fading. From the quaint village, we flew up narrow alleyways to the honey and white Benedictine fortress dominating the skyline. At the ticket office, we made our "pitch" for a pilgrim's room, but learned the Pater was out and wouldn't return until two o'clock. So we shuffled over to their restaurant, made a quick tour of their Park and Garden Pavilion, and then returned. For another thirty minutes we cowered, soaked and shivering in a foyer, until eventually the ticket clerk fetched us, led us through automatic sliding glass doors to a glass elevator, and then up three floors to their guest rooms. Ours was a simple but spacious chamber for four with much-appreciated hot showers and a heater that actually worked. It was a rare luxury, since many Austrian *zimmers* shut off their heat at the end of winter, even in years like this when it was still nearly freezing outdoors.

We were also thankful for the free tickets to tour the monastery and view its treasures, including a relic from the Holy Cross, then roam their library with its thousands of medieval volumes. Its Baroque church was especially remarkable. When we entered, the monks were conducting Mass in Gregorian chants from the altar. Resplendent gold leaf shone through-out and its ceiling frescos were sublime. However, we were most intrigued by two bizarre male skeletons dressed in their finest jewels and silk and posed in glass boxes for all to admire. They were thought to be early Chris-tian martyrs found in the Roman catacombs. Empress Maria Theresia and an Italian Cardinal had presented "Clemens" and "Friedrich" to the monastery in the 18th century when saint and martyr worship was in vogue.

The abbey itself dated back to 1089, when Leopold II gave the castle to the Benedictine monks from Lambach. It was difficult in our modern age to conceive the power and wealth such a monastery once possessed, indeed, enough to survive a thousand years through numerous wars—but I had a glimpse. Crossing the upper terrace between the museum and library, I was overcome by a magnificent panoramic view of the Donau and surround-ing countryside. I could only imagine the wonder a weather-beaten peasant must have felt gazing up at the grandeur from his poor dirt fields far below.

Again, I was so grateful the monks had opened their doors to us. A few hours earlier we were wet and miserable like that farmer—but were now warm, content and fulfilled yet another day.

We woke at 5:00 a.m. to that most rare occurrence—sunshine. It only lasted a few minutes though, and by the time we were ready to leave it was pouring again. It had rained eighteen of the last twenty-one days, almost our entire stay in Austria and much of Germany. No wonder we were a little frazzled.

The day before, I finally lost my temper. I'd reminded Émile several times to look after our bags whenever I left to take care of business. Well, at the restaurant, I went to the WC and was soon surprised to hear him in there. He'd left our bags. Any traveler knows you never leave your back-pack alone and unsecured. True, it was an abbey, but the restaurant was filled with visitors. If we lost our packs, papers and valuables, our journey, pilgrimage or not, would come to a swift and unfortunate end.

We also had a brief conversation about his plans for Istanbul. Sophie and Émile planned to meet in the legendary city and spend a week together. However, she'd recently decided to hold off on their rendezvous. She didn't know exactly when we'd arrive. Then again, she wasn't comfortable with traveling because of heightened tensions in the Middle East.

"Still, if we arrive early in Istanbul and Sophie decides to come to meet you," I assured my companion, "I can always continue to Ankara and wait for you there."

He wasn't enthused by that option.

We slipped and slid down narrow cobblestone streets on a steep descent from the abbey to the *radweg* tracing the river. It was another day of quick changes. First it drizzled, so we'd stop to put on our rain pants, jackets or ponchos, and I'd get into my old waterproof shoes. Then after just a few minutes, the rain would stop, so we'd take them all off again. We'd walk another fifteen minutes before it'd begin raining again, harder than before. So we'd stop again to suit up. Of course, we could have left our rain gear on, but as any die-hard hiker knows, we'd end up even wetter from perspiration in the ongoing celestial joke.

To top it all off, the trails were packed on another national holiday with bicyclists blasting past in packs of four or six with seldom a "clinga-cling" of their bicycle bell. More bikes skirted us than in all our days in Germany. Perhaps the bad weather had kept them away after all.

After leaving Melk, we found ourselves amid one of Austria's most prolific wine regions, the Wachau, and we passed terraced vineyards and *weinstubes* all afternoon. But for two "*pauvre peregrinos*," it was a case of "Wine, wine everywhere and not a drop to drink." Who could stop and risk arriving too late to find a room? With thirty-five kilometers behind us, we were thirsty, exhausted and ready to call it a night in Dürnstein. But as luck would have it, our plan was soon dashed.

We arrived to find the village swarming with river cruise passengers who toured the site where Duke Leopold V held Richard the Lion-Hearted captive during the Third Crusade. Zigzagging through the throngs, we arrived at the visitor's center, already closed. Working off their accommodations list, we must have called twenty local *privat zimmers* before giving up in frustration. All were filled, so we were forced to continue—maybe as far as Krems, an impossible distance.

For another hour, we dragged through small villages, past one "*complet*" sign after another, until fate delivered us to a *gasthaus* and a sympathetic ear. The owner, a tall, attractive redhead, took pity on our plight. Pulling out her dog-eared address book, she called all her friends with *zimmers*, proba-

bly close to a dozen, before finding us a room back in Oberloiben. Then
our "angel" for the day insisted we hop into her shiny, white BMW so she
could drive us the two kilometers back to the village we'd passed thirty
minutes earlier.

After walking nearly forty kilometers, we were exhausted, but famished
nonetheless. So after checking in, we hobbled on tender feet over to the
local *Heuriger*, an Austrian phenomenon I'd discovered on earlier visits.
They typically serve only their own new wine from their vineyards, along
with a simple buffet or menu of cold meats, sausages or *schnitzel*, cheese
and breads. They're only open at certain times of the year, announced by a
sprig of pine bough hung over their outside gates.

That evening, we entered a terrace awash with picnic tables and a full
house of appreciative diners. Eventually, we found a vacant table where we
ordered a smooth, fruity bottle of their white Veltliner wine, a platter of
cold cuts and Gorgonzola cheese blended with butter into a spread similar
to Liptauer. Soon we were joined by a Czech couple living on their own
island in Montenegro, a nation that had separated only the day before from
Serbia. For a while, we tried speaking in a *ratatouille* of four languages, English, French, Czech and German, until settling on French. Of course, I was
surprised and at first flattered when our attractive dinner companion
cooed, "I can understand your French easier than Émile's."

"Yes," I chuckled, "but that's because you and I are alike. We both speak
simple French very slowly—and very badly."

Hope does float. We awoke to sun and it was never more welcome.
Vienna awaited only two short days away and reaching it would be another
benchmark. Beyond there lay not "dragons," as those Old World maps
once claimed, but the "East." Vienna, center of the once powerful Haps-
burg Empire, was the crossroads of civilizations. It was also where all the
rules changed for us, as well as the food, customs and languages. Maybe the
"going" would get a little tougher, but I, for one, was ready for the more
exotic and eager to push the envelope.

We set off alone through Wachau vineyards, warmly aglow in the early
morning sun. The incessant bicyclists who'd swarmed us the past few days
were absent, as everyone headed home after a long holiday. Life on the trail
could now return to normal—and hopefully we wouldn't run out of rooms
again. That evening, we'd originally planned on staying in Altenwörth, a
small village on the Donau, but when we reached the turnoff by the hydro-

electric dam, we were dismayed to read their community directory. There was only one *privat zimmer* in the village.

After our last debacle, I suggested, "Maybe we should continue on to Zwentendorf? It's supposed to have more rooms, instead of walking a few kilometers out of our way only to discover Altenwörth's inn is *complet*."

But Émile was already dragging and adamant about stopping soon, so I reluctantly followed his lead. As it happened, we never had the chance to find out if there were rooms or not. The river had flooded over the road. It was far too deep to cross. So we were forced to backtrack and head across the dam anyway. By then, it was raining again off and on, so we were nagged by our quick-change routine in and out of raingear while trudging in the rain along the Donau. Finally, near Zwentendorf, again our route was covered with water, but we forded across anyway and emptied our shoes of water (and carp) on the opposite shore.

Then spotting another village information board with the *pensionens* listed, we called the first twenty on the list until we found one with an available room. Luck was with us. We found the apartment with no trouble and our kind hosts met us in the courtyard. Our room was spacious with a kitchen and a steaming hot shower to soak pilgrims' bones. Plus, they even brought over a space heater to dry our soaked clothing and boots.

When I asked our host the price, at first, the professorial-looking fellow in his starched white shirt and oval glasses quoted, "Twenty euros each."

That was more than usual.

"Oh… You see, we're pilgrims walking to Jerusalem," I explained.

After listening to my abbreviated story of our journey, he suggested, "Well, in that case, we have a special pilgrims' price of just fifteen euros. My wife and I have been to Jerusalem twice—although we've never walked there like you," he added, with an understanding smile.

It always amazed me how little it took to make you grateful when you're walking a trail: a little sunshine, dry clothes, a good night's sleep and a civilized breakfast. Furthermore, in the morning, without any prompting, our hosts decided to reduce the cost of our room again to just ten euros each—about the cost of our laundry and breakfast.

It was an easy walk along the river to the pleasant city of Tulln. Once a Roman equestrian camp, "Comagenis" was located there in the first to fourth centuries A.D. Today, that period is fondly remembered with a statue of Roman Emperor Marcus Aurelius on horseback overlooking the

Donau, along with a remaining Roman tower and walls. We, too, would soon be entering Vienna, but without the aid of horses—or legionnaires.

Once again, I made it a point to walk far ahead of my companion, as he'd resumed his broken teakettle whistling. I tried to ignore it and remain patient, but Émile was certainly no Zamfir, Prince of the Pan Flute. When you were trying to find some peace on the trail, his whistle was a pesky mosquito serenading in your ears.

Before long, we arrived in Greifenstein, just outside of Vienna. The first *pensionen* was full, but its owner called the other and we waited for two hours perched on her porch for her to return. Apparently, she'd told us that we could use the room upstairs, but I wasn't comfortable about letting myself into a stranger's home, especially one with a bucket-sized dog dish in the front yard.

Once the owner arrived, we were relieved to find our room was elegant in the stately old home, even if our host was unusually curt. When I told her that we were walking for peace, the ruddy matron dismissed us with an ingratiating "Oh, poor thing," look in her eyes, chortling, "Peace is not possible." She was the first person we'd met who'd been so openly pessimistic.

"Why?" I wondered.

"Because there is not enough land to go around."

That seemed like an odd reply coming from one woman living alone in a twenty-room manor. So I countered, "There appears to be plenty of space to go around—even in your own country."

Walking through the Austrian countryside for the past ten days, sometimes we hadn't seen a house or a soul for hours. No, it seemed the problem was having three percent of the world controlling ninety-seven percent of the globe's resources, and you didn't have to go as far as Africa or Asia to see the dire consequences. It was evident in our own backyard where the standard of living slipped every year for the Middle Class. People worked longer hours and more days for less money. Many watched helplessly as their jobs were outsourced to countries with cheaper labor costs. Pension funds and Social Security were on the skids. Many workers' children were raised by television, since parents were seldom at home. Those who continued on to college found themselves tens-of-thousands of dollars in debt when they finished—and still had no guarantee of a decent job. Of course, they could have part of their debt forgiven by the government. All they had to do was enlist in the military.

Breakfast was rushed and awkward at the villa, as our sad hostess was pre-occupied. As much as her gloomy outlook had repulsed me the night before, all I could feel was pity for her. Her once grand home was tragic and cheerless. Although it had recently been renovated, mere cosmetics didn't make it a happy home. It epitomized the "grief" in Greifenstein.

All morning, we followed the *radweg* beside the Donau, as we drew nearer the metropolis looming large on the horizon. For me, it was a return visit, as I'd spent weeks in Vienna before and it never ceased to impress me with some new treasure. Émile was a newcomer and I looked forward to sharing one of my favorite cities with him. Fortunately, while planning our odyssey, he'd contacted his sister, a nun with a religious order in St. Petersburg, who'd made arrangements for us to stay in their Viennese convent.

When we finally arrived at their doorstep, Elizabeth, Maria and Hermine, the three sisters, greeted us with an outpouring of love and attention, eager to hear all about our journey. As one might expect, they had a superb lunch prepared and helped us plan our four-day break, the first major stop we'd made since leaving Dijon six weeks earlier. Unlike your typical visitor to the once-center of the Habsburg Empire, our stay would be a mixture of practical necessities (doing laundry, finding maps of Hungary, catching up on correspondence), as well as experiencing the best Vienna could offer pilgrims on a modest budget.

We began our exploration downtown in the Old Quarter and St. Stephen's Dom, a Gothic/Romanesque jewel at the heart of the fifth century B.C. city. Surrounded by beautiful Baroque façade buildings and horse-drawn carriages plying cobblestone streets, it was a step back into more elegant times. For us, after so many days on the trail in the rain, the vast cathedral provided quiet respite and an opportunity to thank God for the people and abundance we'd experienced so far on our journey.

Afterward, Émile and I sauntered over to the nearby *Zwölf-Apostelkeller*, or Twelve Apostles Keller, an equally authentic slice of Vienna from a bygone era. We entered the classic wine tavern off the street and down two sets of stairs into a cavernous stone room. It looked like a medieval movie set with vaulted ceilings and stout wooden tables. Although its walls dated back to 1561, its delicious Austrian fare was fresh.

We wasted no time in ordering a small pitcher of white Müller Thurgau wine and a *schnitzel* to celebrate our arrival, while a gypsy violist passed from table to table, serenading diners for tips. An old French proverb says, "In water, one sees one's own face...but in wine, one beholds the heart of an other." Well, after a couple glasses of wine, Émile and I bared ours and began a frank discussion about our trip so far. A few important issues had simmered on the back burner, and I felt it was best to clear the air. His "style" of traveling was much different than I'd expected, especially since we'd walked together on the Camino six years earlier. Since he'd only lightly planned so much of our journey in advance, I'd been forced into a "take-charge" mode, so opposite of Émile's "*laissez-faire*" mind-set. Frankly, it was beginning to bother me. The more I did, the less he offered.

"Your "relaxed" way of traveling is only possible because I end up making most of the decisions," I began, as delicately as possible. "I read the menus and translate, negotiate our room, read the maps (when we have them), ask directions, and always take the lead on the trail."

"So?" he replied, with a carefree facial shrug.

"So? I'm not your tour guide," I gently reminded him. "We're partners on this and we have to share the responsibilities. For example, you studied German in school for six years, yet I always have to use my broken German to communicate for us both."

"*Je suis désolé.* I am sorry, but I don't remember any of it."

"Nothing? Is it fair for me every day to have to translate English to German, then German back into French for you to understand?" After thirty days in German-speaking countries, he still couldn't even order a drink or request a room.

"Look, we're soon entering Hungary, Serbia, Bulgaria, and then Turkey where neither of us speak or read the language. Bulgaria even uses a different alphabet. So you can't rely on me anymore as a translator. We need to work together to figure this out."

He nodded hesitantly. "Is there…anything else?" he cautiously asked.

"Well, now that you mention it…there's your whistling," I laughed. "You half-whistle that military march every morning, over and over for hours."

"It bothers you?"

"Why do you think I speed up each time you begin? I like to meditate in the morning. I find it impossible with "mosquitoes" buzzing in my ears."

"Sorry. I realized that today when you walked so fast. Why didn't you tell me sooner?"

"Because you're my friend, a fellow pilgrim. I respect you and want both of us to reach Jerusalem. So, I've tried to be tolerant of our differences."

Did he understand? Or was I just making a fool of myself—while destroying our friendship? Still, I was convinced that it needed to be said.

"Émile, we need to work together as a team. Right now, when you're hungry, we eat. When you want mineral water, we search for *agua con gaz*. When you're tired, we stop. It's always about Émile."

He quizzically stared. I couldn't tell if my French was good enough for him to understand, so I added, "*C'est toujours Émile*. It's always Émile."

He sat there silently, offering nothing in the way of an explanation or defense. Pouting, he gazed deep into his wine glass.

"Also, I'm worried about you, about us, our safety," I explained. "I have to remind you to close and lock our hotel room door at night. Wear your money pouch inside your shirt, not outside for everyone to see—especially in the metro like you did today. And look and listen for traffic before crossing the street."

I couldn't believe I was having that conversation with an otherwise intelligent human being. And I was sorry to have to bring it up, since I loved Émile like a brother. But it needed to be said, especially since he was almost struck by a car again that afternoon while jaywalking across a busy street. When the driver slammed on his brakes, blaring his horn, my friend made some odd, King Tut-like, stiff wrist-locked wave, as if that'd stop the oncoming BMW.

"This is not Dijon," I reminded him in earnest. "You have to be more diligent—if we're ever going to reach Jerusalem alive."

There I'd said it. Who knew what travel across Asia and the Middle East would bring? But one thing was for certain—it would be challenging in ways we could only begin to fathom.

In the morning, our so-called "rest day" began with a quick visit to the Freytag & Berndt travel shop. I'd long been impressed with their books, maps and supplies on past expeditions and again they didn't let me down. We were relieved to find a Hungarian bicycling guide with extensive maps, as well as a more detailed map of Bulgaria. I still planned on contacting the cycling club in Budapest, but with that necessity checked off our list, Émile and I began our self-guided walking tour of Vienna's Old City.

It was a feast inviting excess, but we enjoyed the over-indulgence. We began at the stately Hofburg Imperial Palace that extended from its original magnificent residence to include the National Library, Imperial Treasury, and the famous Spanish Riding School. Its Medieval Chapel was home to the famous Vienna Boys Choir. Then we wandered through the nearby

Franciscan Minoritenkirch and the flowers of the Volksgarten, before catching the clean and efficient Viennese metro to Prater Park with its world-famous Giant Ferris Wheel (Reisenrad) on the outskirts of town.

Since our subway car was crowded, I was particularly wary. During the first time Cheryl and I had visited Paris, we sat awe-struck on the metro when a band of gypsy girls no older than seven targeted an older, refined Frenchman. As one of them opened a newspaper in front of his face, the others dove for his topcoat, pants and jacket pockets, robbing him blind in about 4.5 seconds, and then scampered through the subway doors just before they slammed shut.

That day in Vienna, I had a close call of my own. As we stood in the center aisle, hanging onto the ceiling strap, I felt an ever-so-slight twitch on my shorts' pocket. Instinctively, I moved my fingers down my side—just in time to watch a tiny hand pull away. Did they get anything? As I checked the contents of my pocket, our car pulled to a silent stop and the pickpocketing urchin easily slid through the door and vanished into the crowd.

'Yea, this isn't Dijon. I guess we must look like visitors even without our backpacks, but this is unsettling. Of course, with the crowds today, we should have expected it. Note to self: Always wear long pants with many small, tight pockets in the subway from now on.'

Nevertheless, the Prater was just as amazing as I remembered. After morphing from hunting grounds to a public park in 1766, it went on to host a World Exposition. Nowadays, it offered a museum, planetarium, stadium, swimming pool, dozens of rides, food booths, and miles of trails and gardens shaded by massive horse chestnut trees. Plus, its two hundred foot high Ferris wheel, dating back to 1897, was still a marvel.

Afterward, we headed back into *zentrum*, relying on my stomach's "muscle memory" to find a *Heuriger* I'd visited more than ten years earlier. I was shocked to actually to find it again, but disappointed it didn't open until the day we were scheduled to leave. So instead, we headed to another next door that paled in comparison; no trellised grape vines overhead, no wine maidens in low-cut Trachten wear, no *gemütlichkeit*, and no roaming minstrels. However, their spinach and feta strudels with sour cream and garlic sauce melted on your tongue. Best of all, after the night before, our conversation was amiable. We'd cleared the air. Our friendship would survive.

The next morning, breakfast conversation with the Sisters centered on visiting opulent Schönbrunn Palace. With the weather clear and warm for a change, I decided to catch the next metro to the outskirts of town by myself.

The Palace had a long and colorful history beginning in the Middle Ages, but its golden age began with Empress Maria Teresa. Nowadays, with its gardens, statues, fountains and zoos, it was one of the most important cultural monuments in Austria. Since I'd toured it on my first visit to Vienna, I was content to just wander its acres of gardens and Grand Parterre, and then climb its hillside past the Neptune Fountain with the half-man, half-fish Tritons and nymphs to the Gloriette, a triumphal arch overlooking the palace and grounds.

On the other hand, beauty, history and art aside, one of my main objectives was to find another sauna and reinvigorate my body—and not to leave the addictive city more tired than I'd arrived. So, after asking around, I discovered where the locals went to relax and sweat: the Kurzentrum Oberlaa and its therapeutic spas. It was a long ride all the way to the end of the bus route, but well worth it. I was immediately impressed. It wasn't like the "hot" spot spas I'd indulged in on earlier visits to Eastern Europe. No, it was a full health and fitness center with medical staff, thermal pools, saunas, swimming pools and everything necessary to soothe away the aches of a modern *peregrino*. It was easy to check into the facility for a few hours, and the staff was helpful in pointing me in the right direction. At fifteen euros, it was well worth the splurge.

My session began with the locker room, normally pretty self-explanatory, right? Well, theirs' featured rows of look-alike changing cabins in the center, after which you searched for a locker. No problem, so far. However, after I closed the locker door, I was stymied. Nothing seemed to lock it, until I figured out you had to swipe your wristband across a scanner built right into the door.

Next, I headed directly to the showers and then the aromatic chamomile sauna. I opened its glass door and a blast of sizzling, scented air hit me with such force that it took my breath away. It was clearly not Grandma's chamomile tea. Gingerly edging my way into the white fog, I found an empty space on the bottom row of wooden bleachers. As my eyes adjusted to the vapor and subdued lighting, I found myself surrounded by fifteen portly, porcelain, elderly Viennese fellows, each wrapped in sweat and vapor. Identical white towels protected their flabby backsides from searing wooden planks, hot enough to burst into flame.

'So far, so good,' I thought. 'I can handle this. Besides, I'll feel so much better when we hit the trail again in two days.'

Before long, one red-faced, chubby fellow walked over to the corner and methodically poured a ladle of cold water from a nearby bucket onto the scarlet coals. Rather than cooling them off, of course, that caused a blanket of mist to flood the sweatbox. Pleased, the sadist gleefully stripped the towel from around his waist, and naked, began vigorously fanning the steam up and down like a boxer's trainer in the corner at a prizefight. As the temperature soared another twenty degrees within as many seconds, the crowd of sweating *weissewurst* burst into applause.

I gasped, ducked my head, and thought cool thoughts: days on the Arctic tundra, rolling in snow, camping at Mt. Everest. Whatever worked.

As I began to regain consciousness, I heard a soft murmur in my ear. Half-turning my head to better focus on the source of the voice just a foot away, I saw an older, white-haired gentleman. He looked like a kindly television family doctor, so I nodded a cordial "Hello."

He smiled and then conspiratorially whispered, "*Ich habe ein grosses…*"

"Huh?" I replied, only half-hearing, waiting for subtitles to appear.

"*Ich habe ein grosses Member.*"

With far from perfect German, I slowly translated it in my mind. "*Ich habe*" is "I have." "*Ein grosses?*" "A big?"

'Ah, no,' I sighed, as his pick-up line sunk in. 'Austria's Dr. Welby has just hit on me. What do I say? "Maybe you should see a doctor about that?"' Witty comebacks are in short supply when you're not fluent in a language. Instead, chuckling at the incongruity of it all, I said in my best Amer-i-can accent, "Sorry, I don't speak German," and left for cooler climes.

The next morning, after a leisurely breakfast with the Sisters, I caught up on my correspondence. One email from a Muslim friend had me particularly concerned. She'd warned that things were heating up again in the Middle East with the recent death of Zacharias Mousawi, the wanted terrorist. In response, Hezbollah was firing missiles at Israel from Syria.

Although I appreciated her heads-up, I was reminded how necessary it is to improvise in life. There are obviously many things outside of our control, and international relations fall under that category. Of course, I was concerned, but it was too soon to make any radical changes. Still, I promised myself (and my ever-worried wife) I'd take a clear look at our options once we reached Istanbul. That was a few months away and so much could happen—one way or the other—in the meantime.

To take my mind off events I couldn't possibly change, I returned to the center of the city to visit Vienna's House of Music and its interesting presentation of memorabilia from the lives of Beethoven, Mozart, Strauss, Schubert, Haydn, Mahler and other Austrian and German native sons. However, its hands-on rooms appealed more. There was an electronic section where you could create music by moving different parts of your body. I especially got the bass line moving. Then there was an interactive video where you "virtually" directed an orchestra. The musicians played to the beat of your baton. If you made them play too fast, they'd quit and make rude remarks. However, if you conducted them at just the right pace, they completed the movement to wild applause.

Afterward, I wandered through another tranquil green space named the Stadtpark. As I meandered its neatly lined pathways past manicured gardens, elegant statues and a lake awash with ducks, I marveled at all I'd seen the past few days in the city: the art and culture, history, music, intelligent design, and more than a fair share of beautiful people. Why couldn't we design such a city? Why did we sacrifice refinement for size, whether it was our cars, our houses, our bodies, or our appetites?

Vienna was a scrumptious torte. You savor a few small bites at a time and let its flavor linger on your tongue, while saving the rest for another meal.

That evening, returning to Heiligenstadt Station, I had a brief conversation with a Tunisian who ran the *shawarma* fast-food stand. I was curious about how he ended up in Vienna and eager to chat about our journey. At first, he was open to talking—until he learned my nationality. Walls instantly went up and our conversation cooled. He didn't speak again until I pointed out that more than half of my countrymen disagreed with the War in Iraq and thought we should withdraw.

"As in your country, not everyone agrees with their leaders."

As he nodded, I wondered aloud if my belief that all people want the same things in life—especially peace—held true for Muslim families as well.

"Yes," he admitted, after thoughtful consideration. "It's true for men all over the world. It's only the politicians and radicals on both sides who get in the way with their own agendas."

As I turned to leave, the simple man wished me a safe journey and asked me to tell Westerners when I returned home what I saw and experienced in the Islamic world. I promised I would and left him with the only Arabic phrase I knew.

"*Salaam alaykum.*" ("Peace be upon you.")

"*Wa alaykum as-salaam*" ("And peace be upon you"), he replied with a smile.

Maybe that was destined to be another added goal for our journey—dispelling prejudices between cultures and religions—one person at a time.

While most of the city still slumbered, we left the convent heading east to the Donau Canal. At last, we could once again wear our pilgrim capes and leave our visitor personae behind. It was a lovely morning as we passed joggers and singles walking their dogs in the cool morning air. Mutts were muzzled and well behaved, as they plowed the ground with their noses looking for old friends or new rivals. On one of the first sunny days of the season, older folks had already staked out their benches for the day, and other sun-starved Weiners lay sprawled in the grass.

Tracing the water, we skirted *zentrum*, passing the incredible Hundert-wasser-designed water tower that looked like an elegant gold-knobbed walking staff. Not far out of town, the *radweg* widened and we began to pass restaurants, nightclubs and bars on the distant shore and encounter scores of bicyclists, roller bladers, and a few elderly walkers, but no other hardcore backpackers. We were alone in our quest. As I reveled in the welcome rays of the sun, we came across a traditional Buddhist *stupa*, the Vienna Peace Pagoda. Dropping into its office, we picked up a brochure announcing its anniversary celebration. Although no one was there, we found auspicious words of encouragement in their brochure:

> "True peace is brought about when man pledges himself never to take the lives of others and abandons the idea of killing. This teaching must now be disseminated throughout the world. It is not difficult. If humanity hopes to survive, we have only to resolve not to kill others. It is false to talk of peace while possessing weapons destined to take life."
> ~ The Most Venerable Nichidatsu Fujii
> Founder of Nipponzan Myohoji

Before long, we entered a park surrounding the Donauinsel, a twenty-one kilometer long manmade island dividing the Donau and part of the river's flood control measures. Passing the Copa Kagrana, a narrow beach, all of a sudden, we felt over-dressed. Our path entered the FKK or *Freikör-perkultur*, a "clothes-free" zone. The popular nude beach continued for several miles along both sides of the canal with couples sprawled naked on pontoon platforms, or lying nonchalantly like seals on rocks. There was no rich or poor, and bad attitudes were shed along with inhibitions. Far from sexual, it was an exercise in liberation. I marveled at the way we were approached by matching pink 500-pound nude couples, smiling as they waddled past. Nudity was the great equalizer. (Although some folks might insist, "Some are more equal than others.")

Even though we'd walked for four hours, more than twenty kilometers at that point, we were shocked to discover we were still in Vienna. Not surprisingly, with all the visual distractions, we missed an unmarked detour and had to backtrack several kilometers to catch our trail through the midst of a chemical complex. And once again, we learned to be very careful what you wish for.

In the long-awaited sunshine, we were slowly sapped of energy and forced to collapse in the grass for a few minutes—until swarms of relentless mosquitoes made us continue. Schönau, our destination, was a mirage. We spotted a sign telling us it was "3 Km.," then passed identical "3 Km." markings several more times over the next six kilometers. It was late afternoon by the time we finally arrived in the village and found what might have been its only *gasthaus*. Luck was with us.

In the morning, it was a long, straight path to Hainburg through the Donau-Auen National Park. On Europe's last, large undeveloped floodplain, the river continued to shape and define life among a wide diversity of plants and animals as it had for centuries. We were alone—with (according to its signage), "700 species of vascular plants, 30 mammal and 100 breeding bird species, 8 reptile and 13 amphibian species and 50 types of fish."

No wonder the woods were so noisy.

Still, for a long time, we were the only humans walking that trail atop a soil levee built to hold back the mighty Danube. We'd briefly glimpse deer or a solitary heron in the midst of his breakfast. Otherwise, no more than a dozen bicyclists passed all day. The trail was so straight and flat you could walk it blindfolded and backward. Although it was a National Park, our new challenge was to ration water, since there were no villages, toilets or cafés to be seen.

To top it off, Émile was out of sorts. He'd lost his cell phone and acted like a teenager going through withdrawal. Sure, I knew it was his lifeline to the outside world. Personally though, I thought of it as a modern intrusion I'd happily do without on the trail, especially when it'd ring and he'd stop to chat awhile.

After a long day, we finally stumbled into the pleasant Hainburg and quickly found a *privat zimmer*, where a robust, middle-aged blonde welcomed us inside.

"Our house is oldest in the area, built in the 1930s and home to four generations," she bragged. "There," she said, pointing to a spot on the wall two meters high, "you can see where the river rose earlier this year."

After showering, Émile set off to find a phone booth to call the Sisters back in Vienna. Yes, they'd found his cell phone. He'd left it there after all. So after we reached Bratislava the next afternoon, he'd hop the train back to retrieve it. Meanwhile, I'd have time to explore the historic city on my own. Only twenty kilometers separated us from the unknown challenges of Eastern Europe.

At first light, we enjoyed our last and best Austrian breakfast, and then followed the Donau to Wolfsthal, the final village before entering Slovakia. As we neared the border, I didn't know quite what to expect. Would there be a series of checkpoints with endless demands to see our "papers"? Or, would we be allowed to waltz right on through—no muss, no fuss?

The mystery was soon solved. First, we passed two Austrian sentries and then another two in uniform as we crossed an open field through what must have been, not so long ago, a no-man's land separating Europe from the communist "hordes." Next, we suddenly came across a tent pitched in the woods, and then we nearly tripped over two more camouflaged soldiers hunkered down in weeds along the *radweg*. Then, we passed another group of soldiers in a parked truck carefully studying cars approaching Austria. Finally, there was another pair at the border post that sent us off the trail, forcing us to walk in the long queue of waiting cars. After all those lines of defense, I still didn't know what to expect from the officials.

"Smile, Émile," I suggested, as we approached.

Much to my surprise, the young female border officer motioned us right on through, not even asking for our passports. That took care of Austria. Fifty yards ahead, we braced ourselves for the same exercise. However, the Slovakian border officials just gave our passports a cursory glance and waved us on.

From there, it was a straight shot on concrete into Bratislava. Its castle-dominated location on the banks of the Donau predestined it to become a meeting point of Celts, Romans and Slavs. Once known as Pressburg, it was one of the most important cities in the Austro-Hungarian Empire and capital of the Kingdom of Hungary for nearly three hundred years beginning in 1536. Queen Maria Theresa and ten kings had all been crowned in its St. Martin's Cathedral.

We were scheduled to meet Émile's friend Balint and stay at his house, but soon discovered we had the wrong cell phone number. The best we could do was leave messages on his home phone and hope he checked.

As you might imagine, by the time we traversed a final bridge across the Donau into Bratislava's *zentrum*, our stress level had begun to climb. I attempted to call Balint again from the ritzy Carlton Hotel, but was unable without a phone card. However, the desk clerk confirmed the phone number we had was no good. In desperation, I left another message on his home phone.

While waiting for his call, we drowned our insecurities in Chinese food. By then, it was raining. Slogging back to the Carlton, we attempted to call our host again and I was finally able to reach his assistant who gave us the correct mobile phone number. Finally, the three of us managed to meet for a coffee. As luck would have it, Balint was headed to Prague on business.

"So, what can I do for you?" he innocently asked.

We were a little surprised, since we'd spoken with him a week earlier about staying at his place. Whether it was our appearance and undeniable road aroma, or simply the fact he was heading out of town, we'd never know. Still, he graciously called his assistant who booked us into a nearby businessman's high-rise.

When I first laid eyes on my room, I had to laugh out loud. Only half in jest, I kept looking for two-way mirrors with hidden cameras. There was the "road-kill" carpet, the bed was a pad on top of a thicker pad within a corduroy frame, a "ghetto blaster" with no rhythm, and windows last cleaned during Lenin's time. Yet we each had our own rooms and much appreciated privacy, so I was especially pleased with his bigheartedness.

The following morning, while Émile returned to Vienna, I combined a little business with pleasure. Grabbing my new Olympus camera, I headed into town with the idea of shooting "a day in the life" portrait of the historic city. Cheryl and I had gone on similar missions in places like Nice, France, where we photographed interesting people, attractions and oddities we came across when seeing a place with fresh eyes. In Bratislava, a refreshing city, I was encouraged to spot many changes since the communists had packed their hammers and sickles and returned home. Storefronts were freshly painted and long-neglected churches were undergoing renovation. There were beautiful public sculptures and art, street performers and parks. Plus, the people were well dressed—and the women were remarkably as gorgeous as their Viennese cousins.

Part of my itinerary revolved around our never-ending quest for Serbian and Bulgarian maps. Since we were now in Eastern Europe, I figured they might be easier to find. Well, not quite. At the first bookshop, they suggested I look in the major shopping complex across the river. So again, I wandered across the vast Donau and had no trouble locating AuPark mall with its dozens of stores. Packed with throngs of happy shoppers, it could have been in an upscale neighborhood at home. Although the bookstore still didn't have the maps, I took the opportunity to talk with one of their clerks, Michael, and his manager about our journey and message of peace.

I was impressed with their ability to speak such good English, although it was said in the old days that a true "Pressburgian" spoke four languages: Slovak, German, Hungarian and Mishmash. They'd say two words in Slovak, two in German, and two in Hungarian—all one sentence. Now, they'd added another language. I could hardly imagine a Slovak coming to our country and finding a store clerk who could communicate with them in their own language, so I couldn't resist asking Michael, "How'd you learn to speak English so well?"

"Oh, from reading books in English," he replied with a bashful grin, "and watching CNN on television."

Ironically, how many future immigrants were learning English courtesy of Lou Dobbs?

Late that afternoon, after walking back across the vast pedestrian bridge, I stumbled onto a free concert in front of the American Embassy. There was a ten-piece "big band" dressed in tuxes and female singers in flapper-era gowns, playing songs from the 1920s and 30s and singing in Slovak and English. The crowd loved it and swayed to the music, while clowns on stilts, mimes, and human "statues" busked for tips. Sure, they still had those quaint, creaky trolley cars, but I was surprised to find lovely Bratislava was vibrant and quickly developing. I could just imagine what an influx of capital would do for its infrastructure.

Still, the more I saw, the more I had to shake my head and wonder. Where was our own national budget being spent? Why did the standard of living in all the countries I'd crossed so far look as good or better than our own? More than that, I'd seen more laughing and contented faces—which ultimately said much more about the quality of life than the size of any shopping bag.

PEST

ZENTMARTON

HUNGARY

LDVAR

ROMANIA

SERBIA

CHAPTER FIVE
Hungary

On the Trail of "Treep"

"Go my sons, burn your books. Buy yourself stout shoes. Get away to the mountains, the deserts and the deepest recesses of the earth. In this way and no other will you gain a true knowledge of things and of their properties."
~ Seter Severinus

After a hearty breakfast buffet at the hotel, we made our way back across the bridge with its well-designed pedestrian level, and followed it east with "*La soleil dans les yeux,*" or "The sun in the eyes," as we'd done in the past. It wasn't nearly as well marked as the *radweg* leaving Wien, but we were out of the city in a mere four hours. Once it connected to a roller-blade highway, toned and tan Slovak beauties passed us all morning. Within a few hours we reached the turn-off for the border and walked right down the center of the road, as few Slovakians had any reason to head to Hungary.

The border official only took a perfunctory glance at our passports before stamping us through, as if people walked through in the car lane all the time. No visas were needed, unlike the last few times I'd visited. After exchanging the last of our Slovak crowns, we caught the bicycle path through a shabby wasteland into the hamlet of Rajka.

Although Émile was already eager to call it a day, I was keen to press on since it was already eighty degrees and even hotter on the asphalt. It took us another two hours of walking on country roads to finally reach Dunakiliti. It was a small village and we stopped at the only "*zimmer frei*" ("free room") sign posted in German we'd spotted since leaving Bratislava.

Calling out to the shifty-looking owner with slick black hair and pencil thin mustache, I asked, "How much for a room for two people, one night?"

He looked us over from head to toe before asking, "Where are you from?"

Some things never change. When Cheryl and I first visited Eastern Europe, it was the first question out of someone's mouth, especially at a guesthouse or restaurant. On one occasion, we visited pristine Lake Bled in the Julian Alps, in what was then Yugoslavia. Wanting to rent a rowboat to cross to the island in the middle of the lake, I innocently asked the boat keeper, "How much?"

He, too, looked us over, until his eyes settled on our shoes. Then he asked the ever-popular question, "Where are you from?"

"Why? Do you have a special price for us?"

"Of course," he admitted in his thick accent. "There is one price for locals, one for East Europeans, one for Russians, one for English, one for Germans and one for Americans," he announced, working his way up what he figured was the affluence chain. Looking at our shoes was one way to tell how much to charge.

Nowadays, it was just irritating. This sliding scale assumed everyone was traveling on a super-sized budget and not a *peregrino's* pittance, as we were. So I explained to the innkeeper, "We're pilgrims from France and Hawaii, walking to Jerusalem."

That stumped him, but just for a second, as he recalled my island's location, and then factored in any sort of pilgrim discount.

"In euros, dollars or forints?" he asked.

"Forints. We're in Hungary, aren't we?"

"Four thousand each, with breakfast," he began.

I'd played that game all too often and countered, "Three thousand each seems more fair."

"Okay, okay," he sighed with an easy smile, and then he showed us to a basement room with bars on the windows. Its king-sized bed was a '63 Pontiac of Posturepedics; a unique relic with speakers built into the headboard and a non-working radio in the middle. Initially, I was reluctant to share a bed with my friend, since we already spent too much time together day after day. But before I could suggest another room, Émile had already thrown down his pack with finality and flopped onto the chenille bedspread. After all, the room did have a television set. Émile, as well as the rest of the civilized world, was glued to the tube each night for the World Cup soccer games.

After cleaning up, we wandered over to a small café where we ordered hamburgers. All went smoothly until our bill came, and my past experience with East European waiters told me to check our tab. Sure enough, I found our waitress had overcharged for our drinks. Of course, after I pointed it out, she feigned surprise and corrected it—but it was such a change from Austria where those things never seemed to happen. Then again, for everyone who made us check our fingers after paying a bill, there was another "angel" waiting in the wings.

That night, I met one at the village's library. She was an eager and charming girl who, after learning about our pilgrimage, spent an hour teaching me key phrases in Hungarian, bound to help smooth our journey ahead. Magyar was one of the most difficult languages I'd ever tried to learn. Some say it traces its roots back to Finnish-Ugric origins. I just fig-ured it'd be helpful to know how to say:

"Hello. How are you?"

"*Szia. Hogy van?*"

"Thank you very much."

"*Köszönöm szépen.*"

"How many forints for a double room?"

"*Mennyibe kerül egy kétszemélyes szoba?*"

"Please pass the goulash."

"*Kérem szépen a gulyás levest.*"

Maybe I should've also learned: "I'm American, but I haven't fallen on my head. Don't try to cheat me."

"*Amerikai vagyok, de nem estem a fejemre. Ne próbáljon becsapni.*"

Although yesterday's sun did a good job of sapping the energy from Émile and me, before we knew it, we were walking again in the early morn-ing haze. There was a welcome solitude on Hungary's roads and only the infrequent car passed, or a tractor-driving farmer who'd nod and flash a smile once I did the same. At one point, we were relieved to find a bicycle path along a still tributary of the Danube, or Duna as it was called there. It led us up onto a dirt levee, as it had in Austria. However, we soon learned it wasn't a wise trade-off, since walking on the deep gravel took twice as much energy, and the insects made it impossible to stop for even the shortest rest. Once we came upon a lone shepherd and his flock and thought we'd stop and, if nothing else, compare walking staffs. Within twenty seconds, mosquitoes blanketed us like that old television commercial where the man knowingly stuck his arm into a box of bloodsuckers—except we'd forgotten our "new, improved" protective spray.

It was nearly eighty degrees by late morning when we searched in vain for a restaurant. Bars, yes. But restaurants were as hard to find as duck's teeth until we reached Lipót. It was easier to find a room there. We again paid three thousand forints, and I was now convinced that was the going rate in Hungary, since our kind hostess was also a *peregrina* who'd walked the Camino.

While sitting in the family's restaurant, waiting to sign the register, Émile and I suddenly realized the reason we'd recently seen less wildlife. The lime green walls were covered with nearly a dozen wild boar, goat, and small deer heads. There was even a black bear in a ferocious pose, lurking in the corner. As we savored the atmosphere of that forest mausoleum, he and I briefly discussed the increasing heat and our progress. As much as I preferred to set off at a more civilized hour, we knew we'd have to start earlier to avoid trekking so long in the heat. If that meant a five o'clock reveille, so be it.

Lipót's claim to fame was its recreation center with a swimming pool, thermals, restaurant and pub, so we decided to check it out that afternoon. All of the surrounding villagers were also there for the cool waters and World Cup games. Burly, dark men with bellies hanging over microscopic nylon trunks paraded past, balancing beers in one hand and plates of fried fish and ribs in the other, as they ogled lithe eighteen-year-olds sporting dental floss-sized thongs.

People *are* the same everywhere.

At dawn, we easily found our way out of town on its one road and caught a bicycle path through fields of brilliant crimson poppies. It was already hot and steamy by 10:00 a.m. when we ducked into a café for some ice cream. As I enjoyed its coolness, my conversation with the owner soon turned to local wine. At his urging, I bought a small sample glass for thirty cents, then coaxing, "*Íz a fehér bor,*" he treated me to a thirst-quenching white wine to toast our journey.

The locals' hospitality was equally refreshing. As we continued on the trail, we were greeted by everyone who passed on foot or by bike with either a "*Morgen,*" "*Grus Gott,*" (since they thought we were Germans), a universal "Hello," or its Magyar equivalent. At the same time, passengers packed tighter than pickled peppers in a pot invariably waved as they skidded past in rumbling Skodas and tiny Trabants, ducking and weaving potholes pocking the country roads.

All along our route, the houses were sturdy and constructed of energy efficient terracotta tile block and covered with plaster or concrete to withstand the frigid winters, similar to what we'd seen in Austria. Most had small gardens and fruit trees, yet the concept of the perfectly manicured lawn thankfully hadn't caught on, so streets had a slightly disheveled appearance. Still, each yard came with its own snarling, bad-attitude German Shepherd or Hungarian Puli sheepdog hiding beneath a wild white set of Rasta-locks.

With the heat, it was mid-afternoon by the time we reached Györ, the "city of rivers," and townsfolk were in the midst of cleaning up after a Saturday market. It had been a long day and thankfully the tourist information office was still open in the fine old Baroque city. Even with our limited budget, they found us a room at the hotel across from the train station. On first sight, with its imposing carved façade, I imagined it had once been a classic monument to travel. Nowadays, it wallowed in faded glory. Our room was monastery-sized—without a prayer. A solitary window faced the church and square far below where picnic tables, concession stands and a Jumbo-tron screen were set up to broadcast the nightly World Cup. There was an open co-ed shower down the hall with no curtains and few showerheads. Plus, we'd have to make do without our traditional hearty breakfast.

'It just doesn't matter,' I kept reminding myself, 'as long as we can find a decent meal,' but even that turned out to be a challenge. After eating the world's worst burgers, we trudged back to the square to watch the match. Later that evening, Émile was anxious to return for another, which was fine with me, as I planned on studying our bicycle maps to look for a better route to Budapest. I was convinced we could save a day by heading a more direct route south off the Donau Radweg, instead of following it to Esztergom.

Before Émile left for the crowded square, however, I strongly suggested he leave his money pouch behind in our room, since he projected a certain "*Je ne sais quoi*" decked out in his leather cowboy hat and khaki shorts.

The music in the square just below our room started after the games were over at 1:30 a.m. and lasted for two hours. Then, just as I finally drifted off to sleep, Émile's alarm went off at 5:00—so I wasn't in the best of moods. Creaking open a groggy eye, I suggested, "Hey, why don't we get a few more hours sleep, especially since it's Sunday and there's no breakfast. Nothing will be open."

Émile either wouldn't hear of it—or simply didn't hear, since he often didn't wear his hearing aid first thing in the morning. So I repeated louder, "I really need to get more sleep. I was awake until midnight last night studying the maps."

But Émile was in his own world, already dressed and wolfing down an apple and cheese he'd bought. Reluctantly I pulled on my clothes, stuffed the rest in my pack, filled my water bottle and stood waiting at the door for him when he was finally ready to leave at 5:30. We descended the hotel stairs and reached the square. For once, I refused to take the lead and just waited to see what he'd do. He shot off like a rocket and then slammed to a halt, as soon as he realized he didn't know where he was—let alone where he was going.

"You never listen to me," I groaned. Was it because he chose not to pay attention—even though I was forced to speak French all the time? Or did he simply not hear much of what I said? Either way, it was more than that.

"It's always about Émile. Like I told you in Vienna, this is a team effort, yet I'm still waiting for you to take more initiative; read the maps, learn the language and pitch in."

"I am sorry," he deadpanned. I was far from convinced.

With my spleen vented, I led us down backstreets through the seedy part of Győr and into the countryside. All went smoothly, until a few hours later I missed hearing the constant clop, clop, clop of his heavy boots on the pavement behind me. Spinning around, I was shocked to see my companion sitting forlorn by the side of the road. Thinking something serious must be wrong, I rushed the fifty yards back to his side and asked, "What's the problem?"

"I don't have much water," he sighed, as he munched saltine crackers.

"Why not? We won't pass many towns today." He'd known that if he'd taken time to look at our maps. "Besides, won't those crackers only make you thirstier?"

Terror flashed in his eyes and for an instant he looked as if he wanted to cry. For all my exasperation, I felt deeply sorry for Émile. Although I admired his courage and stamina at his age and with his health conditions, I had to wonder how long he could continue at our pace and with the heat. Then again, how long could I keep picking up the slack?

Before long, as predicted, it was sweltering on the blacktop, close to ninety degrees. With our water bottles empty, we were at last relieved to spot a woman spraying her garden. She was equally surprised to see us and happy to fill our bottles from her garden hose. I figured it was much safer than the hotel's tap water, which was the color of run-off.

From there, it was a straight shot down a scorching country road. After six and a half hours, we finally reached Bábolna, a town famous for its Arabian horses, museum and stud farm. It was eerily quiet on that Sunday and everything was closed—except for the bars, of course. We stopped at a family's *panzió*, or pension, where a couple led us to a spacious room with a full kitchen, and even brought us a bottle of mineral water, cold enough to take our breath away. We were thankful we didn't have to trudge another twenty-four kilometers to the next village with a hotel. Then again, after two days of surviving on little more than micro-thin hamburgers, I was especially grateful to find a grocery where we could stock up on ingredients for a full-fledged Italian feast. With that meal and a good night's rest, the following day would look much brighter.

By sunrise, the road virtually sizzled when we veered off the Donau Radweg, following the more direct route I'd discovered to Budapest. Unfortunately, it was also at that inopportune time that Émile decided to walk on the right hand side of the road, instead of the left. Now, I could understand his need for shade, but it caused a major problem. For instance, if two Skodas coming from opposite directions reached us at the same time, the car in the left hand lane steered toward me, not wanting to hit the one on the right head-on. That forced me completely off the road and into the weeds—as Émile marched along—la-dee-da—oblivious to it all.

Despite the heat, we marched down cracked and weed-choked roads until we reached the outskirts of Tata. Cradled in a lush valley between the Gerecse and Vértes Mountains, it was once the capital of Hungary during the early 1500s. After stopping at a slip of a shop for water, we continued walking into town and weren't gone more than ten minutes when Émile suddenly remembered he'd left his walking staff behind. In a panic, he cried, "*Bourdon!*" and stormed back toward the market. Meanwhile, figuring it didn't take two of us to retrieve his stick, I found a shady spot under a tree nearby and stretched out, not knowing for certain whether he'd actually left it at the last store—or way back in Koçs.

If it were the latter, would he return to even tell me?

Well, fifteen minutes passed before I spotted Émile, still clearly upset and flushed. He couldn't find the shop. How odd. Knowing it was just down the road to the right, I led him back to the store where the shop girl had already tucked it away for safekeeping. Émile, of course, was greatly relieved to find his beloved *bourdon*, but my concerns grew.

Sure, anyone could mistakenly leave their walking stick behind—but to forget where you'd stopped just a few minutes earlier really had me worried.

A crash of thunder rattled us from our beds the next morning. It was the first we'd heard in weeks, and it reminded me of a summer Cheryl and I spent in Carolina's Lowcountry. Daily thunderstorms, powerful enough to shake our house on stilts, occurred as regular as clockwork. In both places, however, it did wonders to disperse the stifling humidity. After the storm passed, it was an easy hike out of the town along Old Lake, then up an undulating hill past the pristine Augustin Arboretum.

When we eventually stopped for water, I was finally able to find a phone booth and call Cheryl, who was convinced I was ignoring her. Even though I'd sent weekly emails, she didn't understand how difficult it was to find phone cards or a booth in which to use them. However, after several attempts and disconnections, we were able to catch up on our lives over those past few months. By the time we said our last "alohas," we were both nearly in tears. I'd missed her so much on the journey, since she was the ideal trekking partner, but work had kept her back in the islands.

Luckily, it was a short trek to Tarján. Since the next town of any size was more than twenty kilometers farther, considering the unbearable heat, we decided to split the distance. Besides, Cheryl wouldn't arrive in Budapest until the 25th, so there was no reason to arrive too early.

Our *panzió* turned out to be a real treat for Émile, since he was delighted to find tripe on their restaurant's menu. His love of honey-combed cow's stomach was an on-going joke between us, dating back to our days on the Camino together. He used to chide me for refusing to venture "whole cow" into the world of organ parts.

"You don't eat "*treep?*" he asked in amazement.

"My stomach churns at the thought."

"Tongue?"

"No, the texture makes me think I'm chewing my own. Do you eat kidneys and liver?" I asked.

"*Mais oui.* Yes, yes."

"Brains?"

"Of course! They're delicious fried in butter."

The closest I'd come was when I'd eaten sea cucumbers or *bêche de mare* and fried jellyfish at a Taiwanese wedding. A huge, fresh fish followed those delicacies, and the lady seated next to me gushed, "Do you want the eyes?"

"No, I'll pass," I said, as their vacant stare met my own.

"It's the best part!" Gleefully she plunged her chopsticks at them with unabashed delight.

Since then, many evenings I'd asked my friend if they had "*treep*" on the menu, just to watch his eyes light up. Then again, I was convinced the otherwise gentle fellow would attack any food with gusto. He once described it as the result of his childhood spent in a family with five kids in Morocco. They lived without electricity and water was toted two kilometers from a well each day. As he explained, "He who hesitated—lost."

We left the *panzió* at sunrise, strolling past the church and monument in the town square dedicated to the fallen local soldiers who'd served in World War I and its deadly sequel. Many of the names weren't Hungarian. I imagined they must have been from German families who'd emigrated there in the 1800s. I had to admire the resiliency of people who'd survived two catastrophic wars on their soil, plus fifty years of communist occupation—all in one short century. Could we handle it so well?

As we walked through rolling farmland, Émile lagged a good hundred yards behind, even though I set a relaxed pace. He had a hard time climbing hills, while I found them a refreshing break from the Donau flatlands. At least, I got to stretch a different set of muscles.

After stopping for a break in the quaint village of Gyemely, we were amazed at a rare sight as we wandered out of town. It was a quaint old cottage with a thatched straw roof, colorful window boxes planted in red geraniums, and whitewashed plaster walls. With its low doorway, I instantly thought, "Hobbit." However, we soon met the owner, a lanky fellow about my own height, who was touching up the paint outside.

"Say, I really like your house!" I exclaimed, without knowing (or really caring) if he understood.

"Thanks, it's about three hundred years old" he replied to my surprise, and he promptly invited us inside to take a closer look. Well, no sooner did we enter, than he asked, "Would you like some wine?" and he began to pull a bottle of red from the rafters.

Normally, on a hot day like that, neither of us would hesitate to take him up on his offer. Still, it was only 9:30 in the morning—and we had a long way to go if we expected to reach Zsámbek before it became too hot. So he eagerly gave us the grand tour instead.

It didn't take long, as his cottage was maybe six hundred square feet in size. But it had real character and charm, thoughtfully designed for practical comfort. There was a cozy living room with fireplace, a kitchen with a connecting workshop, and two tiny bedrooms upstairs. What impressed me most was the energy efficiency of its traditional design. There was a woodstove for heat, meter-thick walls to keep it cool on scorching summer days, and a substantial thatched roof lasting ten years or more before it needed to be replaced.

Regrettably, we couldn't stay long, but he understood. On our way out, we noticed a framed photograph of a man in uniform. It was hung beside golden-framed etchings of Hungarian heroes.

"It's my father," he proudly beamed. "He helped liberate Stalingrad in World War II."

The Battle of Stalingrad was often considered the bloodiest fight in human history with over two million casualties. The life expectancy of a Soviet soldier was less than a day. I hoped his father survived.

The rest of the morning we ducked and wove amid cars and a bevy of huge trucks barreling down the two-lane country road, and were relieved to reach Zsámbek before noon. It was our good fortune to meet a sweet woman at the mayor's office that took us under her wing. Even though she spoke no English or French, she made a few calls to her friends. Before long, we were escorted to the German Friendship House, a beautiful place with guest rooms, a kitchen and a festival hall used by local families of German origin and relatives visiting them. Its walls were lined with photographs of parades with everyone decked out in their finery, as well as three aerial Luftwaffe photos of the village from WWII. Noticing us studying them, our hostess explained in German that the Nazis used Buda as an operational center during the war. Since we were just fifty kilometers away, Zsámbek must have played a prominent role as well.

After checking into our rooms, for dinner we splurged and found a traditional restaurant specializing in wild game. It resembled a peasant cottage with tables set among antique farm implements. Baskets and wooden buckets hung from open rafters. Back when we were first in Eger, Hungary, Cheryl and I'd planned for days to celebrate my birthday with a venison dinner. However, when the big day came, we were sad to learn the wild game restaurant was closed. So after nearly a decade and a half, I finally had my plate of fresh Hungarian venison served with little fried dough balls, similar to French *bagnettes*, and Eger's acclaimed hearty red wine, *Egri Bikaver* ("Bulls Blood"), my favorite.

It wasn't "treep," but it'd certainly do in a pinch.

The air was still when we awoke. Menacing dark clouds gathered to the west, and I prayed rain might break the wall of oppressive humidity surrounding those hills. Once we dropped off the key to the Friendship House, it took us no time to arrive back in the countryside where we resumed dodging potholes and oncoming vehicles. It was certainly more dangerous, as the traffic dramatically increased, and we were relieved to reach Budakeszi, Budapest's bustling burb, late that morning.

At one point, I stopped to take a quick photograph of an interesting wall mural on a wine cave. With sweat rolling like a flash flood down my swollen, Michelin Man hands, my camera flew into the air and landed lens first in the dirt! At first, the zoom wouldn't retract, and then after I jiggled and wiggled it closed, it wouldn't open. However, there was bound to be a repair shop in Budapest—I hoped.

We easily found a room in a *panzió*, but were eager to reach the metropolis and spend a few days sightseeing with Cheryl. The cousin of Zsuzsana, my Hungarian-born friend, lived in Budapest and had already reserved rooms for us at a boat hotel or "boatel," so we had the choice of either checking-in there for our five-day visit, going to Tourinform, Hungary's tourist organization, or heading to the Budapest train station where elderly ladies used to offer their spare rooms to visitors back in the old days. We could decide all that after we arrived.

Leaving Budakeszi early the next morning, we walked though a forest parallel to the road for an hour, until we eventually spotted the distant dome of the Parliament building. From there, it was only another ninety minutes before we reached the historic Chain Bridge that spanned the Duna.

For me, it was a relief to be back in Budapest, like seeing an old friend again. So much was happening the first time we visited in the fall of 1989, with the ouster of the communist regime close at hand. In fact, the gardeners were already busy trimming the red stars facing the Parliament building into circles, and the Berlin Wall's downfall was a few short weeks away. Since then, on two subsequent visits, I'd marveled at her changes. She was like an old Hollywood film star growing better with age—with no need for Botox.

Upon reaching the historic downtown, we made a beeline to the Tourinform office on Deak tér that had been so helpful in the past, only to discover they no longer made room reservations. Instead, they referred us next door to private entrepreneurs where Beatrix, a charming and witty girl, came through with shining colors. I wanted our room to be especially nice, since Cheryl and I were celebrating our anniversary. Slightly off the river and behind the plush chain hotel, our apartment was everything we might hope for.

Entering through a huge, non-descript door off the street, we passed a beautifully tiled courtyard complete with an art deco statue, and then climbed stairs to a quiet unit offering a large living room/kitchen with a refrigerator, stove, microwave and washer/dryer, a full bath and a large bedroom looking out to the Duna below. There was even a pullout sofa for Émile. Cheryl would be impressed.

Next, anxious to get my camera repaired, I located the authorized dealer and was shocked it would take three weeks. However, sensing the urgency, they directed me to a shop just down the street that fixed it that afternoon.

The next morning, ready for pleasure and rejuvenation, I suggested to Émile that we head over to the Széchenyi Bath or *furdö*. It was east of town near the circus, home to the "Rubber Girl" and other memorable acts. Budapest has had a long love affair with water. Even 2,000 years ago, the area called Ak-ink by Celtic settlers was known for its waters. The Romans later called it Aquincum, as their aqueducts were fed by its thermal springs. Hospitals in the Middle Ages, and then invading Turks, used the waters for healing and purification. It only seemed natural that the tradition continued with two modern pilgrims.

Émile was surprisingly excited at the idea, so we set off on the fast and efficient metro (buying tickets this time). We exited at Hosök tér, Hero's Square, with its 47-ton Millennium Monument marking the thousand year anniversary of the Magyar conquest. It consisted of an impressive circle of columns with statues of some of the great kings, princes and commanders of their history. Archangel Gabriel stood atop a 36-meter column, holding the Hungarian holy crown and the apostolic double cross. It was a truly regal setting, with the Palace of Arts and Museum of Fine Arts facing each other on opposite sides.

That's just one of the things I admired about Budapest. Its splendor, art and culture were accessible to everyone, although a little more expensive than during the communist era when we could go to the symphony one night, then the opera, ballet, a Broadway road show and a concert the following nights for about five dollars each. We could even upgrade our seats to front-row center—when a pack of Kent cigarettes changed hands.

Nearby Széchenyi Baths were equally impressive. The neo-Baroque baths, one of the largest bathing complexes in Europe, were one of the city's more recent additions, dating from just 1913. After entering from the City Park into a foyer topped by an outstanding mosaic tile rotunda, we quickly bought a ticket for less than $10. It allowed us to use all their facilities, beginning with the thermal pool, whose warm healing waters performed minor miracles on a pilgrim's aching legs and feet. It was followed by a trip to the eucalyptus dry sauna to clarify our lungs, then by a jaunt to the outdoor thermal pools.

On that particular sunny summer day, a cross-section of Budapest society soaked up the healing waters and rays. It was egalitarian, open and accessible to all—not our New Age "Day at the Spa" experience, reserved only for the well-heeled or special occasion. No, we were surrounded by an odd mixture: the elderly and infirmed taking the waters on doctor's orders, young families with children in tow, twenty-somethings on a date, the over-weight, the anorexic, the rich and far-from-flush. Why, you could even play chess while soaking in its 150-degree water.

Furdös had a long and distinguished history in Eastern Europe. On our first visit, Cheryl and I were spa junkies. On cold autumn days, a hot *furdö* provided the perfect tonic to restore body and soul. In the process, we sampled Hungary's 16th century Rudas Turkish Baths, Rác, the regal Gellért, Király, Balaton and Hévíz thermal lake, as well as Karlovy Vary in Czechoslovakia and Bulgaria's Bankya Spa.

However, I think it was Émile's first visit to a health spa, and it was good to see the sparkle back in his blue eyes. He particularly liked the central thermal whirlpool. Once you let go of the railing, its waters swept you round and round at considerable speed until you were drained—or felt like you were being sucked down its drain. Then again, it was a relief to finally expose our fish belly-white upper arms, legs and torsos to the sun, in an attempt to even-out our odd pilgrim tans.

On the day our rendezvous with Cheryl finally arrived, Émile and I set-off via the metro and then took a bus to meet her at the airport. Her

Austrian Air flight was on time, of course, and after tender hugs all around our trio headed back to the city. It was a relief to have our "missing" team member aboard to inject new blood into the experience. Just as importantly, she'd brought fresh supplies: a poncho, a smaller, lighter GoLite backpack, fresh socks and a memory card for my new camera. She'd be taking even more home. With the hot weather and increasing distance between towns, it became even more important to travel "ultra-lite."

Budapest had always been a special place full of memories for us. Yet as much as I was overjoyed to see my beautiful partner, this time the city was just another stop along our long road to Jerusalem. Thoughtfully, Émile planned to give us time alone to catch up, as he became swept up in the mounting World Cup frenzy.

Early the next morning, we headed down to the Hungarian Bicycle Association and returned twice before we were able to find someone in their office. Unfortunately, they had no information about bike paths in neighboring Serbia, and were only able to supply us with the name of a contact in Sofia, slightly better than nothing. Of course, I'd tried to find the same information before leaving home via the Internet and national tourism offices, but with the same results.

A little discouraged after all our efforts, we met Émile and headed back across the neo-classical Chain Bridge over the Duna, then walked up the hill on the Buda side of the city to the Fisherman's Bastion. Of course, we could have also taken a funicular up the hill to the Castle District, but why bother after we'd already walked that far?

The Fisherman's Bastion provided the ultimate panoramic view of the river, Parliament, and the Pest side of the metropolis. Its neo-Gothic turrets and walkways were constructed in 1901 atop some of the remaining original stones of the castle walls. Later, when the Nazis made Castle Hill one of their last holdouts during the Second World War, it suffered considerable damage during a two-month siege until the city was "liberated" by the Soviet Red Army.

Next, we skirted the hordes of tour groups to admire the nearby equestrian statue of St. Stephen I, first king of Hungary, and the Matthias Church or Church of Our Lady, the site of royal weddings, coronations and frequent concerts.

Then, eager to escape the blazing heat, we retreated to the cool serenity of the Labyrinth, a recent addition to the city's attractions, although the location dated back to prehistoric times. Its 1,200 meters of caves and tunnels beneath Buda Castle once sheltered up to 10,000 during WWII, and then it was a secret military installation during the Cold War. Nowadays, it's a dark, mysterious refuge inhabited by bizarre statues and artwork framed by a smattering of history and music. For an hour, we wandered through an underground catacomb of sections named the Labyrinth of Courage, the Labyrinth of the Magic Deer and Labyrinth of Another World. I particularly enjoyed their wine fountain—but would suggest sampling Hungary's fine wine elsewhere.

The following morning, we set off on a little more business. For months, I'd been suggesting to Émile, "Why don't you lighten up your gear? That's too much weight for you to carry day in and day out for months." At last, he heard my plea. After mailing some of his heavier clothing back to Dijon, we wandered off to an outfitter shop where he bought a lighter rain jacket and pants.

Afterward, since Cheryl would leave us on July 4th and return to Budapest alone, we took a quick field trip to the unique, three-star Fortuna "boatel" to check out their facilities. It was in a serene location, anchored on the Duna, right across from Margaret Island. After taking the cook's tour, we were relieved to discover it was funky but clean and affordable. Better still, they offered to arrange a mini-bus to take Cheryl to the airport when the time came.

Finally, for those who've ever wondered where old statues go to die (and no, it's not the happy hunting ground), in Budapest it's called Statue Park. It took us a metro, a tram, and then a bus ride to finally reach one of the world's largest conglomerations of communist-era statuary, featuring the red trinity: Marx, Lenin and Engels, as well as heroes and martyrs, comrade workers and soldiers all in forgettable poses. At least, many of the locals hoped so.

The road leading out of Budapest was slow and already steamy by 9:00 a.m. the next morning. By then, we'd officially completed all 1,367 kilometers of the Donau Radweg. So after following a bicycle path along the River Duna through town, we were forced to divert into an industrial complex, home to all the multinational corporations who'd relocated there over the past fifteen years. I was all for progress, but Budapest in the old days was more accessible for budget travelers—and residents as well. One of my favorite European cities had been all "tarted up," heaving with package tourists and the well-heeled who eagerly paid inflated prices equal to what they spent at home.

For example, one night to toast Cheryl's arrival, I dropped into a nearby wine cave for my usual 450-forint bottle of *Egri Bikaver*.

"Sorry. This 1,800-forint bottle is all that's available," the clerk sighed. When I shot him one of those "You must be kidding" looks, he replied, "Don't you know you're in a tourist area?" Then he whispered with a sly grin, "Look, you just have to walk a block toward the river to find what you're looking for."

It was "open season" on visitors in over-popular places like Budapest— and wearing an orange vest wouldn't help.

After walking through a sleazy section of the city, or what the guide-books might call, "the section the tours don't show ya," we crossed the Duna and stopped for a cool drink. After we asked for directions, the help-ful café manager pointed us to a bicycle path along the river that wound past a secret underground installation.

"Don't let the private security people find you there," he warned with a wink. "They've been known to arrest people for trespassing."

Sure enough, we were only on the trail for thirty minutes before two motorcycle rent-a-cops approached. They told us in no uncertain terms that we couldn't walk on the perfectly good bicycle path and needed to immediately divert into town. As we headed off in that direction, Cheryl conspiratorially whispered, "Why listen to them? They've already left and we're not even sure this will lead us to another trail."

"True, but that doesn't mean they won't return. We don't want to end up in some goulash gulag now, do we?"

As we plodded along in the searing heat atop another sod levee, we made futile attempts to bat away swarms of mosquitoes or *moustiques*, as Émile called them. Eventually we connected with busy Highway 51—only to resume our battle with the equally persistent cars and trucks until we reached Szigetszentmárton. Spotting a German restaurant, we were relieved to finally be able to ask someone for the nearest *panzió* or *zimmer frei*. So we dragged ourselves inside and plopped down around a wooden table. Imagine our surprise to find probably the only "authentic" German restau-rant within a three-country area—where no one spoke German.

However, good things come to those who walk. When we stopped far-ther down the road at the market for water, I approached an older, kindly looking fellow loading milk into the trunk of his car.

"Is there a *panzió* nearby?"

At first, he tried to explain in Hungarian. Then noticing our bewildered looks, he motioned for us to load our packs into his tiny Skoda and then drove us right to the front steps of a riverside inn. At first glance, the refuge by the river looked closed for renovations, but the young managers welcomed us inside, as much as we welcomed their hot showers and respite after a long day back on the trail.

Cheryl's first day was an especially long one, yet it had already exposed her to the diversity of our journey: trails with mosquitoes, levee hiking, road rambling, and town trekking—followed by out-and-out exhaustion.

As the sun's first magenta rays crept over the still-sleepy river, we were eager to continue. Szigetszentmárton was a tiny riverfront community of mostly holiday cabins. We made good time walking Carolina-like red dirt roads among mosquitoes as thick as a country drawl. Soon drenched and sporting chomps upon bites, we reached a main thoroughfare and then headed along another sod dike surrounded by dense forest. Amid a deafening cacophony of birds and frogs serenading lethargic fishermen, we blindly following the path with only a vague assurance it would lead us back across the river. But we had faith and were eventually rewarded when we reached a lock allowing us to pass to the other side. Otherwise, it would have meant a painful two-hour diversion. Those country roads ultimately led us to farmlands near Tass on the Southern Great Plain and a busy intersection, where we were anxious to find a place to eat (preferably one with tripe).

Just outside of town, as one Darth Vader of a storm front approached from the south, we stumbled into a country restaurant with both "treep" and chicken breasts in mushroom sauce. Right after we sat down, all of a sudden, there was a series of booming, cannon-like cracks of thunder. The deluge struck. Winds grew to gale force strength. Trees bent at odd angles. Limbs snapped and flew across the road. I expected to see airborne heifers spinning past. The rains pounded against the modest eatery with incredible fury. A pool soon formed in the middle of the dining room floor. Although one of the waitresses rushed to mop it up, it was a losing battle. Another took its place each time a customer made a mad dash through the front door to their waiting vehicle. And then, to add to the tension, the electricity went out.

In the interim, we had plenty of time to eat and drink our fill by candlelight, hesitant to venture back into the madness; taking time to count our blessings that we'd made it there when we did. Five minutes later and we'd have been stuck in the middle of all the madness.

It was ninety minutes before the storm abated momentarily and we gingerly poked our heads out the door. Without a moment to lose, we set off again with anxious anticipation, since by the look of things it could begin again at any second. Even still, the huge semis plying those slick roads on the busy north-south corridor had me more worried. There was no shoulder.

'Can they see us in time? Will they give us wide berth? How far will we be forced to walk off the road when they approach? And what if two trucks meet from opposite directions? Do we have time to lunge into the fields at the last second?'

To me, it seemed far too dangerous, and I called out to the others, "Hey, we need to pour on some steam and get to the next town. *Tout suite!*"

At that, we set off as fast as our legs (and lunch) would carry us toward Szalkszentmárton and its one *panzió*. Fortunately, at that speed, it didn't take too long. As it turned out, their motel was right along the road and, for some reason, they only reluctantly agreed to rent us rooms. Maybe it was because their electricity had shut off and their kitchen was closed. Regrettably, there was no other *étterem* or restaurant in town, so we made do with a dinner of chips, candy bars and drinks from the gas station across the street.

Although reluctant, we later joined Émile to mosey into town in one final search for a store or restaurant. It was futile. We simply provided fresh human hors d'oeuvres for hordes of hungry bloodsuckers.

Leaving early the next morning before breakfast, Émile was already sluggish. I didn't know whether his diabetes was acting up, or it was just hunger. Nevertheless, food was always a great motivator for our friend. So we were relieved to eventually find an open café and then continue, even though it was back onto a busy highway. Again, the mosquitoes prevented us from walking atop the levee where it would have been safer. However, before long, we found another country road and conditions became infinitely better—until it started raining again. I felt sorry that Cheryl had to spend her precious vacation days slogging along with us in foul weather, but she didn't seem to mind. Each time I glanced over at her, she looked as pleased as a Labrador on a field trip and kept up with dogged determination.

Thankfully, before long, we reached Dunaföldvár, still decked out in our rain gear. The visitor office was open and their friendly volunteer was happy to find us a cabin at a campground beside the Duna. More importantly, she warned us that Paks, our next destination, was in the midst of a music festival. It was impossible to find a room. I was worried we'd have no place to stay, so I decided I'd call Laszló, Zsuzsana's father, who lived in Dombóvár. We just had to hold out hope that tomorrow we'd meet another "angel," as they'd recently been in short supply.

No tempting breakfast awaited us at daybreak, but we managed to leave without a grumble. The mosquitoes were already as thick as piranhas in the Amazon, but we marveled at the bounty of the countryside surrounding us. The houses were tidy and freshly painted; gardens abundant with vegetables of nearly every type. Fields overflowed with cherry and apricot trees that also draped over the road, so temptingly close you could reach up and eat your fill.

Still, as the morning progressed, Émile slipped farther behind until he stopped to buy water at a store. We waited ten minutes for him and then decided to continue on a straight line to Paks where Laszló was to meet us. Exactly where and when we didn't know for certain, since he'd promised to telephone.

When Émile was finally within sight again, I heard the familiar Vivaldi ring tone on his phone. Since he couldn't understand the caller, he told Zsuzsana's father to call us back in ten minutes. Learning this, I poured on speed to reach the intersection with Highway 6 on the edge of Paks, since I figured it would be a good place to meet. Well, just as I reached the crossroads, I caught sight of a cheerful-looking man with a white beard and green Trachten hat. He smoked his pipe in a car by the roadside. Noticing the Canadian flag sticker on the Ford's window (and his fellow gnome-like features), I figured it must be Laszló.

Looking up, he caught me waving at him, just as he began to phone us again. Grinning from ear to ear like some mischievous elf, he gave us a cheery welcome, and then we piled into his car and set off for the center of town. Still worried about finding a room, we immediately began calling every place listed in the tourist office's brochure. Fortunately, Laszló was there to speak Magyar, but with the festival, nothing was available. Finally, as a last resort, I suggested we ask at the Catholic Church. Of course, that was easier said than done. It started to rain again. After parking, Laszló and I sprinted across the street to the church. No luck. The priest's office eluded us another fifteen minutes, until finally, soaked to the skin, we stumbled upon it—a block from where we'd originally parked.

Hoping for the best, Lazlo pounded on its heavy wooden door, until a young priest answered and invited us into his study.

"What can I do for you?" he asked.

"We're pilgrims walking from France to Jerusalem," I began, dripping onto his carpet, while László translated. "We hoped to spend the night here in Paks, but all the rooms are full because of the Gastroblues Festival."

"Yes, I know," he replied with a bashful smile. "We are the ones putting on the concert."

"Well, by now it's too late for us to continue to the next town. So we were hoping you had a place for us here. We have a letter of introduction, if that will help," I added, drawing the Vatican letter from my pocket for his inspection.

He studied it for a minute and then ducked out the door. Next, I heard him on the phone, but didn't understand what he was saying, of course. Even though it was an unusual request, we had to make it work. After all, what other choice did we have?

When the young priest returned, all he could say was, "We need to wait for Father to awake from his nap."

For an hour, we sat uncomfortably in his office making small talk, while I tried to form contingency plans. I figured László would've already invited us back to his house if it were convenient, so I didn't consider that alternative. Our only other option was to ask him to drive us ahead to the next town, and then we'd hitchhike back to Paks in the morning. That might prove to be difficult on a Sunday.

Finally, an older disheveled priest arrived and welcomed us in English. After assuring me there was no problem for the three of us to spend the night, he graciously handed me clean sheets and the keys to two rooms with a smile.

By then, Cheryl and Émile had waited in the car for nearly two hours, and although they were greatly relieved to have a place to sleep, they were even more eager to find a place to enjoy lunch. With panache, László led us across the street to probably the finest restaurant in town where he guided us through one of the largest menus I'd ever seen in my life. Then he helped us order local specialties and wines until we settled on gypsy steaks with garlic, wild mushrooms—and tripe for Émile. (*Mais, oui.*)

László had an infectious laugh and was the most congenial of hosts. For a while, he talked about life in Hungary before and after the communist regime, since he'd left for Canada and only returned in 1996. Although things had vastly improved since then and the standard of living was much higher, unemployment and the cost of living still made life difficult. They had a long way to go before they caught up to Germany. As some might say, "Freedom isn't free."

All told, Hungary had never had a finer ambassador. Our lunch was truly unforgettable and I couldn't remember when I'd laughed so hard. Eventually, when the time came to say our "good-byes," Laszló appeared genuinely sad to send us on our way. As Émile took photos of the three of us together, I assured our new friend, "You are our "angel" for the day."

Hearing that, he beamed and his eyes welled up. "Well, that explains all the itching and pain in my back. It's just my wings sprouting!"

The next day was one of well-intended bad starts. Leaving the church office, we backtracked north a few kilometers toward where we'd met Laszló. Even though it was overcast, we looked forward to taking the ferry across the Duna, and rejoining our trail south on the other side. The ferry dock was easy to find and we only had a short wait, as it left every hour on its ten-minute voyage. Following a much too-short float, we disembarked and spotted the supposed bicycle path to our left. After leading us into a swampy forest, the trail deteriorated into a muddy mess. We took that as a sign to retreat to the boat landing with the *szunyogok*, or mosquitoes, in swift pursuit. Instead, we chose the country road and soon found ourselves walking past fields of corn, squash, red peppers and poppies—not the red flowering variety, but the bulbed ones, source of all those delicious seeds.

As Cheryl and I walked hand-in-hand, we tried to forget it was our last day together for the next several months. She'd head back to Budapest in the morning.

Although we'd hoped to make it farther, intermittent rain dampened our spirits. It began slowly and we hoped it would pass, but it was soon pounding heavily again. Cheryl was only dressed in a poncho, shorts and trail runners, and she quickly became soaked.

I couldn't help but tease her, "You have to be careful what you wish for on this trail. A few days ago, you were the one who had to say, 'Well, it's pretty here, but a little rain would cool things off.' You may have noticed it's rained every day since."

Fortunately, in short order we reached Kalocsa, the world's capital of paprika or *paprikás*, a Hungarian mainstay called "red gold" in that area. Spotting a *panzió*, perhaps the only one in town, we stopped for a bite to eat, thinking the rains might let up in the meantime. As we picked at our breakfast, I decided it was foolish to continue in that storm and looked for some excuse to spend the night.

"Well for one, we don't know if the next village has any place for us to stay. Two, it's raining like crazy and doesn't show any sign of letting up. And three, Cheryl's leaving tomorrow…"

Putting those reasons together, all of us were relieved to stay in the cozy family inn. There was always tomorrow.

Cheryl and I were especially content to spend the afternoon cuddling in the privacy of our own room. Then again, we also felt compelled to join Émile for his nightly food search at exactly 6:00 p.m., regular as clockwork. It was also a good excuse to look for the bus station, a rough little joint, and then sample the local cherry brandy or *cseresznye pálinka*. Afterward, back in the room, we picked up where we left off.

Five-thirty came all too soon. There was a light drizzle outside, but it was nothing compared to the tempest in my heart. I'm the type of person who can do without long, painful goodbyes, so we'd already decided that Émile and I would head out at first light, while Cheryl could stroll to the station just before her bus to Budapest arrived. The less time she spent there, the better. Lingering kisses would have to sustain us.

We left by 6:30 and I set a faster pace, since I'd swapped my backpack and carried a few pounds less. Every little bit helped. I sent home my cold weather gear, as well as my rain jacket, replacing it with Cheryl's blueberry poncho. Much of the paperwork, guides and maps also went home. So at long last, my gear was whittled down to just the raw essentials.

Émile, however, still carried much more weight in his bulky pack and was soon left in the dust, as I tried to outrun my own demons and doubts, to re-examine what I was doing—and its folly.

'Every day now, I'm putting life and limb in danger by walking these busy country roads. And it will probably only get worse. Sure, this walk for peace is well intentioned, but does anyone really care? Will it make a difference? So far, we've just received polite curiosity from those we've met. I only hope things will be different once we cross those poorer regions more wracked by constant wars.'

I walked alone all day, turning to check on Émile's progress every fifteen minutes or so. Occasionally I'd stop long enough for him to catch up, but his pace confounded me. Even with rest and plenty to eat, he walked at a snail's pace. Although he tried out new, lighter trail shoes he'd bought the day before, he soon switched back to his cumbersome hiking boots with mumbled complaints.

All in all, it was a ten-hour slog to Baja and we encountered more traffic as we grew nearer, as well as flowers and memorials to the dead every five kilometers along the ragged road. Somewhere along the way, Émile disappeared in my rearview mirror. At one point, I heard what sounded like a motorcycle, loud and obnoxious, as its driver raced between gears and revved his engine. All of a sudden, a car whipped past my right shoulder—so close that if I'd turned around I would have become another fatality on the Great Hungarian Plain. Life was just that tenuous.

By mid-afternoon, upon entering the suburbs of Baja, I collapsed next to a pharmacy to wait for my friend. It was a good fifteen minutes before I spotted his bushy white beard. Émile was sweating heavily. The dye from his leather cowboy hat etched crimson rivulets down his flushed cheeks. Although I offered to wait a bit and allow him to rest, he insisted we continue to the visitor office, then to our room above a small café in the center of town.

After a shower, Émile met me downstairs on the snack bar terrace with his itinerary and auto maps in tow. Pulling up a chair, he began, "I am sorry. I want to spend two days here."

"Here? Why?"

"I am very tired," he sighed with a defeated shrug.

"I know. It's been a long day. I'm exhausted too, but we've just spent five days resting in Budapest and three light days afterward."

Suddenly, without warning, he screamed, "I want to spend two days… because I will never reach Jerusalem at this rate!"

I'd never seen him so agitated. I just stared at him, dumbfounded, as he sullenly tugged a trip itinerary out of his green notebook. After looking at it a moment, I realized it was different from the one he'd sent me before our trip. His was based on that useless auto roadmap he carried—not on where we might actually find a place to stay each night. I still couldn't believe he'd planned our journey for six years and come so unprepared. I couldn't believe I'd put my faith in his planning and was now saddled with the job of pulling it together every day, while he was content to merely follow in my footsteps and rely on me to find our room, our path, and translate along the way.

"Look, we need to talk about priorities," he continued, in a more conciliatory tone. "I have always dreamed of seeing Belgrade, Sofia and Istanbul along the way to Jerusalem. Everything else is negotiable."

"That's fine with me," I replied, although I'd already visited them. "What's most important is for us to arrive alive and in one piece. After today's traffic and my near miss, we need to make an extra effort to find bicycle paths or at least smaller roads. I do *not* want to end my life here." I knew the best adventure travelers weren't reckless—quite the contrary. They take an extraordinary amount of time for planning and weighing the options. Risks are well calculated, so they can live to tell the tale.

"*Ah, bon*," he nodded with a grim smile.

"*Ah, bon*" was a French idiom that didn't literally mean, "Yes, that's good," as much as it meant, "I've heard what you're saying." Earlier on our journey, I'd kidded Émile that his frequent expression reminded me of the old sexist cartoon where the wife explained her daily triumphs to her husband, while his nose was stuck in his evening newspaper.

"Honey, I went shopping with friends today and bought a new outfit."
"*Ah, bon.*"

"Then I picked up the kids at school and took them to soccer practice."
"*Ah, bon.*"

"Then I fixed a wonderful meal and bought this sexy negligee to wear while I eat cherries off your stomach."
"*Ah, bon.*"

"Then I totaled the car, slept with your brother and cooked the cat."
"*Ah, bon.*"

Why did I feel like we were some dysfunctional couple? Did he really hear my concerns? Or was his "*Ah, bon*" merely meant to placate me?

Nevertheless, we spent an hour discussing our itinerary and reached agreement on villages to spend each night in Serbia and Bulgaria—based on as much as we knew at the time. For the harmony of the group, I agreed to stay the extra day in Baja, even though it left me short on money. Down to my last forints, I'd survive on pasta another night.

Paradoxically, later that evening, the same "I am very tired" Émile managed to stay awake past midnight watching the World Cup match in double overtime.

MANIA

PIROT

GRAD

BULGARIA

IA

CHAPTER SIX
Serbian Border to Belgrade

World War III?

"The real and lasting victories are those of peace, and not of war."
~ Ralph Waldo Emerson

As Émile and I sauntered through town, Baja slumbered. We'd decided to leave at 5:00 a.m. after hearing rumors the temperature would be back up to eighty-five degrees. Tramping out of town on Highway 51, passing through the last few Magyar villages, we were mostly alone, except for one earthy, dark woman on a rickety bicycle. In broken English, she asked us about our journey, and then radiantly glowed as she wished us *"Fortuna!"* with a wave.

Traffic was nearly nonexistent by the time we arrived at Hungary's southern border. No one was going to Serbia; fewer were leaving. So we quickly cleared the Hungarian side and ambled over to the booth on the Serbian frontier. For once, the situation was a little different. The officer looked us up and down with a skeptical eye, then studied our passports and typed something into his computer. Finally, he picked up the phone and called his supervisor.

Now Émile, for some strange reason, found it all too hilarious and started snickering, until I quickly reminded him, "This might be serious, so please show a little respect." I'd had more than one problem in the past at lonely border crossings. In Tanzania, Cheryl and I had our bags and bodies thoroughly searched and then we were interrogated—until we agreed to a little border extortion and finally paid to exit into Malawi.

The Serbian officer's supervisor soon appeared and took one look at us, settling on Émile's rather lethal looking, flag-draped baton. Noting his concern, in his best professorial tone, Émile began naming all the countries we'd passed, as he lifted their flags one by one.

"France, Switzerland, Germany, Austria, Slovakia, Hungary…" his voice trailed off.

"Yes, we're walking to Jerusalem," I added, without confusing the issue with the subject of peace.

After deciding Émile's baton posed no threat to national security, the officers welcomed us to war-torn Serbia and summarily waved us through. Backi-Breg straddled the Serbian side of the border. Thirty kilometers from Baja, it was supposed to be our destination. However, fate had other plans. We saw and sensed an immediate change once we crossed the frontier—and it was far more than dinars and language. As poor as Hungary appeared at times, Serbia was in far worse condition. Already there were fewer cars (a blessing for us) and the Trabants were replaced by rattling Yugos. Streets were smaller and more pocked with potholes, housing was more rundown, and people already looked a little less prosperous.

It didn't take long before we stumbled upon a sign in German that read "*gasthaus*" and followed it into a dark bar. However, any hope of staying there was dashed when they explained in German that they weren't open, and the nearest room was still ten kilometers away in Bezdan. Even so, they proceeded to draw us a map with directions to the hotel. All that remained was for me to get another ten kilometers out of my companion. At least, it was still early.

Fortunately, it only took us another ninety minutes to reach Bezdan, and after more directions and a hearty, "*Dobar dan,*" we headed down its dusty main street. Still needing to change money into Serbian dinars, we stopped a local woman who led us to the town's only bank, luckily still open at that hour. Stepping into its coolness, I tugged a sweaty hundred-dollar bill from my moneybelt and shyly handed it along with my U. S. passport to the teller, who accepted the soggy Benjamin.

As she began to count out my change, Émile stepped forward and blurted out, "Can I get dinars with my Visa card?"

"No. I'm sorry," the bank clerk apologetically replied in English.

"Then I want to exchange a traveler's check."

"Sorry, we do not accept them here."

Well, hearing that, the normally mild-mannered pilgrim pitched a fit, screaming, "Then I will call the police. Yes, that is what I will do. You have to take them. They are accepted all over the world. This is part of Europe, isn't it? Ah, this would never happen in Dijon."

As he paused in his tirade, the Iron Curtain fell. The woman was not accustomed to being yelled at by foreigners. As luck would have it, not speaking English well, she assumed he, too, was American, since she still held my passport. In typical Eastern European fashion, she icily replied, "This is *not* America, sir. You must go to Sombor."

"No, *he* is French," I explained, eager to set the record straight, since I still didn't have my dinars in-hand. Before Émile could come back for a second round, I intercepted him and whispered, "Look. We'll be in Sombor tomorrow and I have enough money for us tonight." Besides, I knew he'd already exchanged his leftover forints for dinars back at the border, so he was far from destitute.

After making small talk and apologizing to the teller, I eventually received my money, and then led my still flustered and fuming friend into the street.

"Yes, that is what I will do," he vowed under his breath. "I will call the police and report them."

"And do what? Complain that their "cousin" refuses to cash your check? Émile, this is a small town and everyone is probably related or are long-time friends. It's not a good idea to insult the only person in town who can give us money for a room and food, now is it?"

Fortunately, our inn was nearby, just next to a thermal treatment center. As we entered its courtyard, I joked, "*Bienvenue au deuxième-monde, mon ami.* Welcome to the second-world."

No, we were no longer in the West. Already signs were in Cyrillic, as well as Roman. The music had changed, along with the rules and way of life. However, I was elated, ready for a change and for the exotic comfort of Eastern Europe.

Our room, on the other hand, was Spartan and shabby without the "chic." Although its bathroom had a Lenin-era shower curtain with green mold to match, I was simply grateful to have found a place to sleep—short of walking another eighteen kilometers to Sombor. As we relaxed, I realized another bit of odd coincidence. The name of our hotel, "*Fortuna*," was exactly what the gypsy lady had said when she left us earlier on the street that morning.

We left the village at dawn amid a few gentle waves from townsfolk as we passed, despite our near riot at the bank. We looked forward to an easier trek to make up for the past two days that were necessarily longer. But to fuel the fires, we first found a simple café where the coffee was strong with grounds a half-inch thick on the bottom, a pleasant vestige of the painful Turkish occupation lasting from the 15th century to 1878.

As we walked pitted and neglected roads, I couldn't help but think about the ravages of war. All around I saw visions of the Eastern Europe I'd known fifteen years earlier. There were few signs of Western commercialism or growth. The war had delayed all that. How futile it all was; how many lives were wasted; how much a nation's development had been delayed. Civilizations such as theirs had been laid waste for centuries. Families, lives, and futures were ruined in the process. Yet many were still so eager to don a uniform, pick up a gun and "fight long and hard for a bit of colored ribbon," as Napoleon once boasted.

We arrived in Sombor by noon. Cruising down its beautiful oak-lined streets, we wended our way to the center of town and the local Yugoslav Air office. After introductions, at first they tried to convince us to stay at their modern international high-rise hotel—at only six times what we'd spent the night before. But after we explained the reason for our journey, they treated us more as friends than customers and found us a spacious room in the new visitor wing of their geriatric center for just $15 a night. Before leaving, as we guzzled icy water from their office cooler, their office manager sidled up and asked, "Would you consider speaking to our local television station about your trip?"

"Of course. We'd be happy to meet them." I'd always hoped we'd attract media attention on our trip, and reach larger audiences with a message of choosing peace as an alternative to never-ending wars.

"Excellent. I'll let them know where you're staying. I'm sure they'll come by tonight."

Buoyed by the opportunity, we trekked to the senior center within thirty minutes. As we crossed the street to enter, a car swerved in front of us blocking our path, and then an enthusiastic newsperson and her photographer hopped out.

"I'm Ljudmila of Spektar Television. And we'd like to talk to you and your friend about your trip."

With that, they proceeded to shoot a five-minute interview segment for *TV Spektar News* that would air three times and reach maybe 100,000 people in the area, plus others in nearby Hungary.

"Can you tell us where you're from?" she began in heavily accented English.

"I'm from Hawaii and my friend is from Dijon, France."

"I understand you're walking to Jerusalem?"

"Yes. We left on April 23rd and we're following the old Templar trail and Roman *Militaris* road to Jerusalem for peace."

"What countries are you passing through?"

"We've already walked across France, Switzerland, Germany, Austria, Slovakia and Hungary." As I mentioned these, Émile held out the appropriate flags tied to his baton. "Now we're walking through Serbia of course, and then Bulgaria, Turkey, Syria, Jordan and Israel."

"Isn't that dangerous?"

"So far, people have been very kind to us."

"What do you hope to accomplish by this trip?"

"First, we're taking this journey as a personal pilgrimage. But more than that, it is a journey for peace. Countries and especially the common people have suffered too much. There have been too many tears shed by mothers for their sons, wives for their husbands and children for their fathers. Yes, it takes courage to face an enemy—but it requires just as much bravery to say "No" and refuse to capitulate to war. The time has come. This is now a global imperative."

"Why are you taking this particular route?"

"This pathway was once followed by Templars and soldiers on their way to Jerusalem. Now, I would like to see it developed as an international trail of peace for people of all nationalities and religions. I believe once you walk, eat, drink and share dreams with each other, you realize how much we have in common—how much we are truly "brothers." And once you realize that, it becomes so much harder to pick up arms and kill each other."

"Thank you so much," she concluded. "We welcome you to Serbia and wish you continued luck on your journey."

The camera lights went out. Only time would tell if more than the seniors eavesdropping in the lobby had heard our message.

Later that night, before we shut off our lights, I reminded Émile that we had a thirty-five kilometer segment to walk the next day. He didn't take the news well. His face grew gloomy and distant. I'd become more worried about his mental attitude lately.

"Look," I gently reminded him, "You and I set this new schedule together. We both know why we have to walk so far. There's nothing in between. Remember, our days in Germany and Austria were preparation for all this, and conditions will only become harder over the next three months, especially in the deserts of Turkey. So, think of this as further training."

He looked unconvinced and afraid.

Personally, I still couldn't view our journey in one major seven-month stretch. It was simply too daunting. We needed to look at reaching our destination one day at a time. Besides, many of the challenges were now in our own minds. Control those and our bodies were sure to follow.

After downing the center's invigorating breakfast of "stand the spoon up in the cup" coffee, we began our march out of town. Recently, we'd changed our saying, "The sun in your eyes" to "The sun on the left side of your face." It wasn't nearly as catchy, but we were heading south once we left Budapest. As we walked tree-lined streets back into the countryside, we were startled when people honked their car horns or waved as they passed. One lady even leaned out of her car to shout, "Thank you!" in English. Apparently, some folks had seen the news segment after all. With any luck, our message of peace would spread.

For us, their enthusiasm and encouragement lifted our sagging spirits, as we walked through one small village differing little from the last five. Even though many homes had broken windowpanes, most had extensive gardens with women toiling in them. Unlike Hungary, it appeared much of the work was still done by hand and not machinery. We were surprised when a few horse-drawn carts passed toting hay. Still, everyone, no matter how poor they might appear, waved at us or returned our salutes.

Unexpectedly, the high point of our day came just after lunch. A well-dressed lady in a station wagon slowed down as she grew near, crying out in a thick accent as she leaned out her window, "Hello! I'd like to talk and I have something for you."

"Sure. Pull over just ahead," I suggested, not knowing what to expect.

She did and as we approached, she introduced herself, adding, "I saw you on the news last night in Sombor. I was very moved by what you had to say."

"Well, I believe it's time for people to insist that their leaders find other solutions to our problems instead of resorting to war."

"Here, I have something for you," she announced. With that, she swung open the gate of her station wagon and tugged out a huge watermelon. It turned out that she was the one who'd yelled when she passed us the first time, and she'd driven ahead to the market and returned. After borrowing my Swiss Army knife, she cut us both cool, thick slices in the high grass. Fame had never tasted so good.

"Do you belong to any organization, or do you have backing for this?" she asked, raising her sunglasses.

"No, we're doing this on our own, as concerned individuals."

"I just wondered since my husband is with a peace group working in Sri Lanka. What about publicity? Are you publicizing your journey along the way?"

"We could do very little in advance," I admitted between slurps. "But we're willing to talk to whoever will listen. Maybe the television station in Belgrade would be interested in a story?" I suggested, dropping a hint. "We like to believe two people with a message can make a difference."

"Yes. It is an important one and very needed in the world today." Then she added with a quiver to her voice, "I hope it will echo along your trail so many will hear."

"Thank you. It's time we realize, no matter what our culture, country or religion, we basically have the same needs."

She nodded in agreement and then led us back to her car where she presented us with a final gift—a fresh cantaloupe.

"Do you speak to groups?" she asked, closing her car door.

"I'll speak to anyone," I promised with a grin, "anyone willing to listen."

With that, she firmly shook our hands and sped off.

That chance meeting was a first for us. More than any fleeting fifteen minutes of fame, it confirmed we had a message that touched some people; one that some were (literally) dying to hear. Maybe there was something more to our trek than first met the eye. Perhaps something more was in store when the time was right.

We continued our long trek to Odzaci, buoyed by the afternoon's affirmation. Still, reaching it, we also had to deal with the daily uncertainty of where we'd spend the night. The city's hotel was now a disco. The ladies working there refused to even crack open the door to direct us to another. Instead, one woman in her waitress outfit, an uncomfortable proletariat costume with khaki high-heeled *espadrilles* that hadn't changed since the 1980s, screamed at us through a heavy glass door over the din of street noise. As luck would have it, as they say, "One door didn't close without another one opening." Right around the corner, we approached two bank security guards and asked for their advice in finding a room.

"*Nem, nem,*" they replied, but added, "There is one back toward Sombor three kilometers from here."

"But are they open? Could you please give them a call, so we don't walk all that way for nothing?"

At that, the skinny kid who'd been listening next door ducked into the soccer club to call. Meanwhile, a guard went into the bank to fetch his boss, an attractive blonde. Snezana spoke no English, but graciously insisted on loading us and our gear into her Skoda, and then drove us all the way back to the hotel above the restaurant. We'd passed it, but hadn't seen its sign. As a tour group wrapped up their late lunch, the owner and his family prepared a room for us and treated us to cool drinks. Obviously, some type of celebration was planned, but at that point we didn't care. If anything, the day's events reminded me to tap into and trust in a Universal plan.

As it turned out, the night presented a few surprises. There was a class reunion in the bar directly under our room, complete with a fleshy singer sporting several days of beard and dressed in jeans and a ready-to-pop denim work shirt. His partner accompanied him on an organ with its rhythm machine pounding a mariachi beat. Imagine a goat bleating karaoke for ten hours non-stop—and you begin to get a picture of our restless night. Or *my* restless night, I should say, as Émile conveniently took out his hearing aid. I was awake off and on until we flopped out of bed at 5:30 the next morning.

As if to make up for our musical torture, our hostess went all out for breakfast, serving us four eggs each along with four types of ham or sausage—a high calorie, artery-clogging cholesterol bomb—washed down by strong Turkish coffee.

The day's route was long and steamy, as we passed only four villages amid miles of corn, bean and pepper fields. It was a Saturday and the roads teamed with rickety farm equipment, as well as VWs and Yugos weaving in and out, whizzing by at 100 kilometers an hour. The worst, however, was when two semis met on the two-lane road. Oftentimes, the one on the left refused to move toward the center to give us space, because the one on the right was already there, avoiding crater-sized potholes. So we practiced "defensive walking," at times jumping entirely off the road into the weeds, while hoping for the best.

There was the scent of death on the highway. Everywhere I looked, there were either memorials or wreaths to loved ones who'd been mowed down on the pockmarked thoroughfare; or the blood spattered, flattened remains of a porcupine, squirrel, bird, dog or other unrecognizable animal. It was dispiriting to see and smell all day, especially knowing with one false step, or one drunk driver, we could be next. At one point, we even had a car full of young guys intentionally head right for us—forcing us off the road—as they laughed and sped away.

"Perhaps they heard our message and didn't agree," Émile quipped.

No, I chose to believe they were simply bored and saw us as easy targets. Besides, another thirty or more people in cars had already waved at us or shown other encouragement.

"Possibly you should use your ten-pound *bourdon* for more than decoration," I snapped back. "If someone aims at us like that, just hold it out like a lance in their direction—and then see how close they come."

At that instant, I remembered a dream I'd had about Émile the other night and woke screaming. We were in a strange city and I was fighting off dark abductors. I shouted to Émile for help. But he stood stock-still, unable to move, with a confused look on his face. He simply gave me a shrug and one of his frequent "I am sorry" lines, as I was hit over the head and dragged away. I hoped it wasn't a premonition.

After the restless night before, it took at least four caffeine stops for strong coffee and energy drinks to get us to Backi Petrovac, where the wife of the innkeeper had reserved us a room at the tennis center. After we checked in, our new hostess kindly drove us a few kilometers to the only open restaurant for mixed grill, and by the time we'd walked back to the tennis center, Anna awaited. A thirty-something, good-looking woman and mother, she'd studied in France and was the perfect companion for Émile. With her soft brown hair and soulful hazel eyes, I was surprised how much she resembled my own wife. They could easily have passed as sisters. All in all, it was a pleasant interlude. We talked with her about our mission, yet she remained in the skeptic's camp when it came to the possibility of peace.

"But don't you see," I explained, "envisioning peace is half the battle. As the world's consciousness changes, the rest is sure to follow."

The following morning, Sunday, traffic was lighter than usual. As we trudged past corn and wheat fields, we clearly "weren't in Kansas anymore," but it was hard to prove by our surroundings. Ultimately we spotted the yellow haze of smog clinging low on the horizon. Novi Sad, Serbia's second largest city, stretched for miles in all directions.

As usual, we made our way through a maze of streets to *centrum* and found a visitor office where the receptionist sent us on a wild-goose chase to student dorms on the far side of town, since everything nearby was supposedly booked. Getting there turned out to be far more complicated than ever imagined, as we wended our way through a crowd of 150,000 concertgoers camped along the Danube, known as the Dunav in Serbia. Writhing fans, rollerskaters, metalheads, punkers, freaks and Frisbee fanatics had come together from all over Europe for the popular Exit Festival.

Ninety minutes later, when we finally located the student housing, they handed us a fistful of forms to fill out. However, the real deal-breaker was when they demanded we leave our passports with them. That was enough. I made it a point to never leave my passport at a front desk. If they wanted to copy it, fine, but I wouldn't leave it at a luxury hotel in Paris, let alone a Serbian dorm.

Frustrated, we headed back to the visitor office where they easily booked us a room in the youth hostel—five blocks away—after we'd just walked all that way in sole-sizzling heat and frog-choking humidity. At last, checked into the bunk bed-filled room, Émile set off to wash his clothes while I scoured the streets for the ever-elusive Internet café.

After logging onto my account, I was shocked I didn't have any messages from Cheryl. She hadn't even checked her mail since Budapest. It was so unlike her and I was worried something had gone wrong back in Hungary. Did she make her connections out of Budapest? Did she even reach the city? Or was someone waiting for her at the bus stop the day she left?

Flying out the door, I frantically searched for a shop to buy a Serbian phone card—only to discover it was impossible to call the U.S. with one. In desperation, I borrowed Émile's cell phone and made a quick call home, thinking she had to be back to work. No answer. Worried, I phoned her mother and uttered those words every parent dreads: "I seem to have misplaced your daughter."

"Hold on a minute," she chirped. "Let me get her for you."

She wasn't due to return home until the following day.

At daybreak, our trek out of Novi Sad took us along the Dunav. Concertgoers were already scampering like lemmings to a synthesized heartbeat rhythm from Sremska Kamenica across Liberty Bridge for another day of fun. The irony wasn't lost on me. That same bridge had been bombed and destroyed by NATO forces during the Kosovo War and it had only recently been rebuilt. Nonetheless, our early start allowed us to leave town before traffic became too heavy and begin our steep climb through the Fruska Gora Range before it grew too hot.

Huffing and puffing as we neared the top, we stopped at a fruit stand in the countryside. It sure looked enticing. When I held out a ten-dinar note, insisting I didn't need a kilo of apricots to carry, the young fruit seller appeared a little put off, but he sold me a few pieces anyway. As Émile rested, I chatted to the fellow for quite awhile about our journey, and eventually asked him about the clear liquid sitting in plain bottles on his table.

"It's apple schnapps. Would you like a taste?"

"Did you make it here?"

"Yes, let me give you some."

At that, he poured me a small glass of the crisp ambrosia, one nearly as good as the homemade apple *most* we'd sampled back in Austria. Then he wouldn't even accept payment. With a "*Hvala!*" we were on our way.

Before long, we reached the crossroads to Beska, and as soon as I mentioned "food," there was a decided bounce to my companion's step.

"Émile, you know when we were walking across Tibet, we took a sturdy Tibetan horse named Sadhu with us from outside Lhasa to Kathmandu. He was a real trooper and we loved him like a brother, but he had his own sluggish pace and was constantly hungry. To him, life was one continual feast. Once he even got into a villager's hay bin and ate all night. In the morning, our host warned us, "Don't feed horse today!"

"Why?" we asked.

"If he eat more…he explode."

Émile smiled enigmatically, leaving me to wonder whether the analogy was lost on him or not? Anyway, we decided to stop at the roadside restaurant whose dining room was in a small pagoda under a parachute canopy. There was a giant stone statue of a Labrador retriever in the yard.

"Say, Émile, I bet he's the first dog on this trip who hasn't barked at you," I joked. It was true. I didn't know if it was his large walking stick, drooping leather hat, (or a canine's sixth sense), but nearly every dog we'd passed since France barked whenever Émile grew near, often rousing his buddies into a canine chorale.

A strong Serbian woman with one of those Marty Feldman-like roving eyes soon joined us. She spoke about ten words in German and no English or French, but we managed to order some grilled *cevapcici*, small spicy beef, pork and lamb sausages, and a cucumber salad, while relaxing out of the relentless sun. Then after lunch, she tried to convince us to spend the night there, claiming it was cheaper than staying at the hotel in Indija, just down the road. However, I'd hoped to sleep in the larger town and then set off for Belgrade in the early morning. So we moved on.

Walking along tractor trails parallel to the road, it took us another hour or so to reach Indija. It was a mid-sized city with an attractive downtown walking mall and new luxury hotel where we were quoted an exorbitant room rate, amounting to 1/7th of their per capita income. For some reason, they also had a "day" rate of only $28.

"Why is it more expensive to sleep at night?" I asked out of curiosity.

The clerk just shrugged his shoulders and went back to his work. As much as I tried to negotiate, it wasn't like the old Eastern Europe where anything was possible for a price. As someone had told me the night before, "As a country, we have moved from communism to capitalism—to fatalism."

Since theirs was the only place to stay in town, we grudgingly back-tracked to the lady in Beska, exhausted, sweaty and ravenous. After quick showers, the friendly woman invited us into her cozy home for hot soup, more *cevapcici*, fries, dried ham, bread, wine and salad, as we watched the nightly news and tried to understand what was happening in the world through video alone. It was impossible, yet we reveled in the relaxing atmosphere and her kindness. We were especially impressed when we finished and timidly asked, "How much?"

"*Gratis!*" our "angel" proclaimed.

Things did have a way of working out for the best.

Later that evening, Émile approached me with a serious look, a throat clearing and a stern, "We need to talk about the plan tomorrow…"

From his defensive body language, I knew he was prepared for an argument about walking to Belgrade, but I had no desire to push either of us beyond our limits. So I headed off a quarrel by promising, "We don't *have* to walk to Belgrade tomorrow, if you're not able." He looked relieved and a grin returned to his normally jolly face. "But don't be surprised if we have to walk a few fifty-kilometer days in Turkey."

His smile vanished.

In the morning, we woke to a huge breakfast of three eggs each and a blood sausage, along with cucumbers, tomatoes and strong Turkish coffee. Then humbled by her generosity once again, we headed back through

Indija toward Belgrade, even though we'd ruled out reaching the capital for another day.

The morning's route took us past more vegetable and sunflower fields, yet traffic was particularly unnerving. I wouldn't wish that part of the trek on anyone. Speed limits were non-existent on the narrow, two-lane roads and drivers pushed their rusted heaps to the limit. If someone was "only" driving a hundred kilometers an hour, others quickly passed on the left going more—even when there was a solid, no passing line. They zoomed within inches of us and we dared not stumble. I found myself wishing I'd brought bicyclist glasses with rearview mirrors protruding out each side to let me know exactly when to leap out of the way.

We stopped for lunch, grease-dripping Serbian hamburgers the size of saucers at a sidewalk café in Nova Pazova. Now, I don't want to make our walk appear more than what it was, but when I casually mentioned our trek for peace to Marta, our raven-haired waitress, she gasped and openly wept. The desire for an end to war struck such a powerful chord in that land so battle weary. Then, learning we needed a place to stay for the night, she eagerly called all her friends. No luck. She called the hotel in St. Pazova where a journalist had earlier ambushed us, conducting an impromptu interview right on the sidewalk. It was *complet*. So even though we'd planned to stop, again, much to Émile's chagrin, the Universe had other plans.

As we prepared to leave, I thanked Marta for her help, but she insisted, "No, it's me who should thank you for taking this trip. Your message will not die when you leave."

Now, I was the one who was moved. "Maybe our message will be like a pebble in the pond and grow larger as you tell someone, and then they tell a friend, and so on."

Batajnica was a slip of a forgotten village. So we were apprehensive as we entered, realizing if we found nothing there we'd have to walk three more hours to Belgrade. For some reason, I felt drawn to the steepled Orthodox Church in the center of town, so we passed through its gates and into a room where ladies sold religious objects. We asked to see the priest, and before long a fellow in his mid-fifties with a grand bushy beard appeared. As I tried to explain and pantomime our predicament, he only looked more confused. Finally, he disappeared for a moment and then returned with his daughter, an innocent girl in her twenties who spoke both English and German. After sharing our letters of pilgrimage, I assured Olivera that any accommodation, no matter how simple, would be greatly appreciated.

One look at Émile, slumped and red-faced from the heat, and me, equally dripping and dusty, would easily convince even the most hardened skeptics. Without a second thought, they provided us with a room, welcomed us into their home for showers, then onto their shady front porch for drinks and green melon. All in all, we spent a peaceful afternoon with the gracious family. Amid friendly conversation, Olivera presented us with oversized postcards of beautiful icons her mother had painted, as well as a Serbian monastery map to help us pick out other places to stay along our route south. Meanwhile, we were plied with cold drinks and invited to a St. Peter and Paul's Day service later that evening.

After relaxing back in our room, we joined the family in their church for Mass. I'd only attended one other Orthodox service in my life and it was Greek, so I was interested to see how it compared.

Upon entering, I noticed straight, high-back chairs lining three walls, as I'd once seen in Canterbury Cathedral lining the nave of the church. This was the area where the congregation stood. As Olivera explained, "It represents a corral for the 'sheep.'" There was also a central gilded iconic panel that reached the ceiling with paintings on four levels: the Stations of the Cross, the Prophets, the Apostles with the Holy Trinity in the center and the angels Seraphim and Cherubim flanking the doors. Behind the door was the main altar with the Host, where, she explained, "The priest or 'shepherd' enters the chancel through doors representing heaven."

I was particularly interested by the paintings of St. Peter and Paul facing the congregation in the nave. Worshippers who entered the church genuflected in front of those five times, and then kissed them several more. Two people had an unusual way of bowing. They dipped so low they nearly touched the ground with their hand before crossing themselves in the opposite direction of the Roman Catholics, as was their tradition.

Olivera and three other young ladies, along with Father Zarko, angelically sang a cappella during the Mass, while the congregation stood for the entire ninety-minute service. Those high-backed chairs turned out to be mostly for show.

Afterward, they led us back to the rectory where they proudly showed us the sublime, traditional icons they painted. Then we shared a simple meal, even though they normally fasted, eating no flesh, dairy or oil on Wednesdays and Fridays, so they could take communion. Still, the wine flowed freely, followed by delicious herbal schnapps. Then, as with families anywhere, photos were passed around. Olivera even generously wrote a letter of introduction in Serbian for us to present to monasteries along our path to Bulgaria.

At one point, I couldn't help but ask, "What were conditions like back in the old days under communist rule when many of the churches were locked and priests sometimes imprisoned?"

"I was just a little girl then," she confided, "but we still had services every day, even if it was only for our family in our own living room. We had to believe that someday things would change."

The sweet girl reminded me of the valuable lesson we'd learned in Tibet—to have faith. God or the Universe had a plan. If patient, we could hear it, and then experience the bounty of the world. Obstacles would be removed; we could accomplish our destiny.

Our hosts met us shortly after sunrise and had us over for a steaming cup of coffee before we left. Then setting off down the road, past commuters lined up to catch their buses, we only took a little over two hours to reach the outskirts of Belgrade, Serbia's capital. I honestly wasn't looking forward to the noise, pollution and traffic—but it was on Émile's must-see list and he had a "friend" there.

It wasn't long before we passed the "Belgrade" metropolis sign and multinational plants just before entering what we thought was the city. Wrong. When I finally stopped a tall fellow with a gold earring and asked for directions to Square of the Republic, he broke the bad news.

"Sorry, but you have another five kilometers. This is Zemun."

Disappointed, I quickly told him about our pilgrimage. Then anxious to continue, we set a fast pace and hustled down the busy sidewalk, until five minutes later when we heard someone screaming behind us. I snapped around, prepared for the worst, only to find the fellow we'd just met. He'd bought a map of Belgrade for us, and then sprinted to catch up.

"Thanks! Say, if you can walk that fast, you wouldn't consider joining us, would you?"

"No," the student replied with a bashful smile. "But thank you for making the walk," he added, before heading off to class.

After crossing the Dunav, we caught a pathway near her banks and I was struck with a brief sadness. We'd soon be leaving our friend, as she'd continue flowing east to the Black Sea, while we headed south to Sofia. And no, we never did see that American girl supposedly swimming its length.

Finally reaching the impressive Square of the Republic, we phoned Émile's friend Borko, our only contact in the city of a million and a half people. When he arrived, driving his Mercedes right up onto the sidewalk in the town square, the gregarious lawyer immediately took charge, whisking us off to the hotel where he'd reserved rooms. Mine was twelve foot square and hot enough to grow tomatoes. It was furnished with two twin beds covered by blankets made of orange tabby cat fur. Still, we were grateful for his generosity.

Even still, we had just twenty minutes to shower and change before we were shuttled off to a bistro in the trendy Skadarlija district. There we were interviewed for over an hour by two of Serbia's largest newspapers, *Glas javnosti* and *Novosti*, who seemed genuinely interested in our journey and eager to run articles.

After they left, we headed down the street to a traditional café or *kafana* for a feast so huge I couldn't finish all the food. Yet between bites, I was curious to hear Borko's impression about the "new" Serbia and life after the break-up of Yugoslavia.

"Well, Belgrade, as you can see, is awash with money these days," he said, proudly motioning up and down the street.

"But how many can afford all the luxury goods?" I wondered aloud.

"Exactly. You'll notice the poverty more and more as you head farther south. But while you are here, I'd like to introduce you to someone very special, my priest. I told him you were coming."

Although exhausted, we joined him on another long walk to the Temple of St. Sava, the largest Serbian Orthodox Church, where we met Borko's amiable priest. He led us on a personal grand tour of the most important church in the Serbian Orthodox faith. Nonetheless, even he was unable to provide a letter of introduction for us to show to the monastery monks to the east—or confirm whether or not they even accepted pilgrim guests. All that remained a mystery.

After a quick hotel breakfast in the morning, we set off in search of more information about Serbian monasteries, beginning with the travel agency of the Serbian Orthodox Church just up the street. Once they understood what we were doing, the ladies provided us with a map and tried to determine which abbeys existed along our route to Sofia. Afterward, we rushed back to the hotel where Borko had set up interviews with two more Belgrade newspapers.

Before long, the female reporter for Serbia's largest daily journal arrived and asked us questions in perfect English about our journey for over an hour. Suddenly, right in the middle of a long explanation about fostering peace, Borko's cell phone rang. From the look on his face, something was terribly wrong.

"Excuse me," he interrupted. "That was a call from my friend in Lebanon. Israel has just bombed Beirut Airport!"

There was an awkward silence at our table, as we each weighed the implications. Would it mean a swift and violent retaliation by Lebanon and its Arab neighbors? Would it be the fuse that ignited World War Three?

For us, it meant we would have to re-examine our pilgrimage, or at least our route. Syria was already on America's "terrorist-sponsor" list, and it often appeared our government looked for any excuse to draw them into a fight. On the other hand, it made me believe that what we were doing was more important than ever. So we decided to take a "wait and see" attitude. We'd weigh our options once we reached Istanbul when the fall-out would be more apparent.

After posing for the news photographers with our backpacks in front of the hotel, Émile and I headed down Terazije, Belgrade's main walking mall. I felt like a bumpkin just off the farm, as Serbian girls sashayed past in crop-tops, low-slung, tight skirts and impossibly high heels. Fashion had thankfully come a long way since those days when badly stocked state-run stores ruled the roost, and Serbian hair was routinely fried from bad perms and coloring.

As usual, Émile was hungry and I let him take the lead in finding us a place for lunch. That was a painful exercise, as we stopped in one touristic umbrella-bar after another. Most served no food, yet after a cursory look at their menu, he'd say, "Well, this is no more than I'd pay at home."

"Yes, but this is Serbia."

For months, I'd tried to gently impart a little travel savvy based on my twenty years on the road, but I'd nearly given up trying. For example, our latest trip to the bank to change traveler's checks turned into a fiasco.

At first, Émile went in alone, then came shuffling back as I waited in the mall.

"Can you interpret for me?" he asked.

"Interpret? At a bank?"

Nonetheless, I followed him inside a nearby bank where, he said, "The lady is very nice." As luck would have it, it happened to be a Serbian bank and not a more accommodating German or Austrian one. In Serbia, as we'd already learned, only certain banks cashed traveler's checks. So we had to jump through a series of hoops while the "lady" played the music.

"Dance monkeys, dance!"

She immediately pushed us off to her henchman, who demanded, "Show me your original purchase receipts."

"They're at home with his wife for safety," I explained.

Although she accepted that logic, it still took us twenty nail-chewing minutes and a steep commission to cash his checks. Once outside, I reminded my friend, "They'll become even harder to change in Turkey, since we'll be in smaller villages. Next time, just bring your bank debit card as I originally suggested."

For lunch, tiring of the hunt, I eventually guided us to a café one block off the mall (with umbrellas) for 1/3 the cost. Émile was delighted to find his favorite tripe soup on the menu and I had tasty Serbian *moussaka* with *shopska* salad, similar to a Greek farmer salad with cucumber, tomato, onion, peppers and feta cheese. It was certainly a more congenial setting. The fellow sitting next to us, a local businessman, even shared his dish of wild mushrooms.

After a relaxed lunch, we split up. Émile returned to his room for a "*petite siesta*" while I headed up Terazije to the 11th century Kalemegdan Citadel, a hilltop fortress overlooking the Dunav and Sava Rivers. The battlement dated back to the days when Belgrade was a Celtic settlement and the Roman village of Singidunum lay below. Nowadays, it held a serene tree-filled park with tennis and basketball courts, as well as military tanks in the former moats. Entering its gates, I came face to face with Ivan Mestrovic's *Monument of Gratitude to France for Their Help in World War I*. His other statue, *The Victor*, the symbol of the city, overlooked the rivers below. All in all, the gardens provided a tranquil sanctuary to cool off from the summer heat. Eventually, storm clouds moved in and thunder resonated across the hilltop.

CHAPTER SEVEN
Belgrade to Bulgaria

"It is Our Custom Here"

"Poverty is the worst form of violence."
~ Mohandas K. Gandhi

The following day was one of small miracles. We were on the road by dawn, trudging the long expanse out of Belgrade. Once you left its central core, life became far less manicured and you could see how the real city denizens lived. Traffic congestion was high and air pollution intense. At times, there was a Third-World feel to it all. I could have been back in India, weaving from the disintegrating sidewalk to the road and back again, around buses and trucks belching smoke.

Then again, just as we arrived on the outskirts of town, our first surprise of the day came when a white van skidded to a halt right in front of us. A muscular man with close-cropped hair leapt out and ran over to greet us like long-lost friends. Vigorously shaking our hands, he welcomed us and then reached into his pants pocket and tried to hand us a 100-dinar note.

"That's not necessary," I protested.

He insisted, saying, "It is our custom here."

"No," I repeated. "We can't accept this." But he wouldn't take "no" for an answer and thrust the money at Émile until he gingerly took it.

At that point, the doors to the fellow's van burst open and we were surprised to see six tiny children huddled together inside with their mother and a beautiful teenaged daughter with long, braided hair. Her lively eyes danced as she spoke English with us, asking all about our journey. As she did, her father reached into his van and gave us a brochure for a holy site in their city.

130

"We belong to an organization here that practices medieval weaponry," she explained. "Each year we stage a festival with full costumes and mock battles. There is quite a good turnout and many people come from all over Europe."

As she spoke, a pickup suddenly swerved off the road in front of theirs' and four more powerful "knights" with short hair piled out. One fellow handed us each a 1,000-dinar bill, despite our wild protests. "It is our way," he passionately argued, while one of his friends ducked inside their truck and returned with a club t-shirt for each of us.

Nearly speechless at their generosity, I tried my best to explain our journey, but it wasn't needed. They already knew us—and not by the newspaper interview, since it hadn't appeared yet. They just knew.

"Yes, you are walking the old path to Istanbul and Jerusalem," another gregarious fellow confirmed. "We call it the Via Roman."

Back in the 1st century A.D. when it was first constructed, the Romans called it the *Via Militaris* or *Via Diagonalis*. Six meters wide, wide enough for two wagons or chariots, it once stretched 1,054 kilometers and connected Belgrade, Nis, Sofia, Plovdiv and Edirne to Constantinople (that later became Istanbul).

After making small talk with them for a short time, for once, I was sorry to have to move on so soon, as I felt like I was among brothers. When we sadly turned to leave, I gushed, "Your kindness really made our day."

His daughter, with the most beatific smile, replied, "No, you made *our* day more beautiful. Thank you for what you are doing."

"It's our pleasure," I said, humbled by it all.

"Pray for us in Jerusalem," her father added.

"We certainly will."

Even though we had a long, smog-filled climb up those surrounding hills east of the sprawling city, their chance encounter strengthened our resolve. However, it was only the first. Nearing Grocka, the Dunav gorge came into view once again. As we paused on the roadside, two fellows hailed us from across the street. The sandy-haired father appeared to be in his forties and his son was taller and in his twenties. Approaching, they shook our hands warmly and asked, "Where are you from?"

"France!" Émile answered, as if holding the winning lottery ticket.

"Ah!" the father exclaimed, clasping his hands together in a universal sign of brotherhood. "France and Serbia—brothers!"

At that, he and his son insisted we follow them a short distance back to their hillside home where they made us comfortable on their terrace under the shade of their grape arbor. The father immediately ducked into their modest house and returned with cold orange juice followed by thick Turkish-style coffee and fresh apples from their yard. As we gathered around their table, the son, who spoke a little English, translated the details of our trip. Then his father spoke of the bombs raking his village not so long ago, and openly wept with heartfelt emotion when he spoke of the friendship and assistance they'd received from the French during World War I. Serbia had a long memory when it came to such things.

To illustrate, he brought out a treasured photograph of his grandfather in uniform. From what I could tell, after devastating battles, 125,000 retreating Serbian soldiers reached the Adriatic coast and were saved at the last minute from advancing German troops by French ships that carried them to Greek islands. Today, their valor was still remembered in song, statues like the one I'd seen in Belgrade's park, and in a father's tearful memories.

Would there be similar songs about our country in Iraq someday?

Afterward, the son presented us an equally cherished photo of Serbia's most holy icon on which he wrote his family's address and phone numbers, should we need any help on our journey. Then his father returned to the kitchen and prepared huge *sandvichs* of flat bread with feta cheese and thick smoked bacon tucked into a bag along with apples, tomatoes, cucumbers and onions for our journey.

Sensing it was best to move on, as we still might have another eighteen kilometers to walk to the next village, Smederevo, we stood to go. Passionately the father embraced us with tears in his eyes and kissed us three times on our cheeks. I only wish I could have spoken Serbian to better understand his story. Nevertheless, his eyes and heartfelt emotion told a tale all their own.

All day our luck continued. We found a "tourist hotel" just six or seven kilometers away on the other side of Grocka; a welcome surprise, since walking another twelve would have made it a fifty-kilometer day. The hotel was vacant and better than most we'd seen. Beside the Dunav, it was a little pricey, but there was no traffic, horn honking or smog, so we looked forward to a night in the country.

As coolness enveloped the mighty river, I reflected on the amazing people we'd already met since coming to the war-torn, impoverished land —and I was so thankful for their generosity and camaraderie.

In the morning, we said a final goodbye to the Dunav when we reached Smederevo. After an initial tough climb from Grocka, we spotted American steel smokestacks on the horizon, reminding me of the crimson-orange flames from Pittsburgh's steel plants that pierced the night sky of my youth. Back then, in childhood innocence, they fascinated me in a primitive way. As we drove past them each week on the way to the store, I marveled at their magical intensity. It wasn't until years later, as we approached the same spot, my sisters and I let out a collective, "Yeww!" at their overpowering stench. I used to wonder how people could live next door to them? How could they breathe the air that burned their lungs? Or let their children play outside with industrial waste so close by?

Back in the 1980s, those same factories abruptly closed and relocated elsewhere. Where? We didn't know. Did it really matter? All we knew was that our friends and neighbors, loyal "Mill Hunkies" for twenty, thirty, forty years were suddenly on the street, out of work, with little marketable skills. It was devastating to the entire region and some might say that Pittsburgh nowadays still worked hard to heal from that betrayal. Seeing those same factories in similar rolling green hills, set beside water so alike to our own Ohio River, I now knew. It was all about the bottom-line. Corporations moved factories where they could pay workers less with fewer unions and less environmental regulation. What would that small Serbian village do when the company decided they could forge steel cheaper in Brazil, China or Timbuktu? Surely, more lives would be ruined.

We walked in silent contemplation, until we reached the far side of town. Next to the second steel plant, we stopped for water. Émile and I were instantly mobbed by a group of engaging kids in front of their run-down schoolhouse. After I took a photo of their grinning, grimy faces, they tagged alongside for a while, tripping through a shantytown of worker's housing.

Kids aside, we were seldom alone. Our latest interview had appeared in the Belgrade paper and we were serenaded by horn blasts from passing motorists and even offered a ride. In Smederevo, one friendly, stout fellow at a sandwich shop bought us food, and then spoke with me in German about our pilgrimage. Otherwise on Saturday, it was difficult to find an open restaurant. A bar? Yes, plenty. At one point, we stopped into a small market and watched in dismay as a bleary-eyed man downed shot after shot of schnapps. Then, barely able to walk, he stumbled outside to his tractor, cranked it up, and careened down the road—our road.

The streets were patched together like an ugly, gray, communist quilt, rife with moth-eaten holes. It had more bulges than a fat lady in Spandex. The corridor was strewn with trash, rotting animals, and those ever-present plastic liter bottles. Even more disturbing, on one single day, I counted more than twenty memorials and wreaths to those killed on the highway.

Meanwhile, the trucks relished their fast and dangerous games. On one occasion when I was fifty yards or so in front of Émile, I heard a low beep of the horn and assumed it was just another well-wisher responding to Émile's frequent regal waves. I didn't realize it was an eighteen-wheeler barreling in the left-hand lane past another semi and headed right at me. I was already walking on the narrow dirt shoulder when I felt it rush past. Just inches from my arm, it sent me reeling into the brush. My companion lagged far behind. All he could have done was offer a pathetic "Sorry" and then call my grieving widow.

Later that afternoon, we arrived in Osipanoica where we hoped to find a room. After discovering its one motel was closed, Émile took the initiative for once to approach a curly-haired, middle-aged fellow watering his yard. Maybe it was because a car sporting French license plates sat parked in his driveway.

"Oh, it's my daughter's car," the man quickly explained. "She is studying in Paris. But please, come and join our family. We stay nearby."

Relieved, we piled our packs into his car and drove the few blocks to his home, trusting the Francophile would have a place on his floor for two weary pilgrims. Over the next hour, I listened to Émile spin the tale of our adventure, as we cooled off on their terrace. However, for some reason, I sensed they weren't eager for our company—and I was right. Eventually, they commanded, "Come," and loaded us back into their car.

"We will take you to the motel. It is only eight kilometers away on the other side of the *autoput* or freeway ."

After one quick glance at Émile, I knew what I had to say.

"No, no thank you," I insisted, half-surprising myself.

The driver squinted with bewildered eyes through his rearview mirror.

"No, but thanks anyway. We're pilgrims and we have to walk to Jerusalem."

Émile was equally baffled, but I whispered, "Look, if we accept a ride now, it will ruin the integrity of our pilgrimage." Then borrowing his well-worn line, I added, "I am sorry."

As difficult a decision as it was, it made perfect sense to me at the time. Reluctantly Émile and I climbed out of the Renault at nearly 4:00 and began trudging the remaining eight kilometers to Lozovik, which on a typical day might take us two hours. But just one kilometer later we had a reprieve. I spotted a restaurant where we'd been told they might have rooms. Although there was a party going on, as soon as we entered, we were swarmed by waiters decked out in white shirts and black bowties, the gregarious owner, curious kids and partiers. They'd read the article in the newspaper, so everyone was eager to buy us a drink—but no one had a room since it was a wedding party and folks planned to spend the night. We were crestfallen. That was until Alexandra appeared.

A voluptuous, curly-haired, twenty-five year old blonde in low-cut black satin party dress and heels, she was a glamorous 1940s film goddess of the Serbian hinterlands.

"Plus, she speaks perfect French," smirked Émile.

Hearing our predicament, Alexandra was quick to suggest, "You can stay in our house with my mother and grandmother, if you don't mind?"

Mind? We were elated.

"Besides, it's just seven kilometers from here," she added with an endearing smile—one that could make a man say "yes" to nearly anything.

Still, our hearts sank. We'd already walked more than a typical day over difficult roads. But what choice did we have? As she called her mother to let her know we were coming, we thanked the group, and then tapped deep into the last of our depleted energy reserves to reach Lozovik before nighttime fell.

It was nearly dark by the time we reached the crossroads and my friend was dragging his tail. We only had a vague idea where Alexandra's mother's house might be, as her directions were sketchy in a farm country way.

"Turn left at the crossroads, and then left again at the big oak tree, and look for the white house. Everyone knows it," was hardly like having a GPS reading.

Forty-five minutes later, half-starved and panting like racehorses, we ran into two women in the middle of the dirt road. One was a stout blonde pushing a baby stroller. On a hunch, I sidled up next to her and gasped, "By any chance, are you Alexandra's mother?"

"Of course. We've been waiting for you."

Verica immediately took us under her motherly wing and led us back to her large home where she and her aged mother laid out a tasty spread on her kitchen table, as if we were long-lost relatives. After eleven hours on the trail, one of our longest days yet, we were exhausted and sore, but would be fine in the morning—thanks to more unexpected "angels" along the trail.

Leaving early the next morning, Émile was predictably hungry and already in a disagreeable mood. So before long, we plopped down at a rustic roadside bar in a nearby village. While my friend gleefully pulled his extensive food cache of cheese, chocolate and bread out of his pack, I ducked next door for a Turkish coffee and a delicious feta cheese tart, or *syr burek*, made of layers of phyllo dough. It was a typical breakfast throughout the Balkans and Slavic countries, as well as Greece and Israel. Regrettably though, even after this quick break, Émile lagged farther behind. Finally, concerned for his health, I waited for him in Velika Plana.

"Why don't you just walk ahead," he gasped, red-faced and puffing. "We can meet at the hotel in Markovac."

It made perfect sense, since we could each walk at our own pace—and there was no chance of becoming lost. So, for once, I had a more relaxed day, not having to walk slowly, wait, or worry about losing my "navigator," who carried our map due to the sole fact that his pockets were bigger than mine. I sensed walking separately would become more common from then on, as days grew longer and distances farther between accommodations. We were destined to become Lewis without Clark, Marquette *sans* Jolliet.

The road was equally abandoned. Whether it was because of the weekend (or unpopularity of Markovac), it came as a welcome relief. At one point, a man on a bicycle stopped and chatted in an animated way about our journey, and then invited me back to his house for a drink. Nevertheless, I declined his offer as it was still early, and frankly I enjoyed walking solo for a change. Yet even with the delay, I arrived at Markovac's roadside motel by early afternoon. A friend of Borko's had offered us a complimentary room.

In my absence, Émile had an adventure all his own. While walking through Velika Plana, he was approached by a reporter. Unable to speak English, German or Serbian, all he could do was show him the news article from Belgrade and hope it answered any questions. If so, it would already be the sixth time our peace pilgrimage had received media coverage in the tiny, war torn country.

At daybreak, breakfast was meager at the old motel: one tomato wedge, butter, a roll, two thin slices of hard cheese and tiny wedges of feta, followed by a cup of weak tea. Émile was quick to signal his dissatisfaction by loudly trumpeting his nose at our table—then standing to perform his dramatic "clearing the throat" routine—to our fellow diners' chagrin.

Since it was a straight beeline for thirty-four kilometers to the Hotel Jagodina, our day's destination, I thought it better to walk solo again and meet at the inn. After more than seventy days on the trail together, pilgrims or not, it would give our relationship a break. Besides, it would allow us the luxury of stopping whenever we wanted for food, water, or rest without consensus.

We followed the *autoput* south, tracing the old Roman road. Compared to the modern Europe I knew, what I saw was closer to a third-world reality. I passed tattered villages of dilapidated cottages with hogs or turkeys roaming the yards, and Ladas sputtering past in a haze of smog. Ancient men in frayed suits occasionally creaked past on rusted bicycles. One fellow stopped by the roadside long enough to sift through the mountain of trash others had discarded. Since leaving the capital, we'd passed an endless stream of roadside garbage: plastic bottles, worn-out appliances, cardboard boxes and stuffed trash bags. Some had been recently burned, but most was just strewn. It was recycling gone mad. If a plastic bottle took, what, 450-years to decompose, Serbia would be covered to its mountaintops by then, if nothing were done.

It wasn't all poverty and filth though. In that land of rusted jalopies, quite a few sleek, black Mercedes also passed. Occasionally I spotted brand new, tidy homes, and even mansions surrounded by high spiked fences with Rottweiler pictures posted to their gates. Those signs, by the way, were no bluff, as I was snapped and snarled at by several of the largest dogs I'd ever seen. I guess it was like I'd been told. Russians were flooding in with money and snapping up real estate with a passion. In fact, I'd already had an interesting conversation with a teenager who bemoaned the invasion of the Russian mafia and the drugs and guns coming into his country, plus the high inflation and skyrocketing cost of living. At fifteen, he was studying English with hopes of moving to Switzerland someday. Tragically, in his short lifetime, he'd already been through four wars since his family relocated from Hungary eleven years earlier. That was enough to make anyone yearn for peace.

Dasvedanya, Serbia, baby.

Traffic increased as I grew nearer to Jagodina. For hours, I climbed steep hills out of the gorge, but nothing was insurmountable. Émile was nowhere to be seen all morning, but I figured he was just walking at his own pace. Finally, as I rounded one last bend, a city of red-tiled roofs materialized below, as did an even more tempting vision—a motel with a restaurant. It wasn't Hotel Jagodina where we'd planned to meet, but I didn't think my friend would mind, since it was closer and even had a swimming pool, an unheard of luxury.

Walking into its lobby, I met a tall, friendly fellow at the reception desk and briefly mentioned our peace walk to him. He wished us both a safe journey before driving off. It was only later that I learned he'd bought both of us a welcome drink. It was forty minutes before I finally spotted my comrade trudging over the crest of the hill. When I flagged him down, a look of satisfied relief filled his face.

After enjoying one of Serbia's monumental-sized hamburgers, I decided to spend a little time catnapping around their pool. For once, Émile was too tired even to eat, although he did join me later, shuffling poolside in his black bun-huggers and leather cowboy hat—only to wake me up and ask for our key.

We were up and away at dawn and walking down the long hill to the city of Jagodina or "Strawberry," set on the banks of the Belica River. Although a good-sized town, it was easy for us to maneuver. After wolfing down our typical Serbian breakfast of espresso and *syr burek*, it was a straight, no-nonsense trek for the next six hours along a two-lane country road parallel to the *autoput*. Once again, we passed ten roadside memorials marking fatalities in as many kilometers. It was no wonder. Cars and trucks barreled down those awful roads at break-neck speed, weaving in and out between tractors, horse-drawn carts and plodding pilgrims, all without any regard to velocity or such nuisances as "passing zones."

By early afternoon we reached Pojate, a petrol station and motel off the freeway. In retrospect, we should have followed our original plan and continued on to Hotel Pojate, especially since the folks at the last lodging had called ahead to ensure a space for us. But no, we stopped at the other motel, simply because it was the first place we spotted. Initially, its manager was curious about us, especially when he discovered a new article about our journey in his daily newspaper. Maybe we should have known better when he admitted to being an ardent supporter of Serbian strongman Slobodan Milosevic, who'd recently died in prison. All the same, after he'd revealed another route to Aleksinac omitted from our map, we accepted the sociable innkeeper's invitation to join him for a glass of wine.

"Are you hungry?" he asked in passing.

"Of course. Always. Do you have a menu?"

"I only serve hamburgers right now."

"How much?" I asked, as I'd done with the wine. Both times, he gave no response. Looking back, that was our first warning sign. However, for once, I chose to ignore it and trust his honesty, although I did whisper my concern to Émile. As usual, he shrugged it off, thinking me far too mistrustful.

When our food finally arrived, we gleefully polished off those burgers. Imagine our surprise when the bill was presented—and our meal cost nearly as much as our room. Shocked by his chutzpah, we confronted the manager. Well, he quickly deducted 250 dinars from our tab, although we knew he was still overcharging us for his "Welcome to Pojate" glass of wine, charging twice what we'd paid for an entire bottle. Then with an unruffled shrug, he went back to his work. Again, it was all part of the game.

Rising with the sun, we followed a roadway parallel to the *autoput* over hills and mounds of trash all day. Temperatures became blistering. Villages, even at our speed, passed within the blink of an eye. Émile kept pace for a change, footstep for footstep, until by mid-afternoon we reached Aleksinac, a settlement dating back to Neolithic times. Astride a hilltop, it overlooked a valley of corn and pepper farms. Stepping into a restaurant to ask directions to the Hotel Balkan (then closed), we were adopted by a happy-chappy that spoke German. Even though he was visiting town himself, he knew of an inn nearby and went out of his way to lead us there. Unmarked and on a backstreet, we'd never have found it without his help.

After settling in, he insisted on treating us to drinks while we talked about our pilgrimage, as well as Israel's recent bombing within Beirut. We knew that would make our journey more difficult, forcing us to walk through areas of increased tension. Eventually, the fighting might even spread as far as Turkey. Although we still had two months for the situation in the Middle East to cool down, public opinion throughout Europe had already run strongly against our invasion of Iraq and Israel's ongoing violence. In fact, the shyster the night before even went so far as to claim, "Bush, Blair and Bin Laden are all in this together." I couldn't quite fathom their *ménage a trois*, although the image of the three of them in bed together was enough to make me chuckle.

Politics did make strange bedfellows.

What a difference a day could make. Only the night before, I'd confided to Émile that I needed to stop at a bank. I had exactly two dinars to my name—not even enough to even buy water along the way.

Our day began with a climb into the surrounding hills where a bright-eyed teenager on a bicycle soon joined us, pedaling alongside. With controlled emotion and in very good English, he told me how he and his family had recently escaped Kosovo, and how he'd already seen so much killing at his tender age. "My aunt and uncle live in Switzerland," he confided. "Maybe I can join them some day."

"Yes, it's too bad that wars keep countries poor," I replied. "It's only when people decide they've had enough fighting that recovery and rebuilding can begin." The evidence surrounded us every day for weeks. "Look at Switzerland, for example. Their neutrality has allowed them to have one of the highest standards of living in the world."

"My uncle says that's because they have all the money," the kid joked, wise beyond his years. "That's why it's not bombed."

"True, but there are also places like Canada, Norway, New Zealand and Iceland where war has become a relic. I believe it takes a shift in people's attitude and tolerance," I explained. "They have to insist on peace and elect representatives with the courage to settle for nothing less."

There were no towns after we reached the top of the hill, so our clever companion coasted back down to his village. Our throats were parched and we were out of water by the time we finally spotted a café. Sitting down in the coolness of its terrace, we ordered coffees, a bottle of mineral water and another for later. Finally, when we asked the ultimate question, "How much?" we had a shock to remember.

"For you, there is no charge," the owner and his son, the waiter, proudly announced with broad grins.

After yesterday's "misunderstanding," we were flabbergasted. They'd heard about our mission and insisted on helping. After taking our photos, they warmly shook our hands. Then as one final gesture, the bighearted owner ducked into his kitchen and presented us with a loaf of steaming, freshly baked bread for the road.

As much as their hospitality did wonders to raise our lagging spirits, just a few hours later, we had a similar incident at a gas station when we stopped for water. A muscular fellow who looked Moroccan struck up a conversation. He told us he'd lived in France as a child, and insisted on buying us sodas. So, there we were, thirsty—only two dinars in my pocket—and we'd already had two people quench our thirst. What synchronicity.

After battling heat, dust, exhaust and exhaustion all day, we reached historic Nis, a university town and Serbia's third largest city. The birthplace of Constantine the Great occupied nearly 600-square kilometers of low, red-tile roofed houses along the River Nisava and historic Constantinople road. It took us hours to finally maneuver into the main square, boasting yet another statue of a man on a horse. It was there we met Milan, another "friend" of Émile's, who loaded us into his white sedan and drove us to his private clinic. Worn out, we looked forward to taking a day off. Finally, we could sleep late, catch up on correspondence, do laundry, and sample more Serbian delicacies. Then again, Milan had already arranged an interview with Nis Television.

Later that evening, after a week of Internet silence, I had a chance to catch-up on emails from friends and family. Back home, talk of World War III was escalating. It was already being pre-sold as the new, improved "shock and awe" sequel by less-reputable American media. Israeli troops had entered Lebanon, and Iran's president Mahmoud Ahmadinejad was rattling his scimitar, vowing to continue his nuclear development program. Although my family urged me to immediately fly home, I felt we'd be safe—at least until we reached Istanbul. After that, all bets were off.

The techno-music throbbing from the house next door to the clinic pounded all night, until sunrise when it finally abated. Then Émile's alarm sounded at 5:30. So much for sleeping-in.

For hours, we puttered around the clinic doing errands until early afternoon when the NTV producer and her crew finally arrived to shoot their segment. As they set up their lights, she confided that our interview would be seen by perhaps a million viewers throughout Serbia that evening, and the following as well. Our wishes had been answered.

For once, compared to the other interviewers, the pert brunette took her time and conducted a more in-depth look at our journey. I had a chance to discuss Templar history in the area, as well as the idea of establishing our route as a peace trail. As a final point, after twenty minutes, she wrapped up our interview with one last question for Émile.

"You are sixty-eight. How does your family feel about you being away on this long journey?"

My friend, a man of few words, choked up and his eyes grew misty. "They fear for me." A solitary tear rolled down his cheek.

Afterward, Émile and I caught a taxi into town to the visitor information office with hopes of gleaning details about the route to Bela Palanka, as well as any information about hotels there. We were flying blind. Surprisingly they knew very little other than to tell us there was no hotel (not true), and then sketch a map for our exit out of town.

Meanwhile, the world continued to turn and burn. One British newspaper reported that 500,000 people were being evacuated from southern Lebanon in preparation for a full-scale ground attack by Israel, who wanted to create a twenty-kilometer buffer zone along its northern border.

Later that evening, after meeting Milan's family and his very large American bulldog, we went to a stylish outdoor restaurant for dinner where Milan's friend Goran met us. He spoke French, so Émile was delighted. With élan, Milan ordered a feast of grilled meats, *cevapcici* and peppers, *shopska* salad, and a delicious Serbian red wine. As he explained, the cucumber, tomato, feta cheese, olive or pepper salads, known by slightly different names, were as common as sunshine in Bulgaria, Greece, Macedonia and Turkey. Depending on the country, it was often served with *rakia*, *raki*, or *ouzo*, the anise-flavored liquor. As we enjoyed our banquet, we also feasted on what Milan called "Serbia's natural resources"—a neverending parade of stunning women who made grand entrances into the restaurant. At one point, two dark-haired beauties, Balkan Shakiras, belly danced together at their table, captivating diners with their erotic shimmies to Turkish-inspired music performed by the live band.

After an hour of great conversation, another friend of Milan's, "a very successful businessman" joined us. The fellow was perhaps thirty years old, six foot-five and weighed 280 pounds. As soon as he sat down, he began bragging about himself, his properties, and his plans to "make a million dollars this year and retire." I politely listened for over thirty minutes. What choice did I have? Sitting next to him, I was a captive audience. Eventually, when he came up for air, I simply asked one question.

"With all your money, what will you do for the people here to make their life better?"

"I'm going to play and have fun," he boasted without a second's pause.

"But what will you do for Serbians?" I'd seen plenty of people over the past week living little better than peasant lives.

Well, that was the wrong question to ask.

"What did American bombs do to make lives better?" he demanded, poking a finger in my face.

"I'm talking about *you* as an individual—not your government or mine," I replied. "What about you?"

He took that as his cue to begin a tiresome tirade that persisted until I slowly turned away. Milan gave me a "what can I say" look. Without a word, we all rose to leave. An invisible barrier had been breached, and it was best to leave the seething Serbian bulldog lie where he may.

Unfortunately, many governments take actions reprehensible to the rest of the world. As much as we were told Iran, Iraq, Syria, North Korea, and others were "terrorist" nations, other countries viewed America in a dangerous light. In fact, a November 2006 survey conducted by Pew Global Attitudes Project found 75% of Britons (our staunchest ally) considered President George W. Bush a "great or moderate threat to peace"—compared to 69% for North Korean strongman Kim Jong-Il.

We were up and out of the clinic by dawn, ready for a long day and still uncertain where we'd spend the night in Bela Palanka. On the way out of town, we passed the Skull Tower, one of the world's more "heady" monuments. During an 1809 fight for liberation from the Ottoman Empire, an outnumbered group of Serbian freedom fights were cornered there. Instead of surrender, their leader, Stevan Sindelic, fired a shot into their gunpowder magazine, blowing up his men along with the Turks. Later, after squashing the rebellion, the Turkish commander ordered 952 Serbian skulls to be mounted on a tower at the site to discourage any further revolt. In 1892, the skulls were enclosed in the chapel as a memorial to man's heroic quest for freedom.

Catching a small bypass, Émile and I climbed east through a gorge on the traditional Roman route to Sofia. All morning we set a fast pace, climbing for hours through a ravine encircled by sheer cliffs to the south and rolling meadows, orchards and valleys to the north. The road was paved at times, and then it was only gravel, until it eventually disintegrated into dirt. Still, it was the most physically beautiful part of Serbia we'd seen. Even the traffic was light, as most drivers chose to take the busy E-80 highway southeast, so they didn't have to contend with the mountains.

By late morning, we rapidly descended into the village of Spaj where our road intersected with the main highway. There we were finally able to find something to eat, since we hadn't come across a village of any size all morning. As we polished off the café's rustic burgers, I asked the owner's teenaged son, "Do you know of a smaller road we can walk to Bela Palanka? This main highway is just too busy to walk safely."

"Sure," he answered in English, eager to help. "There is an unmarked road running beside the railroad tracks all the way. It is smart to take this path, since the Turks are returning from their vacations now. They try to drive non-stop from Germany and the main highway becomes very dangerous."

We easily found his trail beside the tracks, although it also led us down by the muddy river for a while. Nevertheless, we reached Bela Palanka within two hours and stumbled upon a truck stop renting rooms. It was far from luxurious with cell-like quarters still dirty from the last travelers. Then again, they had a restaurant offering Balkan trucker tucker, and a large television featuring non-stop football. Personally though, I was more eager to clean up in their concrete block shower, twenty yards outside in the back.

Stepping inside the windowless, closet-sized cubicle, I shut the creaking wooden door behind me, locked it, and then jumped up and down long enough to keep my blood moving during the frosty coldwater cascade. Despite my violent shivering, I paid particular attention not to drop my soap, since bending down could pose a real problem. Then drying off with my paper-like pack towel, I grinned in satisfaction, clean for another day. The small victories give you the most pleasure on such a journey. With a triumphant feeling, I turned the key to unlock the door—only to hear a "snap" as it broke off in my hand.

"Ah. What's next?" I tried screaming, "Émile, Émile!" to rouse my buddy, but figured it was useless. I knew he was already enjoying his *petite siesta* with visions of *petits fromages* dancing in his head. Or he'd taken out his hearing aid and hung up a personal "*Ne dérangez pas*" (Do Not Disturb) sign. Then remembering the kids playing in the yard, I began pounding and screaming loud enough to draw them near. Eventually, I heard a timid voice squeak, "Hello?" on the other side.

"Will you get your father," I asked, unsure whether they understood.

Fortunately they did. Before long, the manager appeared with another key and with a hearty laugh set the humbled pilgrim free. When I returned to our room, Émile dreamily cocked open one eye and sighed, "I was wondering where you've been…"

Leaving Bela Palanka at first light, we caught a nondescript road leading up the mountainside to a rustic village, reminiscent of an earlier time. There was no plumbing or electricity. One stooped woman, her face as furrowed as her fields, led her solitary cow up the hillside to pasture. Another ancient fellow dressed in a tattered suit and cap directed us to the next trail leading steeply upward. En route to the top where we'd supposedly run into the old asphalt road, we passed a family carrying axes and pulling a rickety wooden cart, off to collect firewood. Then finally, we encountered a grizzled shepherd with one front tooth who smiled a cheerful, jack-o-lantern grin, as he gave us directions for the last portion of the trail.

By the time we reached the upper road with its steep, thirteen percent grade, we had it almost entirely to ourselves. Only four or five cars passed all morning. It was a welcome relief. At last we could hear the gentle bird-songs and light scamper of lizards into the parched brush as we approached.

Only once was our solitude interrupted. Six ferocious dogs guarding a gravel pit began barking and baying. As we drew near, they threateningly crept toward us in a pack, snarling with ears set far back. For once, to my great surprise, Émile swung his *bourdon*, pounding it on the ground and waving it in the air. As the dogs scattered, I was relieved to know it could be more than a flagpole, if needed.

I was also thankful we'd stocked up on water before leaving, as we passed no villages or stores until we reached the outskirts of Pirot in early afternoon. At just twenty-six kilometers, it was a relatively short day. Dimitrovgrad, the border town, was another twenty-five kilometers with nothing in between.

Pirot was an unexceptional village of more red tile-roofed houses nes-tled in a valley. We quickly found its one and only hotel in the town's tallest building, boasting over one hundred rooms, including a vast ballroom with worn carpets decorated by a graduate of the Miss Havisham's School of Interior Design. Although I couldn't imagine too many people staying there, they refused to budge on their hyper-inflated room price, more than we'd ever paid in Serbia. Our only consolation was being awarded their one room with a working television—so we could watch all our favorite Balkan sitcoms, I guess.

Bleary-eyed and half-awake at 6:00 a.m., we caught the village road out of town until it unexpectedly joined the main trucking route from Nis to Sofia. Hectic and hazardous, I was relieved to discover a tractor trail that we followed until we were unceremoniously dumped back onto the main highway. All too soon, we caught up with hundreds of eighteen-wheelers bound for Sofia, Turkey or the Middle East. They were stalled in a serpen-tine procession that coiled through the mountain pass. Border officials only processed a few at a time. The rest had to wait in the queue all night. Oddly enough, for us, that was good news. We nonchalantly wove in and out of the miles of parked semis in Serbia's longest parking lot and waltzed right into downtown Dimitrovgrad. Once checked into an inn, we had plenty of time to wander hushed streets in search of one last humungous Serbian hamburger.

As a crimson cloak draped across the cozy hamlet, Émile and I fondly reminisced about the Serbians we'd met along our way; how generous they'd been, how forgiving. Only then did we confide how we'd both initially been a little nervous about traveling there. But once again, prejudice had been challenged and changed by walking its breadth, and sharing food, wine and dreams together. Come to think of it, would we have been so hospitable to strangers from countries that'd bombed our major cities, as American and NATO forces had done in Serbia a few years earlier?

Seven Million Steps, Three Pairs of Shoes

Welcome Solitude of the Black Forest

Crisp mornings on the French Canals

Intricate Pulpit Carvings, St. Stephen's Dom, Vienna

Danube Crossing, Austria

David Meets Goliath in Regensburg, Germany

Levee Walking, Donau Radweg, Austria

Peace Stupa, Vienna

St. Stephen I and Fisherman's Bastion, Budapest

Roadside Bride in a Box, Serbia

Big Band Beat of Bratislava

A Horse's Dilemma

Mighty Danube, Our Constant Companion, Budapest

Reflections of Times Past, Statue Park

Calligraphy, Eski Cami Mosque (1414), Edirne

Persistent Juice Seller, Istanbul

Good Enough to Eat, Edirne, Turkey

Blue (Sultan Ahmet) Mosque, Istanbul

Interior, Blue Mosque, Istanbul

Christ Golden Mosaic, Haghia Sophia, Istanbul

Smiling Sultan For a Day (pre-circumcision), Turkey

Unique Hazards of Walking in Turkey

Grins and Giggles, Osmaneli, Turkey

Peaceful Alanya Port, Turkey

Grinding Lentils, Çavdarhisar, Turkey

Boy's Big Salute at Hero's Memorial, Bözöyuk, Turkey

Peppers, a Colorful Window Dressing

Dome of the Rock (Mosque of Omar), Jerusalem

Centuries Old Olive Tree

The Future of Turkey

We Are All the Same, Dead Sea, Israel

Western "Wailing" Wall, Jerusalem

The Edicule, Tomb of Christ

Moonrise Over Old Jerusalem

BLACK SEA

RNE

TURKEY

CHAPTER EIGHT
Bulgaria

Balkan Meltdown

*"A nation that continues year after year to spend more money
on military defense than on programs of social uplift
is approaching spiritual death."* ~ Dr. Martin Luther King, Jr.

After our ritual morning feast of cheese *bureks* followed by a muddy slug of Turkish coffee, we wandered across the nearby Serbian frontier to where trucks still stood waiting to cross. For once, we breezed through customs with hardly a glance at our passports. I'd planned on buying mineral water in Dimitrovgrad in the morning but most of the shopkeepers slept in, so I had no food or water with me and was more eager than usual to reach Dragoman, the first major Bulgarian village. That was one of the persistent challenges of traveling "lite" and not carrying several liters of water at all times as hikers have drilled into their heads. Émile had already nicknamed me "the camel," based on my ability to travel all day on little food or water—and I hated to prove him wrong.

All morning, our road snaked through a scenic gorge that was cool and lush with vegetation, as we wove our way through the stalled convoy inching into Bulgaria. In today's marketplace, they carried more than just produce. Occasionally when passing, I could hear hushed human voices in the cargo holds of those lorries, and shuddered to imagine their desperate lives.

By late morning, we reached the run-down village of Dragoman where we found an ATM and a shop selling drinks and chips, but we quickly moved on before the heat and humidity became too unbearable. Barely out of town, we were surprised to discover a striking ancient relic and elusive symbol of our journey. A stone road ran parallel to the main highway for several kilometers, until it split off and led us all the way to Slivnitsa. It was, it appeared, part of the old Roman highway, built more than a thousand years earlier. To me, it appeared in much better condition than the main highway. Its stones still fit together with a craftsman's precision and were polished by all those who'd passed that way over the centuries.

It only took us a few more hours to reach Slivnitsa, and we wandered down its main street looking for a place to sleep. As fate would have it, we stumbled upon a pleasant, well-dressed lady returning home from work. Rima just happened to be a translator and spoke five languages, including French, which made Émile's day. After almost four months, outside of the week we'd spent in France, he'd made little effort to communicate with anyone unless they spoke French—less than ten people.

Coming to our aid, Rima insisted on directing us to a hard-to-find inn that rented rooms in shack-like bungalows facing well-kept gardens. It was far from deluxe. Our small hut had two rooms, each with three metal cots. Walls were constructed of plywood covered with contact paper. The electrical wiring was exposed, both in the hut and in the concrete block showers. Still we had a bed, it was warmer and drier than sleeping outside, and not too far from a store and restaurant. What more could we ask for?

Later that evening, while Émile dined at the restaurant for the second time in about as many hours, I heard a gentle knock and "Hello" at our wooden door. Pulling it open, I was greeted by our smiling afternoon "angel," whom I invited inside. With old-world formality, Rima presented me with a bottle of Bulgarian *raki*, as well as a colossal two-pound tomato to welcome us to her country. Then for quite some time we sat on the simple metal beds talking about Bulgaria and the changes since their liberation from the communists. All the while, I tried to stall her, knowing Émile would be disappointed he'd missed her.

As we became more acquainted, I finally mentioned the one question that begged to be asked: "Are there still two pricing systems here, like in the old days— one for visitors and one for locals?"

A little embarrassed, she sighed, "Yes. You see, Bulgarian people are still very poor, making just $287 a month."

After seeing our "hotel," the rundown vintage train that chugged past, and the terrible condition of the roads, I had suspected that not much had changed since my last visit in the late 1980s. Hopefully, all those would improve after Bulgaria became a member of the European Union and received its influx of euros for development. On the other hand, knowing that made her gift even more special to two weary pilgrims.

Finally, tired after a long day and unable to stay any longer, Rima handed me a note with a map of Bulgaria she'd intended to leave if we were away. On it she had carefully inscribed:

> "Welcome to Bulgaria! I wish you good days for walking.
> Thank you for bringing the rains with your magic stick.
> God bless you."

At dawn, we traced the same Roman road another six kilometers before merging onto the main E-80 highway headed south toward Sofia, Bulgaria's capital of 1.2 million people. Over the next few hours as we approached, the valley unveiled an unexpected beauty and we were stunned to find ourselves walking through vast fields of brilliant wildflowers. By noon, we'd already reached the posted city limits, but continued on foot another hour and a half to reach the modern high-rises that had loomed on the horizon. It was always difficult to arrive into sprawling metropolises on foot and we dreaded it. They stretched forever and you had to deal with crazed drivers and vehicles spewing pollutants. However, for once, the Bulgarians gave us a wide berth, which was a relief after dodging kamikaze motorists throughout Serbia.

At last, out of the blue, an SUV slowed down and pulled alongside us. The window rolled down on its passenger side and a man leaned across asking, "Émile? Émile, is that you?"

"*Oui!*" my friend replied, a bit startled.

"It is Strahil," announced the stocky, dark-haired fellow in his late thirties. Bounding out of his car, he enthusiastically shook our hands and loaded our packs into his trunk. That doctor was the latest of Émile's contacts met via the Internet and telephone.

Within minutes, the gregarious fellow drove us to one of the city's better hotels, certainly a welcome change from last night's "bungalow." After showering and changing, we met downstairs at their fish restaurant to fill our host in on the latest details of our odyssey. We had little time to sample the fine Bulgarian cuisine, since he'd already scheduled an interview for us with *Balkan Bulgarian Television* (BBT) the following hour. Soon we were back in his SUV, tearing through surprisingly affluent neighborhoods to the nation's main television network.

The producers wanted to shoot their story outdoors, so their reporter asked questions as we walked with our backpacks. All went smoothly and we had time to discuss the reasons for our pilgrimage, as well as my hope that the trail would be developed as an international route for peace. As always, we never knew what or how much would actually air once the editing was complete, so we could only hope for the best. As it was, we'd just finished a last take when it began to pour and we made a mad dash for Strahil's car.

As usual, our visits to major cities such as Sofia, Nis and Belgrade were a combination of business and pleasure. It was a long-awaited chance for us to catch up on the neglected, nagging details caused by a life on the road: to answer correspondence, toss dirty clothes into a real washing machine, locate better maps, and do a little sightseeing.

Later that evening, there was a loud knock on my hotel room door. Surprised, since I wasn't expecting anyone (especially room service), I threw it open only to find a hotel security guard standing there.

"You want any girls?" he asked with a sly grin.

"What?" I replied, uncertain I'd heard him right.

"You want any girls tonight?" he repeated more deliberately, like one of those BBC broadcasters slowly reading the news for foreigners learning English.

I had to laugh. "No, I'm just fine."

He obviously hadn't seen the BBT news segment.

Although the following day was chock-a-block full of other errands, my main concern was to find accommodations between Sofia and Turkey. Everything else, as they say, was gravy. Now, in most other Western countries, it was a simple matter of contacting the visitor information office. However, Bulgaria wasn't quite as advanced. Sure, it was easy if you were headed to a major city or visitor destination, but we were walking roads less traveled. Strahil was generous to offer the aid of his assistant, who spent all morning calling ahead to villages for us to confirm inns along our route. As it turned out, our first day would be the most difficult, since we had to trek fifty kilometers to reach Intiman, the next city of any size. It was bound to stretch our stamina, but what choice did we have? There simply weren't any hotels, motels or rooms in between, and we hadn't brought a tent.

Next, at my request, his assistant found us a short-wave radio. Given the increased violence between Lebanon and Israel, it might be a lifesaver.

I looked forward to listening to the news each night, so we could avoid traipsing through any hot spots—if at all possible.

Then finally, after an enjoyable lunch with Yuri, the editor of *La Monde Diplomatique* in Bulgaria, Émile and I had a few hours alone to explore the fascinating city I'd last seen just before the Berlin Wall fell.

Nearby Alexander Nevsky Cathedral was as magnificent as I remembered. Built in the early 20th century, it commemorated the 200,000 Russian soldiers who'd died in the liberation of Bulgaria from the Ottomans. Regal, artistic, and still draped in an incensed cloak of aromatic mystery, it was a national treasure capable of holding 5,000 worshippers. Most impressive to me, though, was its interior of Italian marble, alabaster, onyx and gold, as well as Europe's largest collection of Orthodox icons.

After a quick but earnest prayer for further guidance on our journey, Émile and I headed across the street to the Tomb of the Unknown Soldier and Church of St. Sophia built during the 6th century. According to local legend, St. Sophia's powers had protected it from devastation throughout fourteen centuries. The rest of Sofia was somewhat less miraculous.

At first glance, I was amazed and relieved to see the progress the city had made over the years, all the glass and 21st century glitter. Yet after cruising the nearly vacant high-end boutiques occupying what was once the popular TZUM Department Store, I was left wondering, 'Is all this just another way to sell more high-priced Western goods? After all, who can afford to shop here on a typical Bulgarian's salary?' I'd already heard that the young had deserted the countryside to move there in search of their piece of the economic pie—and another twenty percent of the population had emigrated to find work in other countries. So, I couldn't help but feel the dreams sold by those multinational shops were still inaccessible to most. "Look, but don't touch, unless you're one of the few elite." As I remember, it was the same during the communist days. That might be the hardest *cevapcici* to swallow.

At the crack of dawn, we began walking toward Intiman from the ring road surrounding Sofia. Strahil suggested it would be safer for us to begin our trek on the edge of town, considering all the traffic in the inner city. Besides, walking fifty kilometers would push us to our very limits. As it turned out, unintentionally, we began inside the ring road in a hamlet, trekking kilometers on the old Roman road until it suddenly vaporized in a wheat field. Discouraged and frustrated, with no one around to ask for directions, we backtracked through high, wet grass to the four-lane freeway east, and then were forced to follow it for two hours. It was maddening.

Walking on an *autoput* is something I would never recommend to anyone— for any reason. "Don't try this at home," as they say. Besides the constant drone of passing cars and danger from unpredictable drivers, we were always uneasy about being stopped by the national police. Fortunately, not a moment too soon, the freeway intersected with Highway 8, the old Roman road. Occasionally, I'd glimpse its familiar cobblestone face staring up at me from under three layers of asphalt, cracked and peeling like a bad sunburn.

Finally, nerves frazzled, we were relieved to duck into a gas station on the edge of Novi Han where we met a vibrant eighteen-year-old. She was bursting with questions and spoke English well. She'd gone to school in Virginia at an early age and there was still a look of longing in her tender eyes when she told me of her plans to return some day. As we rested our feet in the gas station's café, the charming girl with bobbed hair and an engaging smile paid us special attention, offering to bring us coffee or tea.

"No, thanks, it's just too hot outside."

"Well, how about *boza* then?"

"Bozo? As in the clown?"

"No, *boza*," she giggled, with a toss of her short hair. "It's our traditional drink. We have it every morning with *banitsa*, like a *burek*."

"Sure, all right, we'll try it," I promised, and she brought us each a small glass of the thick millet and malt drink that we drank with false bravado and forced smiles. Although the nectar certainly wasn't my favorite, her energy and youthful enthusiasm was a cool mountain spring that I eagerly lapped, camel that I was.

It took us little time to pass through Novi Han with its own MIG fighter plane, overgrown with weeds in the town square. Reaching the other side, Route 8 began its steep climb through the mountains with little shade, water or villages. The trees turned to pine and the terrain looked as if we'd stumbled into New Mexico's high chaparral—or onto the Tibetan plains. Trucks were our only companions. Flying past every ten minutes, they showered us with a veil of dust and pebbles. Before long, we reached Vakarel, where we'd once considered staying, but they barely had a restaurant—let alone an inn. So we did the only thing we could. We continued.

It was close to sundown by the time we staggered into Intiman, twelve hours after leaving Sofia. We received many astonished and curious looks from the dark-skinned, black-eyed locals, who looked more East Indian than Bulgarian. In return, we nodded our "hellos," but otherwise paid them little mind. Exhausted, overheated and famished, we were determined to find the one and only hotel in town before nightfall. Fortunately, it was hard to miss.

At sixty-five leva, it was far too expensive for your average *peregrino* who could easily do without their mini-bar, television or swimming pool at that late hour. It was certainly too much for a local to pay, and what could have possibly brought a foreigner to the one-goat town? After settling in, we had just enough time to head across the street to a small *shawarma* café before a blinding bolt of lightning cracked the evening sky and the heavens let loose, as if tomorrow would never come. Unfortunately it did—and all too soon.

As we set off down the pockmarked road in the early morning dew, Brahma bulls grazed in the fields. A fog draped the base of the mountains like an ethereal mantle. An old woman, the patina of the earth and dressed all in black, cautiously pushed a rickety wooden cart toward us. Then two boys, smiling uncomfortably, giddy-upped an equally ancient horse-drawn wagon down the ragged road. If I didn't know better, I could have sworn we were in India.

After yesterday's misdirection, we took extra precaution to follow my "Three Times" rule of travel. If it's absolutely important to receive the correct information, always ask at least three people the same question—then take the consensus. Often times, not wanting to offend you, people will give you the answer they *think* you want to hear. With confirmation that Kostenets was indeed "just down the road," we steamed full speed (4 kph) up the windy mountain road.

"It's beautiful out here, Émile," I shouted back to my friend, who pulled up the rear as usual. "It reminds me a little of northern California."

There was no reply. I could never tell whether he heard me or not. Or if he did, did he understand? At most, I got an "*Ah, bon,*" in response. Yet many times, I heard nothing at all. Émile was a quiet fellow, often in his own world. Then again, I savored the solitude of "walking alone together." Sure, it would have been a bonus to gain more insight into French life or their psyche, since I'd long been a secret Francophile. Still, from what he'd shared, Émile had led a quiet life "living inside the box," and I knew it was too late for the leopard to change his spots.

By late morning, we reached the "town" of Kostenets and asked several people, several different ways, "WHERE is the hotel? Where IS the hotel? Where is the HOTEL?" All we received were blank stares.

Growing tired of the game of charades and famished, we stopped into a restaurant where we discovered the inn was in the "village" of Kostenets another eight kilometers up the valley. So we stayed for lunch and then hitched a lift up into the hills. Of course, we could have walked there in another two hours in ninety-degree heat. But I figured it was within our vows, since it was well off our route and the next hotel in our direction was another forty kilometers away.

The small hotel was set at the end of a valley cul-de-sac festooned with pine-treed mountains still topped by a dollop of snow on their crest. But the real appeal for us was the thermal hot spring just up the road, a perfect prescription for pilgrim's pains. Still, as they say, "The best laid plans..."

Upon checking-in, Émile insisted on taking his *"petite siesta,"* and by the time we finally headed off to the pools they were closed. We did continue farther through a serene valley to a fountain, and then followed an old Roman road back to a waterfall cascading into an enticing pool. On any other day, that would have been reward enough. However, after yesterday's long, forced march, I craved sizzling, steaming, "knock the wind out of you" pools to soothe our aching muscles. Nevertheless, it was worth it to simply enjoy a few peaceful hours in a spectacular setting. I could only imagine what it might look like after the developers hit town. But at that point, the many unfinished hotels made it look like the money had just dried up. Sidewalks could barely be seen beneath brush and wildflowers. Roadways looked like they'd been pulverized by a tank battalion, and a nation of beat-up Ladas trailed a cloud of smoke behind them.

After dinner on the terrace, we turned in, anxious to enjoy a good night's sleep before facing another difficult fifty-kilometer trek. About 2:00 a.m., I stumbled in the dark to the toilet that was separated from our room by a tiny entryway. However, I found the bathroom light already on. Confused, I checked Émile's bed and found it empty. So I waited a few minutes, but there was no sound coming from the WC. Unable to wait any longer, I blurted out, "Émile? Are you in there?"

"*Oui?*"

"I'd really like to use the toilet."

The door flung open. He stood there wearing only *Le Monde* as a fig leaf—along with his silly grin.

Before sunrise, we caught a ride back down the valley and began our promenade through the impoverished countryside. At that point, little did we suspect our day would become extraordinary—not because of any scenery—but because of those who blessed our path.

By late morning, with nearly twenty kilometers behind us, we ambled into Belovo, famous for its beloved paper mill. I'd never visited a place whose claim to fame was its paper products, but travel has a way of opening your eyes to all types of world wonders. At least five shops and stands boasting pyramids of poo-paper bordered the road. The cornucopia of hygiene products might seem garish to untrained Western eyes, but I remembered all too well Eastern Europe's "Time Without Tissue" ("*Les Temps Sans Tissu*"), which if it were a French film would undoubtedly be shot in gritty, film-noir style. It was once a hoarded luxury. I still recalled the adorable little lady we'd stayed with in Warsaw. She sat at her dining room table, cat curled in her lap, and methodically cut newspaper pages into tiny, even squares for us to use, as the snow gently blanketed the streets outside.

Thirsty and stopping at a tiny roadside dive, we were instantly assailed by Dimitri, a giant, brawny man, as straight as a willow.

"Where are you from?" he demanded.

"France," Émile replied with unabashed pride.

Well, that's all we had a chance to say. Dimitri shook each of us like hollow logs in his bear-like paws and then insisted on buying us a round of drinks…then chocolates…then a warehouse store-sized pack of napkins…then bottled water…all in a matter of minutes.

At first, I was deeply touched by his bigheartedness and content with my cold drink. After that, I felt more guilt than anything. His young wife, their newborn baby, and small son that sat at our table looked like they could ill-afford his hospitality. So once the tissues were offered, I stood up to leave before our presents became any more extravagant. What was Émile going to do with a thousand napkins, anyway?

Though Dimitri still insisted we absolutely had to take the *serviettes*, Émile followed my lead and we rushed toward the door before he could offer any more. On the way out though, in one final gesture, the powerful man blocked our path, swept us both in his tight embrace and proclaimed in English, "France, Bulgaria friends!" to which we assured him, "*Oui, oui,* of course, of course."

That oddly heartwarming encounter, however, was just a prelude to events later that afternoon. In the hamlet of Lozen, we once again paused for a cool drink in the Amazonian climate. On days like that, it was the only reward we enjoyed along the way. In the small outdoor café, we met a local who spoke both English and German, having worked once in Baden-Baden, Germany's famous resort. As we collapsed in the shade, he proceeded to introduce us to his local gang, including a sinewy fellow that he described as "a very important guy." (In actuality, he ran the bar that looked as though it had been built from leftover scrap lumber.)

"You know, life in this small town is the same every day," our new best friend lamented, stretching out with a languid smile. "Just like in Hollywood."

Hollywood? Looking around at the crude vegetable and fruit stands lining the derelict streets, and plodding ponies pulling wooden carts, I found his comparison laughable.

But I played along, saying, "Yea, I guess it is. Isn't that right, Mr. De Niro?" I asked the "very important guy," listening in from behind his bar.

Well, he was mighty pleased with the name I'd given him. Amid guffaws, he served us endless plastic cups of his powerful, homemade peach schnapps, until finally, they wished us "*Gut Reisen*" in German, or "Travel well," and sent us merrily on our way.

By the time we covered those last thirteen kilometers to Pazardzhik, I had just one more thing to show for our journey: a new blister on my left foot—after three months. The wet grass outside of Sofia must have caused it. Pazardzhik was also a little down on its heels with unfinished and crumbling buildings. By then, I was convinced all the money and development in Bulgaria had ended up in the capital.

We walked into the center of town before finding the Hotel Trakia. Simply trying to register was challenging. At first, we were told by the pudgy, balding front desk attendant, "The hotel is full unless you have a reservation."

"You mean all these rooms are full?" I asked.

"Yes," he snapped, and then returned to his busy-work.

"Until when?" I interrupted. "It hardly looks full." I found it hard to believe they could fill a hundred rooms in a town that size. There was no one else in the lobby, the parking lot was empty, and there were no passports in the key slots, a telltale sign.

"Oh, until about seven, eight or nine o'clock."

I was unwilling to accept defeat. We were incapable of walking any far-ther. "So, how much are your rooms?"

"Sixty leva." He failed to add, "Special tourist price."

"Fine, we'll take one."

"Okay," he said, in an abrupt about-face. "Fill this out."

I was flabbergasted. What had just happened? It was bizarre. One minute the place was filled, and the next, "Yes, there is a room." I didn't even have to use my time-tested Jedi routine, as I'd once done in Tibet with an obstinate border official that threatened to put Sadhu, our Tibetan horse, into quarantine. I'd just kept repeating, "This horse *is* going to Nepal," until he finally stammered back, "Yes, this horse is going to Nepal."

In the morning, our one hundred day anniversary since beginning our odyssey was filled with anything but celebration. It began with a Spartan breakfast, barely giving us enough energy to reach the edge of town—let alone Bulgaria's second-city, Plovdiv. After following the "Three Times" rule for directions in the square, we made our way out of the crumbling burg amid commuters, buses, bicycles and horse carts. The terrain was nearly flat and we were optimistic at first, since we were far from the *autostrada*. Nonetheless, as it turned out, there was a constant torrent of traffic, since just as many folks took the small E-8 highway. That made walking difficult, if not more downright dangerous.

For some reason, from the very start, Émile was in a particularly foul mood. I didn't know why, unless fatigue was finally catching up with him. His stops were frequent and I set my own pace a good fifty yards ahead. All went as smoothly as could be expected, until at one point I heard a "grum-ble, grumble" in French, and then turned around just in time to watch him stumble across the busy two-lane highway—with cars zooming past at sixty miles per hour. I helplessly watched as a courier truck slammed on its brakes and blared its horn to avoid hitting my companion, who meandered as if he was sleepwalking across a street in Dijon.

Unfazed, Émile continued walking on the right-hand side of the road with his back to oncoming traffic. Of course, by then, I'd already explained to him at least three times why that made it more dangerous. First, he couldn't see who was headed his way. Then, cars swerved away from him toward the center, forcing cars on my side of the road to veer toward me to avoid crashing into them. Still, he remained unfazed, as if his magic hat and baton made him untouchable. To compensate, I had to walk even farther ahead to avoid becoming another statistic. That continued for an hour, although I kept glancing over my shoulder periodically to keep an eye on him. Finally, I stopped and waited for him to catch up. What surprised me most, given his near-death experience, was that he didn't have a clue I might be upset.

"You're lucky to be alive."

He shrugged it off, saying, "They slowed down, didn't they?"

"That's only because it was an American delivery company," I joked. Still, I had to wonder to myself, 'Exactly what *will* it take?'

With water bottles empty, we found a place to eat just down the highway. Then revived, we attacked the last six kilometers into Plovdiv with renewed vigor. It was miserably muggy; hot enough to give a gator heatstroke. Our hands and feet swelled to twice their normal size, plus my new blister made me cringe with each step. Still, before long, we arrived at a gas station. Émile again mumbled something under his breath and staggered inside.

"Hey, what are you doing?" I asked.

"I…am…finished," he groaned, off in his own world.

"'Finished' as in done?' I wondered. 'Or "finished" as in dead on your feet?'

"What do you mean? Do you want to rest a while?"

"No. I want to call my friend to pick us up. Or take a taxi."

I couldn't believe my ears, since we were almost on the edge of town.

Émile collapsed into a Naugahyde chair in the air-conditioned filling station and slowly began dialing his "friend," a cousin of Strahil's that was expecting us.

"Really, Émile, we can rest here if you like, but we're almost there. You can't stop now."

"No," he said with finality. "I am done."

I was both stunned and disappointed that he was giving up so easily. Still, I wasn't in the mood to argue.

"Fine, if that's what you want, but I'm walking into town."

I headed toward the door.

"I don't speak English!" he blustered. "How will I talk to him?"

Looking over at my friend, flushed and upset, I relented out of some sense of obligation or sympathy and agreed to call our host.

"Look, I don't know exactly where we are," I explained to the calm voice on the other end of the phone. "We're coming from Pazardzhik and are somewhere on the edge of town in a gas station. Émile wants you to come pick him up, but I plan on walking the rest of the way into Plovdiv. Here, just a second. The gas station attendant can tell you exactly where we are." I handed off Émile's cell phone to the confused fellow in overalls standing nearby. "There. Have a good trip, Émile! See you in Jerusalem," I sarcastically added, walking out the door.

Sprinting down the road, I already felt lighter, relieved to be free and on my own. As suspected, Plovdiv was nearby and I was startled when I heard the soft tap of a car horn and an apologetic, "Brandon…" coming from my right hand side. I turned to see a white Renault parked across the highway. Émile leaned out the backseat window like a shaggy sheepdog on a family outing.

Reluctantly crossing over, I introduced myself to the driver. "Look Ron, I think it's just best if we meet downtown. Besides, I prefer to continue walking and it can't be far."

"No, it's not," the tan, fit fellow confirmed with an understanding smile. "You can meet us at the café next to the Hotel St. Petersburg."

It only took another fifteen minutes before we were all relaxing together in the shade. Émile already looked better and had begun rehydrating. Fortunately Ron, who'd just returned from a Black Sea vacation, was willing to come to the aid of two slightly damaged *peregrinos*.

At first, he led us to a dreary, local hotel that his friend had recommended, where we stood around for fifteen minutes while the proprietor screamed non-stop into the telephone.

"That's the Bulgarian way of doing business," Ron confided with a wink.

Eventually, they showed us to their vacant room, a "bed" room: one big bed with nothing else. We passed. Next, Ron drove us to the center of town to check out a hostel, but it was full. Then, even though we were frazzled and still had no place to sleep, he decided to give us the chef's tour of the famed city, including its ancient Roman theater and stadium dating back to 2 A.D. and its statue of Phillip II of Macedonia, father of Alexander the Great. The city, once called Philippopolis, was named after him. On the other hand, it was only one of five names the "City of Three Hills" had throughout the ages. (That must have made it difficult for the post office.)

As we dragged through the Old City, a friendly parking lot attendant thrust us a flyer for a nearby house that rented rooms and we headed right over. I was surprised its owner, a sculptor, had already heard about our journey. Although filled, he had an open room in his traditional Bulgarian house the following day and we jumped at the chance to stay there. Before we left, he also promised to call the Plovdiv newspaper, so they could interview us in the morning. Honestly though, after that day's events, it felt hypocritical for me to talk about peace in the world—when I felt so much exasperation with Émile. Still, I trusted a good night's sleep and some food would give us a fresh outlook in the morning.

Eventually, Ron drove us to his friend's Bohemian apartment used exclusively, as he put it, for "romantic liaisons." All the same, we were relieved to have a place to sleep and the price was right. After showering, Émile and I walked across the street to a surprisingly hip restaurant, as if nothing had happened. Then again, once inside, my friend's uncharacteristic behavior continued. He promptly got into an argument with the waiter over French fries, and once more over a simple glass of wine. Clearly something serious was wrong.

Although the following day was a "rest" day, you'd be hard pressed to prove it. Early in the morning, we left the apartment and moved over to Plovdiv's Old Town to a room above the art gallery; an oasis of rustic elegance with dark paneled walls and kilim rugs. Still, there was still no escaping the outside world. Turning on the television, I was shocked to hear that Israel had escalated its bombing in Lebanon, destroying a UN observation post.

Our scheduled interview with *Labor,* one of Plovdiv's major newspapers, went as well as could be expected, considering the lag time for translation after everything we said, as though we had a bad telephone connection.

That afternoon, eager to find some quiet time on my own, I set off with my camera. Threading the maze of narrow alleyways in the Old Town, I attempted to capture the timeless elegance of the Bulgarian Renaissance architecture surrounding me: its vivid colors, manicured courtyards, and rooms overhanging cobblestone streets. Along the way, I ran into our host, the gallery artist, who insisted on showing me the intricate Roman villa mosaics that were carefully preserved in an underground passage. If only the Bulgarian roads were in such fine condition.

Later that evening, Ron treated Émile and me to an authentic Bulgarian meal on an outdoor terrace. As we feasted on grilled cheese, stuffed grape leaves and other appetizers, our kind host regaled us with stories of life in the "Wild West" East. I had to wonder, with all the confusion, drugs and corruption, was Bulgaria ready to join the European Union?

At sunrise, Ron shuttled us to a local eatery, then to where Highway 8 continued on toward Istanbul. Since traffic was already insane on that derelict highway, I was keen to spot an alternative. All morning, I scoured the fields behind dozens of truck farms selling tomatoes, melons, corn and cabbage, but it wasn't until after lunch that I finally spotted a country road detour that might lead us to Parvomaj. "Might" was the operative word, as it was still anyone's guess.

By mid-afternoon, although we were heading in the right direction, we still hadn't found a connecting road and had trudged all day in intense heat. Our nerves were frazzled and we were ready to collapse, when suddenly I spotted something wrapped around a small tree just ahead. What was it? Someone's sack?

When twenty feet away, I finally spotted two pitiful, brown eyes staring back at us. A newborn bull calf, the size of a Labrador retriever, had wrapped its chain so tightly around a group of saplings that it was slowly strangling to death. One of its front legs was caught up in the shackle cutting it to the bone, while his eye was scratched and nearly swollen shut.

"Look Émile, with this heat, we've gotta do something quickly—if this bull's going to survive."

I stooped down and began maneuvering the little fellow to relieve the pressure. As Émile slightly held him up, I slipped the chain off from around his neck. However, he was so close to death, he barely moved. So I started frantically sawing away at the saplings with my Swiss Army knife to allow his chain to loosen a little more.

"Quick Émile, go find the farmer, someone, anyone!"

It was ninety degrees. He was dehydrated and probably close to heat stroke. I poured some of my remaining water onto the little bull's head, and then tried to get him to drink from the palm of my hand, without success. Fortunately, Émile was luckier in finding a farmer who crossed the street to a nearby house where he fetched a heavyset woman who came running in tears. Together, she and I managed to free the bull's front leg, but he still lay motionless.

"Look, he needs water, cold water, right away," I tried to explain, showing her my empty bottle.

So she scurried back to her farm, returning with a full bucket. As soon as she'd poured about half of it over his weakened body, the little guy miraculously sprung to life. Swaying a little back and forth, he rose on unsteady hooves until she could lure him with the rest of the water back across the street to her yard.

As we turned to go, I was surprised to see a young girl running toward us from the farmhouse. She carried a large sack of tomatoes grown in their yard.

"No, that's not necessary," I said, but she insisted we accept them with their gratitude. Personally, I was just relieved and grateful that he had survived.

While walking those final kilometers to Parvomaj, it struck me how everything ultimately happened for a reason. If we'd never taken that detour, or if we'd found the connecting trail, we would never have found the young bull. Chances were pretty good he wouldn't have survived and the family would have been devastated. Maybe there never was a "wrong" path—just one awaiting a new reason for being.

In the morning, unable to find a place to eat, we hiked east on sidewalks choked by weeds and trees. Businesses and infrastructure were in an advanced state of decay. Windowless tobacco factories offered gap-toothed grimaces. Workers glided past on rusted bicycles, groaning "squee-chip, squee-chip" with every turn of the pedal. Cars were of equal vintage and temperament, with the exception of the occasional new Mercedes, testimony to the booming underground economy. We also passed donkey carts driven by grizzled men with *babushka*-draped wives bundled in back with the vegetables. They glared at us with uneasy suspicion, until I offered them a "*Dobro den!*" Then they usually returned a wave or country nod. Sadly, that was the extent of my Bulgarian, except for "*dobro*" (good), "*da*" (yes) and a few tidbits necessary to order food. Émile, of course, knew even less.

By ten o'clock, it was already beastly hot on those shadeless back roads. Villages appeared, as in a mirage, every six kilometers or so. Short of a few telephone lines and cars, they could have come straight out of the last century. Cows roamed the streets and there was the pungent bouquet of manure or burning trash in the air. It reminded me of the sensory explosion we'd experienced arriving into Nepal, after the featureless landscape of the Tibetan Plateau.

All the while, I continued to try to better understand my friend. Émile moped all morning, so I slowed down, hoping he might enjoy our easier pace. At one point, I even suggested following a shorter route alongside the river toward Dimitrovgrad. But he wouldn't hear of it, insisting on taking the longer road, even though it would force us to walk another two hours in the sun. Despite my best intentions, he was still most comfortable "thinking inside the box."

Before long, we stopped for lunch, but even that was easier said than done. There were two bars, but no restaurants. Eventually, we found a market and brought food back to the pub where the locals were interested in hearing about our odyssey. In return, they shared their refreshing watermelon with us on the terrace. Afterward, unable to delay the inevitable any longer, we dragged ourselves out of their shaded bliss and pressed on in the heat of the day.

All was going as well as could be expected, until Émile once again insisted on walking on the right-hand side of the road—for the sake of a few extra feet of shade. Refusing to play that game of "chicken" again, I sped ahead to create at least a hundred yards between us. The next thing I heard was a truck's blaring double horn, as he narrowly missed my friend, flinging him into the weeds. I really didn't look forward to writing a letter to Sophie to tell her about her husband's demise.

By mid afternoon, the weather was taking its toll. Just four kilometers from Dimitrovgrad, I stopped at a gas station and nursed a gallon of ice-cold mineral water. Émile appeared five minutes later, dragging more than usual. He'd sweated profusely all day and breathed through his mouth, which only made him dehydrate more rapidly. I warned him that he was drinking far too little water, yet Émile poo-hooed my advice, accusing me of being "pedantic."

"Sorry," as he might say, but I knew for a fact he drank less than three liters of liquid during our eight to ten hours on the highway. In that ninety-degree weather, it must have been closer to 120 degrees on the asphalt, and he should have been drinking three times as much. Still, Émile was Émile. His obstinacy was both a blessing and a burden. The trait that kept him moving when lesser men would cry "Enough!" was the same one that could threaten his very life. That afternoon, it became all the more evident.

Dimitrovgrad wasn't far. However, reaching it was just part of our daily battle. Finding a place to stay required the usual patience. I asked person after person, but each insisted they were from out of town. Eventually, we stopped at a market to buy more water. Grabbing a bottle from the cooler, Émile asked the friendly clerk, "It is 'swoosh?'" as he didn't know the Bulgarian word for "carbonated."

She nodded, probably having no idea what he was mumbling about.

Unable to read the label, with his ear to the bottle, Émile listened for the sound telling him it was *aqua con gaz. Nada.*

I tried to remind him, "Look Émile, water is water—and you need to drink."

Well, the sweat really hit the fan. Beyond reason, he slammed the bottle of water onto the countertop. Then he refused the startled girl's attempts to give him his money back and stormed out.

Back on the street, things quickly deteriorated from bad to worse. Walking into the center of town, Émile listed to one side like a ship that'd struck an iceberg and was sinking fast. Shortly after crossing the main bridge, he lost his balance and crumpled by the roadside.

"Émile, what's the matter? What can I do?"

"I cannot go any farther," he cried, blankly staring off into space. "You find the room." There was a quiet desperation in his feeble voice.

I believed him. He was beet red, pulled a muscle in his back, had extreme fatigue and was clammy. To me, it looked like the onset of sunstroke. Stopping two locals who'd slowed down to gawk, I confirmed our hotel was actually just five minutes away. So after a moment, I steadied my cohort to his feet and helped carry his pack the few remaining blocks.

Later, as I cooled down my own overheated brain in the cold shower, one question flooded my mind. 'When is it time to say, "I've done my best. I've done enough?"'

Recently, the days had been long and difficult for us, for anyone. Still, with what I'd seen, I couldn't help but wonder if it would be wise for Émile to catch the plane home with Sophie when she joined us in Istanbul? It was a hard call for anyone to make, especially after having come so far, so close to realizing their dream. It was something only he could decide.

That evening, the BBC reported Iraq was on the brink of a civil war. Hamas vowed to bomb Tel Aviv if Israel shelled any farther into Lebanon. Of course, if Tel Aviv were attacked, Israel would step up its bombing and ground campaign. That increased the possibility that Syria would join in. Iran, a major supporter of Hamas, wouldn't be far behind.

That was the insanity threatening to pull the world to the edge of the abyss.

The inevitable happened the next morning. Soon after we began a gradual climb past Dimitrovgrad's nuclear power plant, I heard Émile huffing and puffing behind me, breathing in and out with step after labored step.

'If he keeps this up, he's going to hyperventilate,' I thought, and immediately slowed our pace. All the same, his exaggerated breathing continued for nearly three hours. We even stopped for coffee and cold drinks thinking it would help, but his respiration only grew worse. Finally, five kilometers outside Simeonovgrad, Émile collapsed. Flushed and heavily perspiring, my friend doubled over with searing back pain. It was time for that heart-to-heart talk.

"Émile, look, we've put in a few long days lately…"

He cut me off, hissing, "We walk too far each day."

That was an ongoing battle we had whenever he was tired. We were walking "too far" or "too fast," depending on his mood. As always, I countered, "I agree, but if there's nowhere to stop, what choice do we have but to continue?" For me, if it meant trekking marginally faster or walking two or three extra hours in the sweltering heat, I'd pick the former. "Besides, it's more than the distance now," I explained. "It's the heat. You're dehydrated and losing minerals through your sweat each day. You can't continue like this. You have to drink more fluids—and beer doesn't count. It only makes you more dehydrated."

His skeptical frown told me he was unconvinced, but I knew I was right. He was an intelligent fellow. If he could only think more clearly, he'd realize the same thing. It was obvious. After he spent an hour drinking fluids and relaxing in the shade, he was usually able to start walking again for a little while.

"Plus you need to start taking magnesium tablets like Dr. Milan suggested. Maybe we can find some in a pharmacy. And when you talk to Sophie, please ask her to bring a powdered energy drink from home. A good one will have essential minerals, as well as salt and glucose. That should help balance your electrolytes."

He looked bewildered, as if he had no idea what I was talking about.

"You know, like the powder I've been drinking these past few months?"

I'd poured the magical Zipfizz into my water, especially on the hottest days, and had even shared it a few times with Émile when he looked particularly haggard. However, I tried to save the bulk of it for Turkey when I'd need it most.

He nodded, but it was just to appease me. It was another, "*Ah, bon,*" in disguise. Tactfully, I hesitated to bring up the subject of his too heavy pack and boots, as I'd done from time to time. He still carried twice as much weight as I did, which accounted for much of his back pain. Our trek was no cakewalk for anyone, no matter what their age or conditioning. Yet it "Gaulled" me when he admitted he'd chosen April 23rd for our departure simply because it was his lucky day. Because of that absurd decision, we

were forced to cross Eastern Europe in their hottest summer months—
and Turkey's stark Anatolian Plains, as well.

Even so, as we sat crumpled by the side of the road, I couldn't help but
feel a deep empathy for what he was going through, and regretted I sometimes had to become "pedantic" to feel like I was getting through. His success, our mutual success, depended on him making crucial changes.
Otherwise, our very lives would be endangered.

The next morning, Émile was dressed before dawn, scarfing down his
bread and chocolate sandwich like it was his last meal. Personally, I decided
to hold out for a café on the roadside out of Simeonovgrad, preferring
their fortified coffee and feta cheese pie.

Even as we began, I purposely trekked slower, as my blister was unusu-
ally painful. However, Émile complained I was already walking too fast, so
I slowed even more. It took us forever to reach the next village of any size.
It pulsated with people as far as the eye could see—all shopping at their
Saturday market. There, of all places, Émile demanded to find a pharmacy.

You see, only the night before, he'd admitted that taking magnesium
tablets was a good idea, so I gave him a note with the word "magnesium"
written in English to present to the druggist. Usually, of anyone in town,
they were fluent in several languages and that one was no exception. Still,
he returned empty-handed from the *apteka*, complaining, "She only spoke
English, German and Bulgarian. No French." His note *was* in English.

I was upset at his timing, but said, "Fine. *Allons*. Go!"

He stood stock-still, waiting for me to take the lead as usual. For once,
I refused to play along. I repeated, "Okay, let's go!" and motioned for him
to begin the search.

Still, he didn't budge and began complaining under his breath, until he
finally grumbled, "Fine, we go on," and off we trudged toward the border.

As you might imagine, we were hungry after four hours of hiking and
our water was running low. The traffic was especially heavy on that main
artery to Turkey. It took constant vigilance to walk on the outside highway
line—and to prepare to jump out of the way at the very last second for
trucks who didn't move over. So, eager to get off the main thoroughfare, I
spotted a tractor trail tracing the edge of a watermelon farm. After stopping to re-bandage my foot, we approached a farmer loading produce into
the trunk of his Lada. I complimented him on his melons in an exaggerated way, so he couldn't possibly misunderstand. Well, hunger is a universal problem and he had the solution. Taking out his knife, he cut up his last

watermelon right there on the edge of his field. First, he cut it into quarters, then ran his blade along the rind, and then through the sugary, pink wedges, cutting it into bite-sized pieces. Finally, he handed Émile a slice, one to me, and took one for himself.

"Oh, that's beautiful. How much?" I mimed, rubbing my middle finger against my thumb in the well-known gesture.

"No charge!"

I polished off the quarter as eagerly as a dog lapping water from the toilet bowl. Émile, a man who'd dive headfirst into a bowl of cow's entrails as if he hadn't eaten in months, only picked at his treat. So the kind farmer gestured for me to take the remaining quarter, and after mock refusal I leapt at the chance. Fruit had never tasted so good. I'd lusted after melon and it was especially welcome on a sultry summer day. I gobbled most of the second quarter and was savoring every last bite, when I noticed Émile had already donned his pack and was saying, "*Au revoir.*" Figuring he was still hungry, I offered him what remained of my piece—and was shocked when he took it and then tossed it into the trunk of the farmer's car along with the rinds. I couldn't believe it, but I held my tongue. It obviously did no good.

Given our slower pace, it was mid-afternoon by the time we reached gusty Ljubimec. Its motel was already filled, but we found the Hotel Fantasy, complete with air-conditioning and a television. We were also able to locate a pharmacy where, even though she only spoke Bulgarian, the pharmacist instantly knew what I meant by "magnesium" and showed us three different types to choose from.

Émile looked on, astonished.

Back at the hotel, they were preparing for a wedding party. In anticipation of another all-night, bed quaking serenade, we transferred to a more quiet, windowless room. Afterward, we set off to find dinner away from the celebration and Bulgarian bagpipes already echoing down dusty streets. At that point, no one in the wedding party was dancing to the soulful whining, but those like us off the A-list couldn't help but sway to the infectious music just outside the iron gates.

At daybreak, we crossed a rugged terrain framed by low mountains in the distance. Quickly covering the seventeen kilometers to Svilengrad, and learning that there was another hotel five kilometers closer to the border, we pressed on. That would shorten our next day's trek into Turkey, and surprisingly it took no prodding Émile. Either he was finally catching on—

or his vitamins had miraculously kicked in. It was all going too smoothly for a change. That was until we reached the Summit Hotel and tried to check into the inn perched atop a barren hilltop.

"Passports," squawked the bird-like lady at the reception desk.

As I reached to pull mine from my money pouch, fear lit Émile's face. He was frantic. His passport was missing, but it wasn't a difficult mystery to solve. He'd left it back at our last hotel. After I patiently spoke to the manager's son, he called back to the Fantasy who found Émile's passport. Then he negotiated a taxi ride for us back to Ljubimec to pick it up. For some strange reason, Émile, with his sad, hangdog eyes, insisted I join him on his odd fieldtrip. Why? Surely, he couldn't get lost.

Nonetheless, after forty-four kilometers (and twenty-five leva), my companion had soon retrieved his papers and we could finally relax. In a way, I was relieved we'd discovered it missing then. If it had been at the Turkish border, life would have been much more complicated.

At long last, ready to unwind, we wandered downstairs to the hotel's underground restaurant where I ordered shish kabobs, salads and beers. With typical gusto, Émile threw back his lager and swallowed it in great gulps—until—blam! It shot out his nose and mouth like some water gnome at Vienna's Schönbrunn Palace, cascading all over the table and floor as it had many times over the past few months.

"*Explosif?*" I asked, dabbing the beer from my arms.

He sheepishly grinned. "I am sorry."

RKEY

IRAN

IRAQ

SYRIA

CHAPTER NINE
Turkish Border to Istanbul

Difficult Choices

*"My heart is open to all the winds. Wherever God's caravans turn,
the religion of love shall be my religion. And my faith."*
~ Aribi, 13th century Sufi traveler and mystic

U p with the sun, we flew down from the summit and arrived at
the Bulgarian border in short order. Since Émile, for some
inexplicable reason, had exchanged forty euro at the hotel the
day before, he was intent on changing those back to Turkish lira. Spotting
a currency exchange office, he entered alone while I searched for food.
Oddly enough, by the time I joined him, he'd already exchanged more
euros for Bulgarian leva. Why? He never told the clerk he wanted Turkish
lira, and was clearly upset.

"Look," I explained, trying to defuse the situation, "why would we want
more Bulgarian leva when we're entering Turkey?" But it was too late.
"Okay then, change all these leva into lira," I told her, and I combined his
leftover money with the new, equally worthless bills. Of course, she was
happy to oblige, but didn't provide a receipt until I demanded one. She
reluctantly handed it over—along with five extra leva she'd kept for herself.
Oh, those last glorious impressions of Bulgaria.

With those, we splurged on breakfast. Then I spent the next hour
buying a visa, and then we passed through no less than five Turkish checkpoints for customs, *polizia*, and a car inspection, totally unnecessary for us.
At long last, we were in Turkey.

Its highway was an instant improvement over Bulgaria's. Yes, there was
the same trash and it was awash in plastic bottles, but there were extra-wide

shoulders for bicycles, horse carts and *peregrinos*. We followed the frontier road ten kilometers until catching what I hoped was a short diversion into Edirne. It turned into a sizzling eight-kilometer trek through the country-side, so it was noon before we rolled into the early Thracian town with the famed Selimiye Camii mosque, boasting Turkey's highest minarets.

Before any sightseeing was in order, I first needed to get some Turkish lira, so I stopped at a bank machine on the street. In the past, Émile and I had set up a system where one of us would watch out for other whenever he was at an ATM in a busy city location. It was an easy way to make sure neither of us were robbed or hassled while holding a fistful of money.

"Émile, please watch my back," I reminded him, as I began to punch in my pin numbers. But as soon as I took the cash from the machine, I sensed someone looking over my left shoulder and spun around to face a scruffy local fellow with a crazed look, flashing an equally dirty wad of Turkish lira.

"*Merci*, Émile, for watching!"

My companion was mute, stepping past us both to withdraw cash for himself. Meanwhile, I confronted the man. He whispered something in Turkish that I obviously couldn't understand, but I answered, "No," to cover all the bases, and at the same time slid between him and Émile. He persisted though, fingering his weathered money.

"No, thanks," I repeated more insistently.

He continued moving closer until we were nearly cheek-to-jowl. I grew more tense until I finally grabbed Émile's heavy *bourdon* leaning in the corner and jabbed its metal tip into the sidewalk with a "ping!"

"No, go away!"

It still didn't sink in with the stranger. He kept on jabbering away as I grew ever more irritated, until finally I think he must have told me what terrible people we were and shuffled off in a huff.

"What did he want?" Émile naïvely asked.

"Our money."

"Oh…" he said, with a befuddled look.

With cash in hand, we checked into a nearby hotel featuring well-worn oriental carpets and equally frayed men, shuffling to and fro in slippers. Sipping tea from miniature clear glasses, the Muslim gents sat transfixed by the black and white glare from a small television. A dramatic photo of Ataturk, the revered "father" of modern Turkey, intently passed judgment on it all.

Our room was far from luxurious, yet its balcony with ratty aluminum chairs faced a street that promised to serenade us all night with the fervor of Turkish life.

After touring the mosques and marveling at their outstanding tile work, I met Émile for dinner at a haunt where we were obviously the only foreigners. Its rustic cabin-like setting could have been right out of Wyoming, although the menu was a little different, featuring *köfta* or miniature hamburgers, tomatoes, hot peppers and cold beers. Another difference became clear when the owner passed from one diner to the next, sprinkling their palms with lemon-scented water—hardly my memory of the rugged Wild West. As the rest of the men in the room sat entranced by a Turkish Hollywood-like exposé show, I gazed out the dusty window to watch the city tuck itself in for the night.

Young girls, a few wearing *burkas* covering all but their faces, some in cream-colored topcoats, and others in neat office attire, scurried to the mosque or home for supper. One weary man pushed his watermelon cart down the narrow alleyway; its fruit still piled high in a green pyramid. Meanwhile, the evening call to prayer echoed through our windowpane, as the golden, crescent-topped dome of the nearby mosque sat silhouetted in the final rays of the sun.

Before we turned in for the night, Émile asked, "If my back feels better tomorrow, should we continue walking?"

Earlier, he'd practically demanded we take a day off. Knowing his ragged condition, I was stunned he wouldn't jump at the chance of staying off his feet for a day. So I replied, "Your choice," trying to be agreeable. Imagine my surprise when my answer came back to haunt me.

At 5:30 a.m., Émile was up and raring to go. Unfortunately, I'd been awake until midnight listening to a BBC report on the shortwave about the booming modern slave trade. And then someone tried to barge into our room—until I shouted at them to go away. Émile slept through it all.

After I placed my legs in "sleepwalk" mode, we set off once again. As usual, it was impossible to doze off on that road. Cars chock-a-block with waving locals passed. Bus drivers blasted their horns. They knew nothing about our journey, where we were going or why—only that we were foreigners in their Islamic home. It was refreshing to see their interest and moral support.

Before long, we trekked past statues of wrestlers locked in fierce embrace, as Edirne was also home to the famous olive oil-greased wrestling matches called *Kirkpinar*. According to legend, in 1361, as the Ottoman army advanced to capture the city, their soldiers wrestled during breaks in the fighting. On one occasion, two soldiers fought all night, neither able to win. The next morning, they were found dead, bodies intertwined, and they were buried beneath a fig tree. Today, the world's oldest sanctioned wrestling competition was still re-enacted there annually.

Personally, it was my daily goal to call Cheryl and learn if she'd heard any more news about the precarious situation in the Middle East. However, I couldn't find a telephone until 11:00 when we reached Havsa and found a post office. Although usually dependable places to make an international call, those refused to accept my Hungarian calling card number supposedly "Good in forty countries," and I was forced to buy the local version.

Lately, I'd been thinking more about walking from Istanbul for seven hundred kilometers or so to Antalya on the Turkey's southern coast, and then catching a ferry to Cyprus, once a Templar stronghold. I knew the route was similar to one taken during the later Crusades. Although I still preferred to walk through Syria and Jordan, with the increasing carnage, that possibility appeared more distant with each passing day.

Half a world away, Cheryl knew more about the situation than I'd suspected. The ferry service to Cyprus from Turkey had been indefinitely halted. In fact, they were evacuating families from Lebanon to the island nation to get them out of harm's way. Hotels and other facilities were stretched to the breaking point, and it was anyone's guess how soon the situation would change.

For us, Havsa's one hotel was an inviting change from the night before, and we were welcomed in English and French by Suleiman, the owner of the Internet café just across the street. After a lunch of liver and pepper stew, rice *pilav* and a block of fresh yogurt, I took Suleiman up on his offer and visited him for tea. As Émile retired for his *petite siesta*, Suleiman, who was also a local teacher, and Kosmo, his assistant, treated me to a drink, as we talked about our trek. Sipping tea amid the teeming teen activity, I was reminded of the kindness we'd experienced on past visits to that intriguing country.

Years ago, Cheryl and I had landed in Gallipoli on the Turkish coast late at night. All the hotels were closed. We were forced to endure long hours of sitting on a seaside bench, waiting for daybreak. In spite of this, what could have been a disaster turned into an unforgettable evening when we were adopted by an outgoing Turk, who was closing up his food stand for the night. First, he gave us a blanket to protect us from the cold sea air, then shared fresh lamb kebabs, and regaled us with stories. He even invited us back to join him and his friends the following evening when they pre-pared a feast on the docks, complete with a companion who played a soul-ful violin—and enough *raki*, that head-throbbing anise-flavored liquor, to create warmth in any weather.

Then again, how could I forget our outing to the house of the Virgin Mary, who reputedly lived the last part of her life near Ephesus. Unable to catch a bus to the site, we decided to walk—until we were offered a ride—on the back of a local fire truck. I'll never forget the two of us balancing on the rear platform, hanging on for dear life, bugs in our teeth, as we zoomed up the mountainside.

No, the Turkish people were as kind as I remembered. Before leaving, Suleiman insisted I take his better map of the country, as well as a hotel guide. Once again, I was confident we'd continue to meet our fair share of "angels" along the path—no matter what direction it led.

It's amazing how we create routine in places so foreign and situations that change so much every day. Maybe it's intentional; the mind's way of creating normalcy from chaos. We were up at 5:30 and left at 6:00, after Émile gobbled a pastry roll from his private cache, and then we headed to a café for tea and a *börek*. Our black teas were served in petite, thin glasses called *ince belli*, about 1/3 the size of ours' and almost too hot to handle. They arrived on small silver plates with cheap spoons, looking like they came from a child's tea party set. People dropped one, two or three sugar cubes into the four-ounce flute for a cup of hot, sugary energy. We wolfed them down in non-typical Turkish fashion, stopped for mineral water, and then headed out of town at a good clip amid soft sunlight, muted in an orangish glow.

It turned into a sultry dog day—and we met our share. One curious, stray mutt with a gray, mottled coat and eager blue eyes popped her head out from between stalks of flaxen corn as we passed. For a moment, with her sad, hopeful eyes and cockeyed ears, she reminded me of a friendly "Gollum," the character from Tolkien's *Lord of the Rings*. She hesitantly approached, tail tucked between her legs, as dogs were often fearful of Émile's stick and wild hat. The young female groveled toward me, belly brushing the hot pavement. For that, she got her head scratched and was in nirvana for a blissful moment. Still, we had to leave her all too quickly. She could hardly tag along, just to be deserted once we reached the border.

She patiently sat by the roadside for a long while, waiting to be called to join us, yet it was not meant to be. She sat there alone as we disappeared over the next hill. My heart went out to her.

Although I couldn't help her solitude, as we entered Babaeski, I did have the chance to come to the aid of another lupine brother. When passing the village cemetery, I heard a young pup yelping in terror. Slowing down, I spotted a man tossing something at her and then hosing her down. Every time he did, she cried pitifully.

"That guy's torturing the young dog," I said to Émile.

"*Ah, bon.*"

I hurried back and saw two young German shepherds chained underneath the overhang of a house. The bully continued tossing garbage at the smaller one, then soaking him with water from his hose. I wanted so much to go over and give him a piece of my mind. But having none to spare, especially in Turkish, I approached until he saw me giving him what Hawaiians like to call "one kine stink eye," until he stopped and slunk off. I waited long enough to make sure he didn't return right away, but there was little more I could do. I could only hope I'd brought a little peace to those pups.

Once in Babaeski, we found another hotel, sweltering but clean. As Émile enjoyed his *petite siesta*, I wandered over to the Cedid Ali Pasa Camii mosque dating from the 1500s, where the watchmen were happy to give me a tour in Turkish. Or maybe, they were just making sure, in my ignorance, I didn't accidentally desecrate something.

"You broke it, you bought it."

The following day, we walked a shorter distance to Lüleburgaz, as the next town of any size was Çorlu, forty-seven kilometers east. In the suffocating ninety-degree heat, that was just pushing our luck too much.

Reaching the town of 79,000, we began looking for a room—in something other than the three-star monstrosity dominating the town square. Hoping to find an alternative, we dropped into a sidewalk café. It was always difficult to tell what was on the menu in those places, since they seldom had one. Although Émile was desperate for a cold beer, I tried to break the news gently to my parched friend.

"You're never going to find a lager in a regular café here, except maybe in Istanbul or another tourist town. This is a Muslim country and most Turks don't drink alcohol, at least in public. We have to go to one of those pubs decorated with the beer flags and keg outside, as we did the other night in Edirne."

As he slumped in his chair, a fellow with thick glasses who'd been reading his newspaper at a nearby table adopted us, ordering colas and then teas all around while we shared our predicament.

"Sorry. That big hotel is the only one here," he explained in broken English. "The next one is in Çorlu."

So, with our tails tucked between *our* legs, we approached the high rise and awaited the bad news. It was already obvious the hotel catered to foreigners. You could tell by the empty lobby and parking lots.

"What's the price of a double, two people, one night?" I asked the very "proper" female desk clerk.

"Seventy-five dollars."

"Not dollars, lira. This is Turkey, right?"

"One hundred Turkish lira."

Their rate was four times what we'd spent the night before, and far out of line with Turkish costs of living, but most places were willing to haggle. After all, it was a national pastime. But, for once, she wouldn't budge.

"Is there any other *pension* in town? A local hotel?"

"There is one place just a kilometer from here," she suggested with an understanding smile. "The Park. You may want to try there."

We were grateful and found the perfectly cozy inn a few blocks away. By then, I was anxious to catch up on the news via our hotel television. That was one major advantage of being a modern pilgrim—but in our case, ignorance was bliss.

Britain had just exposed an Al-Qaeda plot to bring a liquid bomb onto ten airplanes and detonate them simultaneously. America raised its terror alert to "red," perhaps for the first time since September 11th. As if that weren't enough, there was an outbreak of Crimean-Congo Hemorrhagic Fever, an Ebola-like virus. It was airborne in central Turkey's Anatolia region—an area we planned to walk across—and had killed at least twenty people. I watched on television as workers in HAZMAT outfits fed chickens through a machine resembling a wood-chipper.

Life had become like the old Chinese blessing (or curse): "May you live in interesting times."

Just when you think that things can't get any worse… Besides the political violence and plagues, in the morning, even our wide road with broad shoulders disintegrated before our eyes. There was absolutely no safe place to walk, and at one point, within ten minutes, a hundred buses passed en masse. The traffic didn't let up all day, which made it especially tough on our forty-seven kilometer marathon. I could scarcely take my eyes off the highway. Traffic zoomed past, just feet away—at best. To top it off, we spent much of the day walking on gravel and rocks, which wasn't any good for shoes that already had 1,500 kilometers behind them. It was another 150 kilometers before I could retrieve my third pair from Sophie in Istanbul.

It took nearly ten hours with just three short breaks in the intense heat to reach Çorlu, and we arrived not a moment too soon. Strength and morale were as scarce as water. It was time for a serious heart-to-heart about our options. After more than a hundred days together, I still hadn't seen any improvement in my companion—quite the opposite. Émile grew weaker and more forgetful. The heat weighed heavily on him and he was ready to quit after a few hours. He still wasn't adequately re-hydrating. As much as I hated to admit it, I couldn't needlessly risk our lives as we approached Turkey's arid plains where the villages and water were farther apart—and we had to cope with pestilence, terrorism and the unknowns of the Middle East to boot.

"Look, when we reach Istanbul in a few days, we need to decide what to do," I reluctantly explained. "Do we continue walking across Anatolia to Syria? Head to Antalya with the hope of somehow continuing to Cypress? Or do we decide it's just too dangerous and head home?" Then I added, "If we continue, is it together—or alone?"

At daybreak, we were spurred on by the prospect of relaxing in Istanbul within a few days. Still, it took us ninety minutes to wend our way past military posts and *gendarmeries*, through what looked like an armed camp just outside of Çorlu. It was home to Turkey's 189th Infantry Regiment, and I hadn't seen such a military presence since Tibet. However, soon we were back to walking past ranks of textile factories extending thirty kilometers through the countryside.

Most people we encountered were curious and welcoming, like the kids at the family *köfta* restaurant who snatched away our empty bottles and plates as soon as we set them down. After asking where we from, Émile's answer of "France" got the usual positive response, as one son was heading off to work in Paris. It was easier than saying "America," which still invariably created a debate about our foreign policy. Plus, it was something Émile could contribute to our cause.

After lunch we reluctantly headed back onto the hot tar highway, feet sinking into the road with each labored step. We'd briefly considered walking at night, but the buzz of 24-hour traffic made that far too dangerous to seriously consider. Before long, we were elated to spot the glimmering Sea of Marmara off on the horizon, and I was tempted to continue walking to our seaside destination. It had been far too long since I'd played in the surf, but Émile doused water on those plans, complaining he was already exhausted. The siren's call of the hotel pool ahead was too strong for him to ignore.

"Okay, I have no problem in stopping now," I assured him, "but I want you to arrange our rooms, okay?" It was high time he increased his confidence, just in case we went our separate ways after reaching Istanbul. Not too surprisingly, Émile managed to do just fine, and we checked into a tangerine-colored room complete with a sunken bathtub and television showing X-rated films. Two pilgrims had wandered into the "little whorehouse on the prairie."

Stumbling downstairs at 6:00 a.m., my suspicions were confirmed when a beautiful "escort" with a distinctly Eastern European accent joined us. It was heartbreaking that many of the countries we'd passed insisted on exporting their young, vivacious women to the rest of the world. The other night on the BBC, I'd learned that Eastern European women were often promised good paying office jobs in London with hopes of sending money home to lift their families out of poverty. In reality, many of them were sold from one owner to the next as sex slaves. In the same lobby, we spotted a sign in six languages providing workers with a "hot-line" (partially funded by the U.S. government) to report employers who refused to pay them, or withheld their passports. Morality aside, it was a sad commentary on the promise of Western capitalism.

It took several hours to leave the outskirts of Silivri, and our brains were sizzling by 10:00 am. I scheduled stops more frequently because of the heat, plus road walking (unlike street walking) took a huge amount of concentration to avoid (not entice) passing cars. By late morning, we stopped into a gas station where workers instantly struck up a conversation about Émile's pendant-draped baton.

"Why no Turkish flag?" they demanded in mock indignation.

"We haven't been able to find one," I explained. "We're hoping to add it to our collection in Istanbul."

Hearing that, one enterprising fellow ducked into their back room and soon returned with a small Turkish pendant, while another brought us a plastic twist-tie to secure it onto the *bourdon*. All in all, it was another spontaneous display of hospitality that invigorated our morale and kept us moving.

Heat radiated off the black tarmac amid mottled brown earth splotched with wildflowers. I felt like I was trudging along the San Diego Freeway. I kept half-expecting to see a large yellow road sign warning drivers to watch out for *peregrinos* (instead of illegal immigrants) scurrying across the highway, but it only existed in my sun-addled imagination.

Shortly after noon, Émile already eyed another high-rise and its inviting pools, declaring, "I'm tired, my feet hurt and I'm stopping here!" We hadn't even reached thirty kilometers, but I wasn't up to an argument, so I played along. Even from the start, warning signs should have convinced us to keep walking.

First: the buxom, blonde Amazons dressed-to-kill that stepped out of a black stretch limousine by the front door.

Second: a metal detector to enter the lobby.

Third: the huge, armed bouncer by the front desk.

Fourth: when we asked for a room, they answered, "We have only one room with one bed. Maybe we'll have one with two beds in an hour."

'An hour? They rent by the hour?'

Now, I'm far from being a prude, but I felt uncomfortable about supporting a hotel that exploited young women while catering to vacationing mafia. So we left. Émile fumed at my decision, but I refused to go into details. When he asked why, I simply answered, "*Complet*. Full."

It took us four more stops and two more hours to reach another string of three and four-star hotels in Kumburgaz, a seaside resort less than fifty kilometers from Istanbul. By then, all the inns were full with the exception of one charging exorbitant rates.

"Are the girls included?" I asked, in my best wide-eyed innocent look. The lady at the reception desk just smiled.

By 3:30, we'd run out of resorts and returned to the desk clerk at an earlier hotel that'd promised to "make some calls" if we didn't find a room. Well, he did and we found one—*sans* metal detectors, weapons, bouncers and bustiers.

At long last, after what turned out to be a grueling day, Émile and I finally had time to relax at a local café *with* a menu. It was a welcome change, since I was beginning to think the others just made it all up depending on who came through their door. As we relaxed in the cool shade, watching all the newcomers look for last-minute rooms, we ordered spicy *Adana dürüms*, thinly sliced lamb rolled into a burrito-like shell. As a finale, to take the edge off, we ordered a *hookah* filled with mellow apple-flavored tobacco.

I'm not a smoker, but I remembered how pleasurable water pipe smoking could be in Arabic countries. It had a long tradition in Turkey as well, during the old days when smoking and sipping coffee were an integral part of social life—until too many *hookah* houses burned down. Once, when Cheryl and I were in Egypt, we had the memorable chance to relax with a few villagers in a café only a hundred yards from the Great Pyramid. As the sun set, we, too, set aside our differences in a fragrant billow of smoke, while the world and its problems passed by.

Since it was Émile's first *hookah*, he didn't know quite what to expect, but was pleasantly surprised as we passed our "peace pipe" back and forth. The restaurant owner brought us fresh coals and then tea to sip along with our smoke. Finally, when we stood to leave, the roly-poly fellow came over to shake our hands, as did the chef, and we were made to feel at home.

We expected the following day to be an easy one, but fate had other plans. Leaving the hotel after breakfast, we headed east toward Istanbul. With the increased traffic, we were initially relieved to catch a smaller road we were told would lead us all the way to the famed metropolis—only it didn't. We ended up zigzagging through a sea of condos on Turkey's version of the Costa del Sol. Frustrated after wasting energy on all those diversions, we took to the main highway again. It was a bizarre scene—us versus a sea of vehicles—one of those "What's wrong with this picture?" drawings. Émile and I climbed a steep mountain pass for over an hour, braving a hornet's nest of swarming cars, amid the cacophony of belching buses and trucks. In all my wanderings, I couldn't imagine a worse place to trek. My walk into Rome paled in comparison. As if that weren't enough, at one point we stopped at a gas station for water and were shocked to hear them say that Istanbul was still fifty-five kilometers away. It wasn't that far when we'd started walking that morning. As consolation, the attendant manning the pumps gave us each a small bottle of what's best described as lemon-scented gas station cologne. It was unleaded—but far from premium.

Finally reaching a small town, we ducked into the pharmacy where a woman with gentle eyes scoured the Internet until she found us a hotel "just five kilometers away," or so she assured us. It was welcome news, since my friend already sat crumpled in the corner.

Well, five kilometers quickly turned into twelve. It would make little difference if you were in a car. "So what?" you might say, but for us it meant the difference of walking one hour vs. two and a half in hundred-degree heat, with the air as humid as a tropical rainforest.

The traffic-crazed highway ran parallel to the tempting sea. As usual, I tried to keep an eye on Émile, crawling at a snail's pace a hundred yards behind. Nevertheless, looking back at one point, I was shocked to find my friend lying flat on his face! I rushed back to see what had happened and was stunned to see he'd tripped over broken pavement and cushioned his fall with his face. His wire-rimmed glasses were broken and had gouged his cheek, which was already swollen. It didn't look serious, but he was clearly shaken. Pouring what was left of my water onto my bandana, I gingerly washed out his bloody gash.

"Look, it could have happened to anybody," I assured him, yet the best medicine was to get him into the shade and off his feet.

With that in mind, we continued on toward the elusive hotel. That proved harder than expected. Even the traffic police, staring at his blood-spattered condition in sympathetic horror, had no idea where it was. Although I tried to convince Émile we were close, it took us more creative effort than usual to find the little-known inn in the center of town.

After cleaning up, we bandaged Émile's battered cheek, but it was as clear as the swelling on his face that he was going to have a sizable "shiner."

"Ever had a black-eye, *mon ami?*"

"No, never," he uneasily admitted.

"Well, they're pretty common with teenaged boys back home. You've joined the club. Congratulations."

Émile frowned, unappreciative of my humor. I couldn't help but wonder what Sophie would think when they met in only two days?

Yet for all the anguish, the afternoon's events were just a prelude to an equally frustrating night. Hungrier and more parched than usual, and ready to lick our wounds in camaraderie, we wandered down to a nearby pub where a sociable group of locals instantly adopted us. They shared their food, we bought beers, and they bought *raki*. We were having fun, even though we barely shared a common language. Their generosity and body language spoke volumes. Haki, a friendly fellow who'd spent years working in Germany, spoke broken English and German for nearly an hour. Émile swapped addresses and then even t-shirts with Biero, a guy who worked there. Then something odd happened.

Suddenly, Haki started rambling on and on only in Turkish. As he became increasingly agitated, I got the distinct impression he was insulting us. Of course, Émile had no idea what he was talking about, yet in his usual friendly manner kept nodding his head "yes" to it all. From personal experience, I knew it was his non-verbal "*Ah, bon,*" and had once warned him it might be taken the wrong way in other cultures.

What if Haki was saying, "You French hate Turks, don't you?"

Nod.

Or, "You invaded Iraq just for the oil."

Nod, nod.

Nodding could have serious consequences, so I just sat there poker-faced, waiting for the storm to pass, not anxious for the argument to escalate. As it grew increasingly tense, at one point I looked over at the cook. He winked, as if to say, "There he goes again. Haki can't hold his *raki*," but that was little consolation if fists began to fly.

Before we knew it, Biero had stripped off Émile's shirt in a huff and thrust it back at him, while our addresses were ceremoniously torn into confetti before our eyes. Then bewildered Émile handed back the prayer beads Biero had given him for his journey. The party was clearly over—and we still didn't know what had been said—or why? We only knew that given the right amount of *raki*, Haki's resentments bubbled to the surface like the La Brea Tar Pits.

Obvious that we'd clearly overstayed our welcome, we stood to leave. Well, imagine my surprise when Biero stepped forward to hug and kiss us on both cheeks, before we retreated into the moonless night. Only later, back in our room, did we discover he'd slipped those prayer beads back into Émile's pocket when they'd embraced.

At dawn, heavy traffic persisted as we trudged the final twenty kilometers into Istanbul or Constantinople, once capital of the Holy Roman, Byzantine and Ottoman Empires. We reached the official "Welcome to Istanbul" sign in less than two hours, yet we continued to weave in and out of smoggy buses and commuter traffic. By 10:00 a.m., hoping we were near the hotel where Émile was scheduled to meet Sophie, we stopped at a construction site to ask directions to Piyerlotti. We were elated when they assured us it wasn't far. However, any jubilation evaporated just as suddenly.

As soon as we started across their site, Émile tripped and fell again, face down in the dirt. Coated in sand, sweat and blood, he let out a pitiful, "I am tired," as I helped him to his feet.

I had no doubt. After a hundred days of walking and facing that challenge together, I knew his willpower was still strong, but the weather and distance had taken their toll on his strength and balance. Together we trudged those last few kilometers into the city until we reached the luxury hotel where he and Sophie would spend the next few days. After a little hesitation, I agreed to spend a night there in celebration, but couldn't justify spending over a hundred euro a night to simply sleep. It might take us another seventy days to reach Jerusalem, and I didn't want to run out of money on the way. So I decided to move to a room nearby, and later had no trouble finding a suitable place for fifteen euros.

As we waited to check into our room, I needed to tell my friend I'd come to an important decision. "Émile," I began, "I want you to know I've thought about this since we talked in Bulgaria, and I've decided to continue to Jerusalem. We've had our differences in the past, but I want you to know I will continue with you—if you need me."

He looked a little shocked I'd actually considered walking it alone, even though we'd spoken of that possibility. Now he had a serious decision to make, especially after those last few, difficult days. Would he continue— either together or alone—or would he return with Sophie? Then again, after she saw his bruised face, bent glasses and bedraggled condition, would she insist he come home?

"Tomorrow I will tell you what I will do," he sighed in deep resignation.

That evening, just outside the famous Blue Mosque, my comrade and I ran into two French twenty-five-year-old bicyclists. They'd just covered 3,600 kilometers in forty days. I was happy for them, but thought, 'We've covered nearly 3,000 kilometers in ninety-nine walking days, so we've done well. It's another 800 kilometers or so to Antalya and at most 150 across Cyprus and maybe 225 across Israel. God willing, we'll reach Jerusalem by my birthday in early October. What a present that will make.'

The following morning, we enjoyed a buffet breakfast in the hotel's rooftop restaurant while admiring panoramic views of the Bosporus Strait. Right after his eggs were polished off, Émile solemnly made an announcement.

"I will not continue. I will go home with Sophie."

"I'm sorry. I understand," was all I could muster at first. I knew it was a difficult choice. He'd invested so much mentally, emotionally, physically in the journey, his dream, for so many years. I could only remind him, "Look, you've walked 3,000 kilometers in four months. Considering your other pilgrimage from Dijon to Finisterre, Spain, you've walked across Europe. That's quite an accomplishment."

Still, I knew my words were little consolation. 'It's his choice,' I reminded myself, 'and I shouldn't try to talk him out of it. This trip, any trip, is not worth killing yourself in the process.'

After breakfast, we asked another diner to take our photograph on the sunny terrace with the sea shimmering behind us in the distance. Asia was a stone's throw away, but it was far from a triumphant moment. Neither of us smiled. We'd soon part company—perhaps never to meet again.

Knowing Sophie and her friend Charlotte were arriving later that day, I decided to tour the Blue Mosque and Haghia Sophia alone. Lost in intro-spection among their towering magnificence, I attempted to put my self-doubts into perspective. With his resignation, I questioned my own sanity—but never my resolve. After studying a new map, I'd discovered the towns were farther apart than expected and the rooms would be more rare. I might have to walk fifty kilometers a day. With the terrain mountainous at times, dry and more desolate, one thing was for certain. The 85-100 degree weather and desert-like conditions would test all my resolve, sur-vival skills…and luck. Would one pilgrim receive the same warm welcome as two, especially without a *bourdon* with banners flying and silly hat? I also remembered all those "angels" who'd supported us along the way, and our promise to send them postcards once we arrived in Jerusalem. If and when I made it, how would I explain Émile's absence?

Later that afternoon, he and I walked along the sea promenade, the eastern edge of Europe, and then wandered to the hotel where Sophie and Charlotte were to meet us. They were late in arriving, but soon the four of us headed to a nearby Italian restaurant for a late dinner. Thoughtful Sophie had brought my replacement Montrail shoes from Dijon, as well as a block of my favorite French cheese.

Still, it was all a little unsettling. I half-expected to talk about Émile's decision and kept studying her face, looking for some sign of her reaction. Was she angry? Disappointed? Relieved? I'd never know, since she and her friend spent an inordinate amount of time discussing the preparation of our food, instead of the crucial decision Émile had just made in his life.

Lying in bed that night, I tossed and turned as I tried to analyze my emotions so I could move on and face the challenges ahead. I knew we'd had our differences at times. I felt a little guilty for those moments I'd lost my patience or been stern in my warnings: "Lock the door to the room," "Bring your money pouch," "Check for traffic before crossing," "Don't walk on the right hand side of the road." Yet I knew they were always well intentioned and for our safety. Perhaps some of our disagreements had been caused by my limited ability to speak with the subtlety of a true Frenchman. For him, it must have been like talking with a ten-year old. Then again, there was Émile's travel inexperience and physical problems that would have prevented many from starting such a journey in the first place.

Still, after traveling 3,000 kilometers together, we'd done pretty well given all our challenges. I'd miss my friend and promised to toast his efforts when I reached Jerusalem. In just two days, I'd begin the hardest part of the journey—alone. God be with me.

Over the following days, I half-heartedly accomplished an obligatory sightseeing tour. Since I'd already visited the vibrant city twice, it was more like visiting an old friend and noticing how much they, or you, had changed. The city had certainly grown—to nearly nine million—as well as blossomed in popularity. I'd never been there before with the summer swarms of tour groups—and they were a scourge.

Nevertheless, the Blue Mosque or Sultan Ahmed Mosque was still exquisite with its magnificent 20,000 handmade tiles, stained glass, and towering minarets that pierced the sky with their "call to prayer" five times a day. It was all the more impressive when you realized it was constructed in the 1600s, directly across from the Byzantine Church of the Holy Wisdom.

That Christian church, called the Haghia Sophia after the Ottoman conquest, was once the seat of the Eastern Orthodox Patriarchy of Constantinople. It was considered one of the finest buildings in the world. In fact, it was the largest cathedral for 1,000 years. Even today it was breathtaking with its expansive dome, marble columns, towering vaults and rich golden mosaics. With their crowds, the sanctuaries were hardly tranquil or contemplative, but with a little creativity you could still imagine the awe they once inspired.

I also revisited Chora Museum, once a church on a less grandiose scale, but renowned for its exquisite tile mosaics and frescoes impressive in their detail and realism. Of all my memories of past visits, those were my most vivid and I had to return.

Later that morning, I crossed the Bosporus Straits in search of the U.S. Embassy. I wanted to give them my travel plans, just in case there was any trouble and they had to evacuate Americans. Reaching the other side, I began the long trek to their mission, weaving in and out of throngs of local teens who would have looked right at home in America, as well as women wearing black *chadors* and carrying upscale boutique shopping bags. Eventually, I reached their location only to discover they'd moved and failed to notify the tourist information office. Nowadays, they were another fifteen kilometers outside of town, so it wasn't worth my effort to try again. I'd have to take my chances.

Not wanting to return empty handed, I easily found the walking mall and resumed my search for more detailed maps of Turkey, a country stretching more than a thousand miles long and half as wide. I found one map for the southern part of the route, but was unable to find a more detailed one for the north, despite checking six different shops. At the last one, out of desperation, I half-jokingly suggested, "Maybe you could just copy the necessary pages from this 300-page Turkish atlas I found on the shelf." I couldn't fathom carrying something so huge, and it seemed a waste to just tear out the ten pages I needed. "I'd gladly pay for them," I suggested.

As you might expect, the salesgirl initially laughed at my idea, but after hearing about my pilgrimage she phoned her manager, who much to my surprise agreed. Imagine trying that at home?

That evening, I met Émile, Sophie and Charlotte in the Sultanahmet district for dinner. He appeared in new clothes Sophie had brought from home: a white hiker's shirt, lightweight trekking shoes (he had heard me), and a smaller backpack, or as he called it, his *sac cadeau*.

"So, now you're ready to finish the trail?" I kidded.

"No, I've bought a ticket to return on the same flight as Sophie. It will be the four month anniversary since our departure." He was all dressed up with nowhere to go—except home.

As the ladies "oohed" and "ahhed" over their place settings, Émile and I ate in near silence, as was our habit. It was all so anticlimactic.

After a painful hour together, he, Sophie and Charlotte left the restaurant for a nighttime promenade along the waterfront. I'd already cruised the area and still had so much left to accomplish before leaving. Besides, the ladies were making the plans now. They'd already scheduled a tour of Topkapi Palace in the morning, and we planned on rendezvousing around noon to cruise the Bosporus together. So I excused myself and headed back to my inn. I walked alone in hushed darkness, crossing the site of the ancient Roman Hippodrome, a chariot-racing track with ancient obelisks. Our goodbyes would be painful. Though Émile's *sans souci* attitude ran counter to my own, I'd miss his gentle ways and grim determination.

Nonetheless, our long goodbye would never come to pass. Our meeting at the hotel at noon never happened, and I was left like the bridegroom at the altar. There was no message, no note, nothing. I waited alone in the silent lobby for an hour, and then left a note of my own suggesting we meet for dinner at 7:00. Then I rushed to catch the last ferry up the beautiful Bosporus.

The sunshine and water were gorgeous and the absence of pleasure yachts and fishing boats was a relief. The banks of the Bosporus and surrounding Dardanelles were terraced with palaces and luxury homes of various architectural styles reminiscent of Newport, Rhode Island. Our ship made seven stops en route to let off commuting locals, until we all finally disembarked at the last port before entering the Black Sea. Then, after indulging in a freshly grilled fish, we headed back to Istanbul just in time for me to take a quick shower and meet everyone at the hotel for dinner.

Imagine my disappointment when the desk clerk handed me a hastily scribbled note that read:

> "Got tired and rested at the Topkapi Palace, so
> unable to come back at noon. Sorry. We are taking
> the night cruise of the Bosporus from 5-9 p.m.
> Good courage. Good luck." ~ Émile

I was stunned. Angry. Saddened. After all we'd been through, I got a brush-off on our final night. Émile pulled what they call a "French exit," where a person leaves early without saying goodbye. It seemed so unlike him. No farewell? "It's been fun. Have a nice life?" Perhaps he thought he might be tempted to rejoin me, or simply it would be too emotionally painful to go our separate ways and never realize his dream of reaching Jerusalem on foot. Maybe it was better for him, but we could have just said our "*adieus*" the night before in front of the Blue Mosque. As far as memories go, it would have been more respectful of what we'd been through together.

'*Ultreia*, my friend. Onward.'

CHAPTER TEN
Istanbul to Kütahya

Turks Bearing Gifts

"War does not determine who is right - only who is left."
~ Bertrand Russell

On the morning I departed Istanbul, I willed my faithful Montrail shoes to the front desk clerk who promised to find them a new life with a poor kid that could use them. They still had some kilometers left in them, and I was grateful to have a new pair for the 1,000-kilometer challenge ahead. Then I set off in a mad dash to the ferry terminal at the bottom of the hill, since I was told it left at 6:30. However, when I arrived, I found the ticket office sealed shut. I could do little more than treat myself to several *çay* and a *tost* sandwich as I paced back and forth awaiting its actual 7:40 departure. As it was, the passenger ferry to Kadicöy on the banks of the vast Asian continent lasted less than thirty minutes, hardly enough time for another tea. Once we docked, I immediately began asking directions to Pendik.

"It's impossible to walk there!" two folks assured me, but after our trek across Tibet, I no longer accepted "Impossible!" as a reason for not doing anything. Next, one lady sent me in the wrong direction. Afterward, I was told the distance to Pendik ranged from six to sixty kilometers. They didn't get around much, I guess. Finally, I set off walking down the road in what I figured was the "sun in your eyes" direction, until I met a young, bearded Spaniard who confirmed, "Yes, you're going the right way." However, he suggested I walk a few blocks south on the more scenic beach road and I was relieved when the simple path turned into a paved bikeway and exercise circuit. It ran behind a strand of luxury hotels and condos for fifteen or twenty kilometers.

That section of Kadicöy was appealing with tranquil coves, islands dotted offshore and a waterfront that put San Diego to shame. It could have been southern California; everything was so lushly green and manicured. As it was Saturday, everyone was jogging, biking, exercising, or walking their dogs. People were fit and decked out in designer training gear—except for a few women in black flowing *burkas* who sashayed back and forth on treadmills. Black really did make them look slimmer.

The beach walk continued all morning until the area eventually became more industrial. I counted at least twenty enormous ships anchored offshore Pendik, a city in startling contrast to the laid-back ambiance of the last. A working-class resort, it had existed for about 4,000 years, yet I couldn't see the attraction.

By the time I arrived in its swarming central marketplace, I found myself in the midst of an unsettling road show. There were huge photos of wounded civilians, shocking videos, and a blaring soundtrack with mothers wailing and babies crying. It displayed in devastating detail the horrors of the war in Palestine and Lebanon, starring Israel and the United States as the villains. To any Muslim sitting on the proverbial fence, it was an effective propaganda tool. To thinking Westerners, it raised serious questions as well, as they weren't images we often saw on television or in newspapers covering a war that had been "sanitized for our protection." To my recollection, unlike the Vietnam War where we dined on death via television every night, we'd seen only one disturbing photo of dead American soldiers returning home from Iraq—let alone many images of the 600,000+ Iraqi civilians reportedly killed at that point. As the mob viewed it with little concealed anger, I maneuvered past, trying to remain as invisible as possible; one blonde, tallish man in a sea of mostly dark, compact people.

On that weekend, Pendik was heaving with beach-goers and rooms were at a premium. The first hotel I visited wanted much more than we'd ever paid in Turkey, while the other, after learning I was American, refused to let me stay. So given the circumstances, I trudged on in the stifling hundred-degree heat and humidity. Tuzla was "only" another ten kilometers away and I easily found a room just outside the village. After another long day in the sun, its air-conditioning was heavenly at any price—and no road show in town meant I wouldn't have to sleep with one eye open.

Yesterday's serene seaside path evaporated with the rising of the sun. It
was replaced by the controlled chaos of Route 100: two lanes of frantic
commuters running in either direction, plus another lane for an onramp,
walkers or horse-drawn carts. I rediscovered my own pace. After walking
so long with Émile, I kept feeling as if I'd forgotten something back at the
hotel, yet I had to admit it was a relief not to have to turn around every
kilometer or so to check if my friend was still there.

Not far down the road, I heard a shout above the traffic roar and
turned to spot a uniformed guard standing outside a factory. He signaled
to me, his hand turning in a circular motion as if stirring something. As I
walked over, the young security guard suggested, "Çay?" "Tea?" and I was
hooked. I rushed to join him and four other guards in their cubbyhole of
an office.

Kürs, my host, spoke a little English, as he'd once worked at an Istanbul hotel. He was curious about my journey, and I took time to field their
questions, leaving out the name of my final destination. After seeing the
crowd's reaction to the road show the day before, did I dare mention
Israel? Or was that inviting trouble?

He and his friends were attentive, sharing their bread and black olives
with the stranger. As I sipped from a small, sizzling glass teacup, I traced a
line from north to south across the map of Turkey hanging on their wall,
as I showed them the path I intended to trek.

"Ah, do not go there," Kürs warned, pointing to six or seven Kurdish
provinces in the southeast. "Terrorists!"

Terrorists? How easy it was to classify an entire people because of the
actions of a few, whether they were Kurds, Palestinians, Jews, Iraqi…or
American. When would we move beyond prejudice and profiling? Yet I
nodded and took note. I didn't plan on heading that far east anyway, since
the Crimean-Congo Hemorrhagic Fever was much more of a deterrent.

As much as I enjoyed their hospitality, I was eager to get started again
in the welcome coolness of the morning. So after swapping email
addresses (a modern custom everywhere), and meeting their aged Labrador
guard dog who appeared stuffed and mounted in the courtyard, I set off
once more down the highway.

The road progressed through a series of steep climbs and descents all
morning, until I reached the futuristic vision of the last hellhole on earth.
Outside of Hereke, a Hieronymus Bosch-like village appeared in an awful
amber haze. Factories belched smoke. I could scarcely breathe. There were

chemical plants, mining operations and a deafening aluminum plant so close to the mosque that you could barely hear yourself think—let alone the call to prayer trumpeted from the graceful minaret.

Not a moment too soon, I again viewed the cobalt-blue Marmara Sea with villages glistening on its distant shore. Then I spotted an equally welcome site: a stucco hotel hugging the hillside just above the water. Considering yesterday's prices, I was certain it exceeded my modest pilgrim's budget, but at least I could savor a few minutes in its cool lobby. As I entered the parking lot, a tall fellow in his twenties shouted an enthusiastic, "Hello, welcome!" in Russian-flavored English. But with a nod I hustled indoors, having already spent far too long in the broiling sun.

My daily joust began when the front desk clerk quoted me fifty liras, as posted on the wall (for the first time in recent history).

"I only have thirty to spend," I countered. I hadn't seen any other guests and was hoping they'd rather have a full room at a reduced rate. They didn't agree. However, just then, the fellow from the parking lot intervened and helped translate. Our negotiations went back and forth before settling on forty liras.

Mikhail or "You can call me Mike," was curious about my arrival and I was happy to talk with him about my trek for peace, if only I could shower first. Wandering down vacant halls, I breezed into my room whose balcony overlooked a vast sea radiating tranquility, except for when the trains rattled past.

After cleaning up and hanging laundry outside to dry, I ambled back down to the lobby, since I hoped to find a restaurant in town. I was shocked to discover it was still several kilometers away, so I settled for theirs instead. As I tried to translate their menu, Mike again came to my rescue and insisted I join him at his table.

"I used to work here at hotel," he explained, between mouthfuls of chicken and rice, "but now, I am…between jobs. They put me up here and feed me until something comes along. Please, help yourself to chicken," he pleaded in his odd accent, passing it my way.

"No, no, I'm fine," I replied, nibbling on my salad, but he obviously thought otherwise.

"Look, you want a plate of chicken? The chef fix too much."

That was probably true, since we were the only ones there. Still, I assured him, "Thanks, this is fine. Really," once, twice, three times before he got up and ducked into the kitchen. His buddy, the cook, appeared a few minutes later and presented me with a huge portion of fried chicken and a plate with four different salads, plus a fresh peach. It was perfection.

"Gifts from your friends," Mike said, with a gracious smile.

Over our impromptu feast, I answered his questions about the purpose for my peace pilgrimage and about life back in Hawaii.

"You know, people are basically the same everywhere," I explained, and was relieved to see him nodding in agreement. "To eliminate wars, we need to eliminate their root cause. When people become so desperate, living in poverty with no jobs, no healthcare, no security, no house, no chance for a better life or even a homeland, with their backs up against a wall, they take desperate measures. After all, at that point, what do they have to lose?"

"I know too well," he whispered, revealing his secret. "I am a Kurd."

He was the first I'd ever met—and he didn't look like a "terrorist"—or act like one for that matter. Mike was simply a man sitting across from me, sharing a chicken. Yet I could see the pain etched in his chiseled face and furrowed brow.

"I just hope to find better life," he slowly explained in broken English. "I am engaged to Scottish girl. We hope to marry soon. She tries to... understand me," he said, with a gentle laugh.

"Well, in many ways, you come from two different worlds."

"Yes, I know."

"Do you plan on emigrating there to work once you get married?"

"No, I stay here in Turkey."

I was surprised, since I figured many foreigners married Western Europeans to be able to work abroad.

"Or, I like to return to my home. Bosses here will not hire me if they know where I am from."

"Really? Is that legal?"

He grinned at my naïvety. "Even when someone is working here, life is hard. Take this hotel. You make five or six hundred Turkish lira a month. Cigarettes alone cost three hundred."

"People *are* the same everywhere. It's similar for hotel workers in Hawaii. They make so little compared to what guests pay for their room."

"How much?"

I hesitated answering, as it would seem even more obscene to him than it did to me. "A hotel worker makes around seven dollars an hour plus tips to service guests who spend $250 to $1500 a night."

He was surprised—especially since I'd just haggled over ten liras.

"It's one thing, Mike, for hotels to gouge the well-heeled visitor who doesn't care—but its workers as well?"

"That's why many Turkish workers go to Germany or England," he insisted.

"Ah, but it gets worse. In our "paradise," many folks often have to work two jobs, both mother and father, while kids seldom see their parents. Their family lives in a cramped house. And many of the sons and daughters can forget about ever owning their own home there. Houses already cost more than many of them will earn in a lifetime."

I could only wonder how long it would be before we bred our own disenfranchised youth with nothing left to lose?

I set off along the coastal highway before sunrise. Already a smothering haze, an amber death shroud, covered the valley and coastline choked with spewing factories. Traffic was horrendous with cars cascading to Istanbul to the west, and trucks continuing east to Ankara, or south to the Middle East. I had to concentrate on the road more than usual and skip my daily meditations, perhaps when I needed them most. As if that weren't enough, by midmorning it was nearly one hundred degrees with little shade. Although I paused for water once or twice, I didn't dare slow down. The heat would only grow more intense as the sun arched higher in the sky.

By early afternoon, feeling like the proverbial ant frying under the magnifying glass, I reached Izmit and found another modest inn. It didn't offer air-conditioning, a pool, ocean views, or "escorts," but it was exactly what I needed, with a Turkish pub right next-door. Usually those places had a cold case with *shish kabobs*, fruit, tomatoes, peppers and cheese. You went to the case and pointed—but not this one. It only served ice-cold beers, nuts and watermelon to a crowd just as intent on watching their football match as any sports nuts in the States.

As much as I enjoyed life with its assorted nuts, I needed something more substantial, so I ended up wandering down the street to the bazaar. Settling down in the courtyard for a spicy *Adana durum* and *ayran*, a refreshing yogurt drink, I ate dinner under the watchful eye of the cadaver of a butcher across the passageway. He was a fellow so stooped that his chin rested on his belly. As he leaned back in his wicker chair against the plaster wall, his son and grandson, younger carbon copies of the master himself, tended his morsel of a shop.

Someday, all that would be theirs.

Traveling alone has a way of making you accessible to the locals and
they're more likely to invite you over to share tea—or a bit of their lives—
as they did the following day.

I cleared Izmit before sunrise and thankfully left the Ankara-bound
traffic behind. Climbing toward the surrounding hills, I made my way
unfettered through a few hamlets, marveling at the livestock, especially one
yard filled with plaster dinosaurs and larger-than-life sized chickens. It was
a scene from *Food of the Gods*, but I didn't stop for a bite, even though their
artistic creators invited me for tea. However, I did pause just down the road
when a group of fifteen truckers, sitting at tables under shade trees, invited
me over. After shaking my hand, pulling out a chair, and pouring me a cup
of steaming *çay* from their samovar, they asked the usual first question.

"Where are you from?"

"Hawaii" I replied, hoping to avoid another political argument. That
usually sufficed. Hawaii still enjoyed a reputation as a tropical isle, and not
everyone, especially the elderly, knew it was part of America. However,
that day was different. As soon as I heard someone mutter, "Oh, American," I knew the jig was up. The mood palpably shifted before I could
finish my first cup of tea.

Mustafa, the road-toughened fellow sitting beside me, declared with a
scowl, "Bush, Blair, Cherac, Putin very bad!" Then he proceeded to count
on his fingers the Muslim countries recently bombed: "Afghanistan, Iraq,
Bosnia, Somalia, and Palestine." Israel and America were considered half-
brothers by much of the world.

There was no use denying it, although I refused to get mired in the
rationale of each. "You're right, but our country is divided now," I pointed
out, as if that were some consolation. "Half of Americans want an end to
this war in Iraq and the number is growing. No sane person wants war.
When we can all sit down and drink tea together like this, we realize how
alike we are. And we learn there are other ways for honorable men to settle
their differences—other than killing each other."

Those common Turks, all simple workingmen, seemed to get the gist of
what I was saying, as they spoke a smattering of English and German
between them and nodded their heads in agreement.

"It is only the politicians who want war," one man cried, his dark eyes
filled with sorrow.

"You're right. War hurts families, mothers, wives, children and countries for years to come. You easily see that in countries like Serbia and Bulgaria that are still so poor while their neighbors prosper."

After lively conversation among themselves, they turned out to be gracious hosts. Their feelings were better described as being more anti-Bush than anti-American.

"After all," I explained with a wink, "whatever our country, whether America—or Turkey, not everyone agrees with their government leaders, right?"

They shook their heads and grinned knowing smiles.

Then feeling safer for the first time since arriving in Turkey, I dared to reveal my ultimate destination. "I'm walking to Israel for peace. I'm on a pilgrimage walk, similar to your *hajj.*"

"Well, Israel certainly needs peace," another fellow sighed.

The reason for my journey appeared to gain their respect, as making a *hajj* was one of the cornerstones of Islam. Every good Muslim was obligated to make the journey to Mecca once in their lifetime, if possible. So it dispelled any remaining doubts in their minds and the tea flowed once more, followed by pieces of cool, juicy watermelon. Between bites, to further illustrate my trek, I pulled out my weathered route map. As truckers well versed in the road to Antalya, they were especially helpful in showing me what towns had places to stay.

Then, amid cups of tea, I pulled out postcards of my island home and passed them around. Mustafa, the fellow who'd originally invited me over, leafed through my pictures, saying, "Oh, like Antalya," since it's on the coast, but he gasped when he saw the dramatic Mars-like photo taken inside Maui's sacred Haleakala Volcano.

"Allah is great!"

I could only agree and smile.

Eventually, I had the nerve to ask the one question that'd been nagging my mind for weeks. "Should I walk through Syria...or catch the boat to Cyprus?"

With furtive glances, they quickly agreed, "Do *not* walk through Syria right now. It is too dangerous." It was just as I'd imagined.

All too soon it grew time to leave the group that had so quickly taken me into their fold. Rising, I presented Mustafa with the photo he'd admired. Beaming broadly, he took my hand and warmly shook it, as did the others who stepped forward to wish me a safe journey. Then reluctantly, I turned and began silently walking down the road again. If nothing else, perhaps I'd lent a face to a country and people probably as misunderstood today as their own. I fervently wished all people, especially the leaders of our world, could walk a trail like that together. Once we dispelled fears and prejudices, it became much easier to wage peace.

Before long, I entered Sapanca and "angels" helped me find a room. Later that night, during my never-ending search for food, I ran into a family outside a tailor shop. The little boy, perhaps seven, was dressed in what's best described as a "Sultan" outfit, complete with ivory suit and cape, bowtie, crown and scepter. His younger sisters were equally charming in their pink and blue frou-frou "princess" gowns. I just had to ask their mother if I could take their photographs and they were delighted to pose. The little girls crowded close to their brother like ducklings, while he wrapped his dashing cape over their shoulders.

"What's the occasion?" I asked his mother. "His birthday?"

"No," she assured me with a coy smile. "*Sünnet Düğünü*. His circumcision."

My four-month anniversary since leaving Dijon began with a steep ascent on a country road out of Sapanca. Although I didn't have to fight for space with the usual crazed vehicles, I did encounter something more dangerous—massive, gray and brown Anatolian Shepherds. Lean and muscular, weighing up to 150-pounds and standing as tall as a wolf, they originally protected shepherds' flocks. Nowadays, sometimes outfitted with sharpened spike collars, they were still capable of bringing down a wolf or bear, and over-qualified to guard local shops, factories and houses. The chained or fenced ones caused me little concern. However, the ones that had escaped and roamed in packs caused my hair to stand at bristly attention.

Early that morning, just as I approached an otherwise tranquil village courtyard, I suddenly heard blood-curdling snarls. As I grew nearer, I saw five of those hunters circle, then viciously attack something in their midst. The alpha male, his head down and ears laid back, would lunge in for a quick bite. Then another would follow, and then another. Like sharks, they each took their turn. I couldn't see their victim, but as I grew nearer, I heard a faint yelping coming from their midst. Since no one else was around to intervene, I knew there wasn't a moment to lose. So I let out my own loud bark—and only hoped they wouldn't turn their wrath on me. Well, my growl took them by surprise. They paused just long enough for a black cockapoo-type dog, their breakfast, to scamper off to safety.

I'd never witnessed such a vicious attack by any pack before, even in Africa. I hoped the little guy would survive. Yet the scene quickly convinced me to pick up a little protection of my own now that Émile and his *bourdon* were history. Alongside the road, I found a five-foot long walking stick about as big around as a silver dollar. It was well seasoned and as tough as old hickory. With my new companion, I felt a little odd at first, like Buford Pusser, the plank-swinging sheriff in the classic film *Walking Tall*. You might laugh, but when I encountered another wild pack on the same trail later that morning, after eyeing my "big stick," they kept a respectful distance.

The country road eventually dropped me back onto the hectic highway where I passed through a beautiful tree-lined valley over the next few hours. As usual, I was determined to find a trail off the main road, especially important if anyone was to walk that path in the future. It was enough to put your "normal" life on hold for months and subject your body to fatigue and extreme weather—without risking life and limb. So with that in mind, after noticing a small track on the other side of the river, I asked a shopkeeper, "Does that path go to Geyve?"

"Yes, just cross the bridge and go to the right."

That wasn't as easy as it sounded, since it was just wide enough for a set of railroad tracks. No sooner did I finish crossing than a train barreled past and flew across the same bridge. That was a little too close. If I'd been twenty seconds later, I'd have been forced to dive into the river, backpack and all.

Before long, I arrived in the charming village of Geyve and for some odd reason was welcomed like a celebrity. I was quickly asked to tea three times, people drove by offering encouragement, and then a friendly senior shopkeeper adopted me. Sabuhattin insisted on leading me to the village's one inn. After unloading my gear, he invited me back to his hardware shop for tea. For nearly an hour, as the world wound down, we sat outside on stools like old friends, drinking tea and sharing stories about our lives. As in small towns everywhere, politics was never very far from anyone's mind. From what I'd seen so far, if Turkey was a member of America's so-called "coalition of the willing," God help us all.

Before turning in for bed, I ran into a bright student I'd met earlier in the afternoon, and we had a more intellectual conversation about religion. Perhaps their similarities became more obvious once we stripped away mutual misconceptions created by a thousand years of war. I was surprised to learn that Islam shared many prophets with Christianity and Judaism, including Jesus, Abraham, Isaac, David, Solomon, John and Moses. He quoted his holy book, saying, "Those who believe in the Qur'an, and those who follow the Jewish scriptures, and the Christians and the Sabians, any who believe in Allah and the Last Day, and work righteousness, shall have their reward with their Lord; on them shall be no fear, nor shall they grieve." That hardly sounded like a call to arms.

Then, he wisely reminded me, "Governments, politics and big business create wars and dissent while the poor sacrifice their lives. Today, more than ever, we need to remember we are all cousins, branches of the same tree. We need to work together to survive."

In the morning, a simple country road carried me past a cornucopia of orchards and fields bursting with pears, plums and pomegranates, corn and collards, apples and figs, watermelons and walnuts, grapes, tomatoes, cabbage, onions and just about any other fruit or vegetable you could imagine. I'd never seen such a bountiful area. A few fields had already been picked clean; others were still being hand-harvested by women garbed in scarves, long sleeved shirts, and skirts or harem pants ("poo pants," as Cheryl liked to call them).

Minute villages appeared every five or six kilometers and disappeared just as swiftly. When I entered most, a cadre of curious geezers at the "sit and spit" corner greeted me, wondering why I was there. Each time, they made that familiar "stirring the tea" gesture and with a smile crooned "Çay?" I was usually delighted to take them up on their kind offers, since by 10:00 a.m. it was already in the mid-eighties and zoomed to over ninety degrees by early afternoon. Although there was little shade, the plains were picturesque.

Mountains, reminiscent of those in Arizona, ringed the gorge. Occasionally, I'd spot caves set high above the valley floor and found myself wondering if early Christians had worshipped there, as they once did in the tenth and eleventh centuries at "Rock Churches" in Turkey's Cappadocia region? I still marveled at the memory of those entire chapels carved out of rock and decorated with brilliant frescoes. I could just imagine untouched paintings up there waiting to be discovered.

In due course, I came across a secluded park with thermal pools that also happened to host a school outing. As I grew near, I was bombarded by a barrage of questions from giggling teenaged girls practicing their English.

"Hello. What is your name? Where are you from?" first one asked and then another repeated. It was like trying to have a conversation with a parrot. I played along with them for a while, until I just had to duck into the shade. Joining the caretaker at his hut, I was startled when he offered me a fresh peach. I devoured it, as if I hadn't eaten in weeks. Then I polished off a liter of water before I was joined once again by five of the charming girls. Those ten-year-olds brimming with smiles were bundles of light wrapped in a rainbow of flowing scarves and shimmering skirts. They were more than eager to pose for a few photos, before all twenty-five of them loaded into the bed of a pick-up truck and sped off amid a chorus of "goodbyes" echoing down the canyon.

They were instantly missed, but others fleetingly crossed paths with me along the empty road. In Selçuk, just outside of Osmaneli, a dump truck driver slowed down to invite me for a ride into town for tea. I refused, but was more than happy to take him up on his offer for a drink at the dusty café ahead. As usual, I attracted a crowd (as I couldn't imagine they saw many visitors there), including a group of students who invited me into the back room. After a fellow who spoke English appeared, we talked for quite some time about the necessity for peace. Then at my urging, since I was still uncertain where I'd sleep, one fellow called ahead to the next town to reserve a room.

The hotel was surely not in the *Michelin Guide*, but it was "local" in every sense of the word. Wherever I travel, I like to immerse myself totally in a culture. Travel as a "local," eat in local haunts and sleep in local rooms, even if they happen to be psychedelic pink like that one, with a shower heated by a wood fire down the hall. After all, as rustic as they might seem at the time, that's the stuff you'll remember.

At daybreak, I just knew the traffic was going to be tough—and it began the moment I stepped out the door of my hotel. Trucks whooshed down the two-lane highway. There was no shoulder to walk on and the lanes were narrow. I wasn't out of town more than forty minutes before one lorry passed another on the left, missing my shoulder by inches. As my life flashed before my eyes, I thought of all those things I hadn't finished and the loved ones who'd be hurt by my passing. I prayed, then had to ask myself, 'Why does this route have to be so dangerous? What am I doing here? What does it matter? Does anyone care?'

And most of all, "The man who said, 'A miss is as good as a mile' never had a close encounter with an eighteen-wheeler."

Determined not to end it all on the lonesome highway, I caught whatever tiny trails, tractor roads and paths I could find heading south over the surrounding high chaparral. Before long, I began the first of a series of major climbs, as I continued to dodge traffic driving too close to the highway's edge. I quickly lost count of the number of times I had to grab my cap from flying off, or hopped off the road into the dust—at just the last second.

Yet ultimately, I reached Vezirhan, but there was no greeting, no *"Çay!"* No one seemed to notice, so I continued another sixteen-kilometer climb at a fifteen percent grade up a winding mountain pass through mountains dotted with pine, juniper and scrub. In my never-ending quest to find the elusive parallel trail (perhaps existing only in the "parallel" universe), I followed a dirt track until I ended up in some fellow's field—in water up over my shoes. It would have been serious if I hadn't kept my original waterproof pair of Montrails, so I took time out to change into them, along with a dry pair of socks. Otherwise, I'm positive I would've sported a new set of painful blisters before sundown—even after having walked three thousand kilometers. Life just wasn't fair.

For the next three hours, truckers were both a curse and a blessing, as I scrambled through the mountains. The same fellows who'd earlier crowded me off the road now saluted me with honks and waves. They were small gestures, I know, but enough to keep my spirits up in the infernal heat.

Eventually, exhausted, I limped into Bilecik, an ancient Hittite stomping ground. For once, I easily found a room and caught up on my correspondence. Cheryl was still double-checking with the Cypriot government about my ability to cross the Green Line in Nicosia from the Turkish controlled northern Cyprus to the south. If all went according to plan, I'd cross the border, then hike to Limassol on its southern tip. From there, I might be able to catch another boat to Haifa on the northern Israeli coast. On the other hand, the Cyprus border had been sealed tight since the invasion in 1974. If that fell through, I didn't know what I'd do. Still, a small voice within kept reminding me to have faith.

Even though one fellow in Bilecik assured me the next day's walk was a "descent," after the first five kilometers I was climbing again all day. In many ways, especially on a miserable one like that, I was relieved Émile had decided not to continue. The steep climb, lack of water and shade, and unbearable heat could have been fatal. It affected me as well. There was absolutely no place to stop after my 9:30 soup and water at a roadside restaurant. Dehydrated and craving protein, I was rapidly losing energy and weight, a deadly combination. Meanwhile, the dust was so thick that I trumpeted into the wind more often than the serenade of the trucks that passed. Ah, the glamour of travel.

All day, I kept searching for the obscure trail that'd deliver me from the two-lane asphalt road to hell—but there was no relief. Trucks passed every few seconds, belching smoke and noxious diesel fumes. Drivers insisted on making kamikaze passes as they approached hilltops or blind turns—only to expect everyone to slam on their brakes at the last possible second to let them swerve in. Given all that, it seemed especially ridiculous when two folks actually warned me against walking *off* the highway, as the trail would be "dangerous with snakes, bears and foxes." I'd rather have taken my chances.

Still, it was all just a rehearsal for the following day, the most difficult yet. It began with all the appearance of being an easy trek (relatively speaking, of course). I only had to walk twenty kilometers to Inönu. I'd confirmed there was a hotel there, asking four people over the past couple of days. Imagine my surprise when I arrived at the turnoff into town and posed that same question one last time to the gas station attendant.

"No," he replied, with his head oddly tilted upward.

Unsure what his body language meant, I asked a trucker standing nearby.

"No. The next hotel is in Kütahya." That was over sixty kilometers.

"Isn't there some type of hotel in Ilica?" I countered, remembering one I'd seen in a guide.

"Yes, but it's very expensive," he explained, rubbing his thumb against his middle finger.

So much for my "easy" day. I either had to continue to Ilica, a thermal village with healing waters, and trust I'd find a room there—or risk wasting an hour looking for a place that probably didn't exist in Inönu. The choice was obvious.

By that point, the unfinished two-lane highway I'd been walking since Böröyuk had morphed back into blacktop, and the traffic was still light since it was Sunday morning. I hoped it would stay that way, but no, it didn't take long before I was climbing up steep mountain passes with no shade, amid a steady stream of semis and cars with vacationers heading to the coast. There was one lone restaurant outside of Inönu—and then nothing for as far as the eye could see; no houses, villages, or water.

Accordingly, I began carefully rationing my fluids, until I started to get a telltale pain in my hips. It was my own early dehydration warning system, the canary in the coalmine. No wonder. It had been more than eighty degrees since 9:30. Although I hadn't eaten anything since my black olives, bread and ounce of cheese at breakfast, water was my major concern. I was down to one cup—with no village in sight.

Just then, when life appeared bleakest, it happened. I spotted a cattle-watering trough beside the wheat field below. A couple of men stood nearby. So I decided to fill my empty water bottle, just in case. As I'd learned while trekking across Norway of all places, contracting parasitic giardia is far from pleasant—but better than dying from dehydration.

As I approached, the Turks' first question was the usual, "Where are you from?"

Gasping "Hawaii," I waited for their anti-American response, but none came. So I asked, "Can you drink this water?"

They shrugged.

"Well, can you please tell me if there's a restaurant or petrol station nearby?"

"No," one well-dressed fellow answered. "Why, are you hungry?"

"More thirsty than hungry," I admitted, dipping my red bandana into the foul water.

"Come, follow us," he replied, and they led me down a dirt road to the other side of some olive trees. Beneath it sprawled four other men of varying ages along with two boys, sitting around a virtual banquet. They motioned for me to join them, and then set half a watermelon and plastic fork in front of me. I was bowled over and didn't know what to say. I'd fantasized about melon for days. Still, the sweet fruit was just the beginning of a feast for a man literally starving in the desert. Bread, feta cheese, olives, tomatoes and cucumbers were all passed my way. As I politely tried to restrain myself, the men were interested in hearing what brought me to the middle of nowhere. I managed to fill them in on all the details of my peace walk—in between bites.

"What mean "peace?"" one older, intense fellow asked.

"No war. No fighting. No guns," I replied in simple English, miming as if I was shooting a rifle.

As my statement was translated from man to man, a couple of the Turks exclaimed "Bravo," while others grinned and enthusiastically applauded. I felt embarrassed, humbled, and yet pleased my message had stuck home.

"So what you do?" another asked.

"I'm a writer. I hope to tell others about this journey when I return, so more people will walk for peace." That also seemed to please them.

"How long you stay in Turkey?"

"Maybe one month. I'm walking to Antalya." They, too, were headed there.

"How you like Turkey?" another asked.

"People are very kind. You know, there are good people and bad people everywhere. But I like to believe there are more good people!"

At this, they laughed heartily and soon began loading cups, plates and silverware into their van. Tearing myself away from the melon, I stood to shake hands with each of them and asked, "What about this food? Don't forget it."

"No," the father calmly replied, "we leave it here."

"Here? Why, I couldn't eat all of this." It was more than I'd eaten all week.

"No, it is for you," he said with finality, dismissing any further debate.

Again, we solemnly shook hands as friends and wished each other "*Salaam*," or "Peace," before they piled into their van and headed down the road.

For once, I was like the family dog left alone at the Thanksgiving Day table. I didn't know what to eat first, but after thirty minutes in the shade of the olive grove, I did a decent job. Then remembering how far I still needed to walk, I reluctantly headed back onto the highway—but at least there was a spring to my step and I made good time to the next gas station five kilometers away.

"How far is it to Ilica?" I asked the *gendarme* who sipped a cola inside.

"Oh, it must be twenty kilometers."

"You sure?" I thought it was only ten.

"Twenty." He was adamant.

"Then where's the next petrol station or restaurant where I can get water?" After all, that was the more important issue.

"Kütahya." That had to be forty kilometers or more.

Things were not looking good. Then again, what choice did I have? I set off at the fastest pace I could muster in mid-afternoon under a cloudless sky, until the sun eventually got the better of me.

By 5:00, after ten hours in the energy-draining inferno, I ducked into a ceramic shop along Porsük Baraji (Lake) and took them up on their kind offer of tea and water. Pushing my luck, I even asked, "Would it be all right if I slept here? It's very hot, I'm exhausted and Ilica is just too far away. I could sleep right here on the floor, if you don't mind."

The cordial artist had a more immediate solution. Producing a Persian rug and pillow, he led me behind his shop to a terrace overlooking the lake. Initially, I was reluctant to take the time out to relax, afraid of running out of daylight before I reached Ilica. Nonetheless, I relented since my back was tender and I thought lying on a hard surface would help. As it turned out, I rested in the shade for nearly an hour, before returning the carpet and pillow back to the potter. Surprised to see me up and ready to go again, he offered to drive me to the hotel, if I'd wait until he closed at 7:30. It was a tempting offer to be sure, yet I insisted on continuing, hoping I could make up for lost time.

Unfortunately, the traffic was as bad as ever. I lost count of the number of times my cap went sailing from gusts of wind as the trucks barreled past. I still didn't know exactly where Ilica was—or how far a hotel might be from the main road. In the worst-case scenario, I figured I might find a restaurant along the way to spend the night. In actuality, I found two cafés, but both told me to continue to Kütahya.

By 7:30, prospects didn't look good. I was discouraged and bedraggled. The sun had set. The only light emanated from a fingernail moon. Although it was a just minute 'til pitch-black, traffic was as heavy as usual. Some trucks even insisted on driving with their headlights off. I was stuck in the middle of high chaparral, somewhere near the Ilica turnoff, without a house or village in sight.

In desperation, I made a prayer for help—and it honestly wasn't a moment until when I heard a high "beep, beep" from across the road. At first, I couldn't even see what it was, or if they were honking at me. But after crossing, I could just barely discern a young guy with a mullet hairdo, waving from atop his motorcycle. I recognized him from the last restaurant where I'd looked for a place to sleep. Even though we had been so faithful about never accepting rides, I took that as a sign.

I was reminded of the old joke about the fellow standing on the rooftop of his house, as the floodwaters rose and threatened to sweep him downstream. He prayed, "God save me from the waters."

First, a man in a rowboat came by and said, "Hop in, I'll get you out of there."

"No," the man answered, "I'm waiting for God to save me." Then to escape the rising waters, he moved to the second floor.

A second boat pulled up and told the fellow to climb on board.

"No, thanks," the man shouted from his window, "I'm waiting for God to save me." Then to escape the floodwaters, he climbed up to his roof.

A little while later, a helicopter flew over his house and they lowered a ladder.

"No, thanks," the man said. "I'm waiting for God to rescue me."

Before long, his tiny house was swept downstream and the man died. Reaching heaven, he was a little upset with God, demanding, "Where were you? I was up there on my roof waiting for you to save me, but you never came. How can you be so cruel?"

"What, cruel? (God had evidently once played the Catskills.) I sent you two men in boats. Then I sent you a helicopter, but you refused them all. What do you want? I answered your prayers, but you didn't hear."

So I accepted the kind stranger's lift, hopping onto the back of his "rice-burner." With my walking stick in one hand like a jousting knight and cap in the other, we zoomed the remaining five kilometers or so, most of it off the main route south. As we sped up the canyon to Ilica, bugs spattered against my face. The wind made my eyes well-up; tears showering my cheek like rain.

As some small penance in the morning, I walked back through the sleepy mountain village, down through the canyon to the main road heading south to Kütahya. Passing through those steep granite canyons, I couldn't help but reflect on the once mighty civilizations who had all called the area home: the Hittites, Phrygians, Persians, Macedonians, Galatians, Romans, Seljuks, Crusaders, Turkmen, Ottomans. Oh, how the mighty had fallen.

Soon the smoky haze of Kütahya rose into view on the horizon, and suddenly I was thrust back into civilization. At nearly 3,000 feet in altitude, lying at the base of a mountain range, the refined city bustled with factories producing porcelain, tiles, ceramics and pottery. There was an air of prosperity, from the men planting trees down a highway median strip to the small businesses flooding the downtown. I'd looked forward to spending two nights there to take in some of the sights, as well as to rest for the strenuous, sizzling days ahead.

After checking into a hotel, I headed over to the local tourism office to get a better handle on where I might stay over the next ten days en route to

Antalya. Their director, a reed-thin man, was courteous and immediately served me the customary tea, even though he spoke little English.

"I'm walking to Antalya," I explained and pantomimed. "Can you tell me if there is a place to sleep, a hotel or *pension* in Afyon and Burdur?"

The crane-like fellow seemed to understand and immediately telephoned the tourism offices in those towns. Hanging up, he confirmed, "Afyon, yes. Burdur, yes." Then came the bad news. "Only one place between Afyon and Burdur."

With the deadly weather, I'd originally planned to take three days to get to Afyon, but his news meant I'd have to cover it in two: one forty-kilometer day—followed by another of sixty. I was not looking forward to that. He'd saved the worst news for last.

"No hotels for 120 kilometers before Antalya."

"Private rooms?"

He shrugged, not knowing for certain. That'd be a real problem. At that point, I was halfway between Istanbul and Antalya—ten days journey—and he only knew of three villages that might have a place to sleep. I could sleep outside, but those huge wild dogs had me a little concerned. After witnessing their shark-like attack on the little ankle-biter, I was hesitant to even consider sleeping under the stars, although I'd done so for five months in Africa amid all sorts of night stalkers.

No, I'd have to rely on my "angels" more than ever. "*Inshallah.*"

That evening, I pored over my maps one last time, looking for other minute towns or a route that might be more trekker-friendly, but I came up empty-handed. Eager to leave no stone unturned, I went to a nearby Internet café and attempted to find better maps than those in the bookstores. In my search, I encountered even more disturbing news.

Cheryl had emailed me from home. Kurds had just exploded a bomb that injured twenty in the resort town of Marmaris on the Turkish coast. Their target was a nightclub filled with tourists and one of those commuter vans or *dolmas* as they're called in Turkey, since they're stuffed like grape leafs. She was worried of course, but since the targets were touristic and not rural, I figured I'd be safe until I reached Antalya, another potential resort target.

The following morning of my "rest" day, I did anything but lollygag around. It wasn't in my nature, especially when an interesting area like Kütahya lay right at my feet. Although the city of 600,000 was best known for its tile production, arts and mosques, a 3000 B.C. city near Çavdarhisar offered a greater temptation. It was just an hour away by bus.

The settlement of Aizanoi was founded on the banks of the Rhyndakos River flowing through a region called Phrygia Epiktetus (Little Phrygia). Conquered by the king of Bithynia, it came under the control of the Kingdom of Pergamon. After its unification with Rome, it became a major market known for its wine, wool and grain production. Then, with its capture by the Crusaders and the spread of Christianity, the city eventually became a center of the patriarchate.

It only took only an hour to cover more ground than I'd usually walk all morning. The bus dropped me off on Main Street, and after a short hike the Temple of Zeus clearly came into view. Built in 117 A.D., it was extraordinary. With 124 remaining columns, it was reportedly the best example of Ionian architecture in Anatolia. (It also featured a bust of Zeus, resembling Jim Morrison of *The Doors*.) After ambling awestruck through its ruins, I walked over to the ancient stadium, impressive in its own right. You could still see medallions from winning athletes carved into its marble posts. It once held 13,500 cheering fans, but today it rang eerily silent. I was the only one there.

The adjoining amphitheatre was equally impressive, yet that was where I met a Turkish family on vacation. I was warmly introduced to a mother and her curly-haired, ten-year-old daughter, the lady's two sisters, and a sister-in-law with her two bright-eyed boys. They generously offered me a soft drink that I was happy to accept in the stifling heat, as I told them about my journey. Although the adults spoke little English, the girl was happy to translate, boasting that she studied it in school. The purpose of my trip met with their wide approval and they asked me to join them as they continued their tour.

Their charming daughter, whose name meant "Kisses" in Turkish, was anxious to practice her English while we paraded through what was the world's first commodity exchange. Its prices were set in stone. One wall read: "One strong slave = two donkeys" and "One horse = two slaves or 30,000 dinars."

The little girl with fawn eyes and wild, wavy hair was full of questions: "Do you have children? Do you have brothers and sisters?" I could tell she was working her way through her textbook, but honored to have the attention.

As we meandered to the *hamman*, or traditional baths, we wove our way past whitewashed adobe homes where villagers still lived above animal stalls on the ground floor. Their windows were festooned with strings of red peppers they'd strung to dry in the sun. One spry village woman sifted lentils by hand and then ground them into yellow meal, while another's hands were dyed in intricate rust-hued henna designs, similar to the women in India. She had just given away her daughter in marriage and still had a blissful glow.

Reaching the conclusion of our self-guided tour (and the end of questions from my charming interrogator), we hugged. I wished them a "good life and good travels," since they were off to explore more ruins in the surrounding countryside. Walking back down the dirt road into the village, I felt an immediate sense of loss. Still, I was so grateful for their friendship—if only for a little while.

As I rode the *dolmas* back into Kütahya, I couldn't help but wonder how many eager, bright-eyed kids like "Kisses" had been recently killed in Iraq, Israel, Lebanon, Palestine, New York City, and around the world by senseless violence.

I had to agree with Howard Zinn who once said, "There is no flag large enough to cover the shame of killing innocent people."

CHAPTER ELEVEN
Kütahya to Alanya

"Sempre Diretto"

"We have it in our power to begin the world over again."
~ *Thomas Paine, Common Sense*

The thoroughfare out of town was well lit by streetlights and I was back in the bucolic countryside by sunrise. After passing the spot where our bus turned off to reach the ruins the day before, I began wending up over the surrounding hills. Passing amongst craggy monoliths on the foreboding desert, I was reminded of the many times I'd driven across America's Southwest; the first when I was only six years old with my father behind the wheel of a classic red and white Chevy with a water-filled burlap bag strapped to the grill. Little could I ever imagine I'd trek across something so remote, so ethereal—but then again, I was on a special quest.

I found serenity in the solitude. In all forty kilometers to reach the turnoff to Altintas, I passed only three or four gas stations and nothing larger than a sprinkling of houses. Throughout my loneliness, the wind was my constant companion, drying my lips until they cracked and bled. Yet even out there in no man's land, I was startled by random acts of kindness. At one point, a road crew boss invited me over for a hot cup of *çay*—right on his brand new highway.

Relieved I'd gotten an earlier start, by 1:00 p.m. I'd already arrived at the turn-off to Altintas. I'd spend the night there, even though it was an eight-kilometer, two-hour detour off the Templar Trail. Besides, it wasn't like I had much choice. It was the only town with a place to stay before Afyon, nearly fifty kilometers away. That was another day's challenge. Eventually, I reached its one lonesome inn where the manager was hospitable—until he saw my passport. He never said another word.

I left before dawn and only walked a few kilometers before a car suddenly stopped, giving me a lift back to the crossroads south. The terrain remained just as desolate. Most villages were several kilometers to the east or west off the highway. Although the wind had died down, by mid-morning it was already over eighty degrees, a dramatic forty-degree shift in only a few hours.

Fortunately, gas stations continued to materialize every ten kilometers or so, and I always stopped to refill my water. Usually I ran into truckers inside. Out of curiosity, they ultimately asked about my trek, and then gave friendly toots of their horn whenever they passed me later on the road. On some days, I suspected that Mustafa and those truckers with whom I'd shared tea under the trees had told others about my journey and the word had spread. I felt a kindred spirit, as they knew only too well the siren's call; the lonely lure of the open road. Their encouragement sustained me, and I tried to pass their kindness along to others.

That morning, I stumbled upon a minibus with engine problems, stalled with its passengers huddled in the shade beside the road. Although I offered to carry a note ahead, they said it wasn't necessary since they had their cell phone. When I saw a police car outside the next gas station, however, I stopped and let them know. Two cops invited me over to their table and insisted on sharing their watermelon, as they listened to my tale. They passed me twice later the same afternoon and each time slowed down to wave.

As bleak as the terrain appeared, I was seldom alone. Once while stopping for water, I ran into five local kids and we sat around talking on the stoop of a deserted shop for a while. Then again, another bright boy in Anitkaya rode his bike over to introduce himself in English, and I shared sweets with him and his sister in a bit of "candy bar diplomacy."

Before long, the outskirts of Afyon appeared in the distance. Once famous as the center for Turkish opium, (in fact, it's name means "Black Castle of Opium"), nowadays it evokes images of a young Las Vegas with high-rise resort hotels and thermal pools set at the base of a mountain range. It even boasts its own 24-hour McDonalds, or "McDo," as Émile called them. Most of all, I was relieved the fellow at the café the night before had been right. There were a couple of hotels at the crossroads where major highways intersected, heading west to Izmir and Istanbul, east to Ankara, or south to Antalya. Fortunately, it wasn't necessary to detour ten kilometers just for a room. The one I found at the intersection was expensive, but I easily negotiated a better price, cheaper by a third, than the one they had listed. I had to laugh. Why did they always insist on playing that game?

When I hit the trail shortly after sunrise, pregnant black clouds, the first in a long time, already shrouded the sky. It was less than fifty degrees outside. Without a moment to spare, I backtracked to the crossroads leading southeast to Cappadocia, Syria and Jordan. Suffering a final moment of self-doubt, I again weighed the logic behind my painful decision to continue south to Antalya on the coast. It was the last chance to change my mind.

'Can I risk losing it all—including possibly my life—by taking on the needless extra danger of heading straight through the midst of the Middle East? With the recent bombings in Lebanon and Israel, Westerners must be prime targets for any wanna-be kidnappers. Sure, I might be able to pass for a German or Scandinavian on the street, (plus I still have my Canadian flag pin), but when I check into a hotel and present my passport, my cover will be blown like it was two nights ago. I doubt they'll take the fact I'm walking for peace into account.'

'Plus, with no Syrian visa, I'd have to sneak in with a tour and vanish. Could I smuggle myself out the other side into Jordan?'

'It makes logistical sense. According to my maps, the villages in central Turkey and the east are farther apart. I just can't walk more than sixty kilometers a day in this weather, and don't expect others to either.'

'Then again, there's the Ebola-like virus and Bird Flu in Anatolia—not a pretty way to die.'

'On the other hand, coastal Antalya was a staging area for the fourth Crusades to Palestine. So the route's still accurate from a historical perspective. It's also rich in Roman ruins, so it's likely a southern terminus.'

'Finally, if part of the ultimate reason for my journey is to open this route to future pilgrims, isn't it best to send them along the "safer" path?'

'It's settled. *Sempre diretto*. Straight ahead.'

There were no villages of any size once I left the outskirts of town where an older gentleman warned me in German to watch out for the trucks. It was timely advice. The wide shoulder that once made walking in Turkey so pleasant had disappeared. I had to balance along the cracked edge of the berm.

Afraid it might be hours before I found another place for water, I risked pausing at one last gas station. The eager attendant instantly brought me a cup of hot *çay* and then acted offended when I refused a second. But there was no time to waste. I was pitted against what looked like an impending deluge—without a single house in sight. Reluctantly I suited up for rain in the new blueberry poncho Cheryl had brought, along with a pack cover, rain pants, and my waterproof Montrail Susitnas. Then again, true to form, the rain clouds changed course. I should have known. It never failed; like washing your car only to create a downpour. Still, the winds continued to howl off the mountain peaks, billowing my poncho until I looked like a blue Michelin Man balloon in a Thanksgiving Day Parade. Yet oddly enough, even that had its advantage. Drivers gave me more room than ever on the road.

After speed walking for hours through bleak hills all morning, I felt a piercing pain just below my ribcage and behind my heart. At first, I figured it was a lingering result of the cracked rib I'd suffered trekking to Mt. Everest. Then I worried, 'Am I having a heart attack? Or is it just hunger?'

There was no sign of civilization, except for a few passing motorists and nondescript buildings far off to my left. As I grew nearer though, I spotted trucks and road equipment parked outside and then saw a few folks milling about. Eager to find something to eat, even if it was just a warm cup of tea, I approached their doorway and made the universal "eat" sign to a fellow working inside. He nodded and motioned for me to go around to the side of the hut. Ducking indoors, I smelled food, real food. Forty people sat at aluminum tables and lined up in front of the kitchen counter. Although they were surprised to see me at first, the road workers helped me off with my pack and then directed me over to the window, where the chef dolloped salad, pilaf and a chicken leg onto my metal tray. As I looked around for a place to sit, one fellow stood to give me his. Then I tore into the food, as if I hadn't eaten in weeks. Between bites, I pantomimed and used simple English to answer their questions while sharing my beliefs about the necessity for peace in these dark times.

Afterward, we exchanged handshakes, and when I rose to pay, they refused, simply pointing at me saying, "Family."

I was touched by their kindness. It made leaving even more difficult, yet Sandikli was still too far away. I didn't want to risk running out of light again, especially with the wild Anatolian Shepherds I'd seen more frequently. I'd never been afraid of dogs. In fact, I felt a sort of kinship, as if we could communicate on an unspoken level. However, those emanated a ferocity that sent a shiver down my spine. Earlier that same day, two huge

Shepherds, the hue and size of wolves, snapped and bared their teeth at me from a yard while straining taut their heavy chains. Then another male dog in the wild snarled, while his bitch and pups shifted into tall grass like lions in the savannah. Later, three others, wearing those S & M sharpened spike collars, growled and left their flock of sheep to creep within charging distance as I passed.

All afternoon I raced the sun. I shuffled across a rough tarmac that devoured the bottoms of my shoes and aching feet. Until finally, just before sundown, Sandikli rose into view, a welcome oasis set at 3,400-feet along the base of the Kumalar Daglari Mountains. Drifting famished and bedraggled into town, I encountered a distinguished-looking Muslim fellow who came to my aid. While fingering his prayer beads, he led me through back alleyways to the Hotel Sönnez, a calm *pension* offering a local welcome and prices to match.

Later that evening, as the final call to prayer echoed into my chamber, I easily came to a decision. After the past week, where four of the last six days were close to fifty kilometers each, I was near collapse. So I promised myself I'd take an extra day to rest with no sightseeing and no excursions, especially since the following days to Antalya promised to be just as demanding. Villages were farther apart and the location of water, food and inns was still mostly unknown.

Two days later, after my one rare day of rest, I'd already become too used to sleeping in and found it difficult to get an early start. But as they say, everything happens for a reason. Mine was an encounter with a fellow I met on the outskirts of town, as he rummaged through a trash dumpster. He wasn't that old, but life had been hard. His clothes were ragged and I especially noticed his feet in tattered leather shoes, lined with plastic bags. Immediately, I knew I'd finally found a home for my waterproof Montrails that had served me so well.

"Could you use these?" I asked, motioning to the shoes lashed to the side of my pack. Seeming to understand the gist of what I said, he nodded. So I quickly unstrapped them from my pack for the last time, saying, "These are still in pretty good shape. They brought me here from France." Then setting them on the ground between us, I hoisted up my pack.

He cautiously approached, cowering like a dog beaten too many times. Then after examining them approvingly, he backed up, tucking them into his sack with the rest of his booty.

At last, I was pleased I'd found them a good home. I'd learned a valuable lesson back on the Camino de Santiago. What you don't need, give away. It lightens your load and helps others.

"What goes around, comes around," was proven to me in spades later the same afternoon. It had been another sun-drenched day with even fewer places to stop to refuel. After six hours trudging across the desert, I began to fret about where I might find something to eat—that was, until an eighteen-wheeler aiming straight for me gave me more immediate cause for concern. At just the last second, as I readied to leap out of its way, the huge lorry skid to a halt. Its driver hopped down with a plastic bag. The elfin fellow jogged over and proudly showed me its contents: tomatoes, cucumbers, bread, feta cheese, and loose salt wrapped in newspaper. Then he thrust it toward me, as if to say, "Here, for you."

"Th...thanks," I stammered, still shaken by my near-death experience. "But I have no room to carry a kilo of food."

The driver persisted, refusing to take "no" for an answer. "Look, I've gone to all this trouble to stop my rig for you," he mimed with a mischievous smile. "You must take it."

"Well, if you insist." And I stuffed his food into the top of my already bulging pack. Then wishing him "*Salaam malakim*," he responded, "*Wa alaykum as-salaam!*" before climbing back into his cab and driving off.

Thank goodness for Turks bearing gifts. All afternoon I was buoyed by his kindness and my load felt surprisingly lighter. Other truckers honked their horns and buses even got into the act, as I climbed one final rise in the Mojave-like landscape, before coasting downhill all the way into Dinar. Immediately, I was relieved to discover a hotel oasis with a pond and waterfall. A sprightly fellow in his sixties rented me a room on the third floor and practically flew up the stairs to show me around. After walking more than fifty kilometers, my steps were a little more measured, but the room and day's kindnesses were never more appreciated.

In the morning I slept-in a little, considering I "only" had about thirty kilometers to cover; at that point, a half-day lark. On the way out of town, I stopped into a *börek* shop to savor *su böregi*, a round pasta-like *börek* with feta, and a sweet tea similar to what I had nearly every morning in Turkey. It was a traditional Muslim shop tended by a young wife who wore a modest scarf or *hijab*, along with a skirt down to her ankles, a baggy sweater, hose and practical sling-back shoes. She timidly gazed at me, as most traditional women averted their eyes. A few stared, and in the past weeks only a couple dared to return the "*Merhaba*" or "Hello" I offered to them.

Soon I was back in the countryside, surrounded by vast mountains. Traffic was light, since most vehicles caught the bypass the day before. Villages were rare and always several kilometers off the highway. Restaurants had vanished along with their *kofta*, and I passed only two gas stations all day. Yet it was cooler in those hills and the morning quickly passed. I was lost in thought and meditation, coming to grips with the fact I'd arrive in Antalya in a few days and soon afterward in Cyprus. When I'd first landed there after a seven-month trip across Africa, the island was captivating with its history, culture, broad beaches and pine-scented mountains. I'd always wanted to see its north and hike from village to village, so I was thrilled to finally have the chance.

All afternoon, I passed hushed fields and harvested trees twisted with the wind. I was alone, except for one moment when a gaunt, wild dog crossed the road. Pausing mid-stride, we examined one another. He was so close I could see the outline of his ribs beneath his short, gray-wheat colored coat. For an instant, he appeared torn between a domestic urge to join me, and another more primitive instinct to avoid human contact. In a primal sense, I felt connected to him; a Steppenwolf torn the same way in my own life—between buying into society's domestication—or trusting in the freedom of the road.

Solo within those barren, dusty hills, I reveled in their solitude: a magnificent sanctuary, endless and timeless. Little had changed over the past thousand years. As much as I had found solace in the cathedral-like holiness of Germany's Black Forest, the desert, too, displayed a testament to the perfect creation of a higher power. I was uplifted by their majesty. For once, my destination, Keçiborlu, arrived all too soon.

Later that evening, I heard on the radio that several travelers had been gunned down at the ancient amphitheatre in Amman, Jordan, one of the cities on our original itinerary. At that point, the police were still uncertain if the gunman was a "terrorist" who'd opened fire on the innocent Kiwis, Brits and Dutch with his automatic weapon—or just one of your more garden-variety fanatics.

But for all the crazies in the world, the trail seemed to have its share of gentle souls. Shortly after leaving town the following morning, I met a lady and her daughter selling fruit at their roadside stand. Her apples looked especially enticing, and I pointed out one with my walking stick, asking, "How much?"

"One lira."

I shot her a glance as if I knew better, but gladly gave her the coin. Her reaction was unexpected. Looking at the apple, then at me, she abruptly had a change of heart. She refused my money, saying "No charge." I was surprised, but what happened next shocked me even more. The woman with a heart as large as her girth started picking out peaches, a pear, and grapes and dropping them into a sack. The harder I protested, the more she added to the bag—until I finally cried, "Enough! My pack can't hold any more." I was impressed by her generosity; embarrassed I'd ever doubted her intentions.

Before long, the road divided. Much of the traffic headed east to Isparta, while I continued south and began a gradual climb until I could view Lake Burdur shimmering on the plains below. Elated, I descended to the village beside the lake, checked into a hotel, and quickly set off in search of the local visitor information office. Its manager., a gregarious, curly-haired fellow, was cordial, offering me cup after cup of sweet tea. Then he shared his box of Turkish delight or *lokum*, a candy delicacy once concocted to calm the tribulations of a sultan's harem. Still, no matter how much sweet "delight" was served, his news remained just as bitter for me to swallow.

"There are no places to stay between Bucak and Antalya."

Of course, he was apologetic and even called ahead to Antalya to make doubly sure, but it was true. I'd have no place to stay for ninety kilometers. I'd suspected as much, but it was still discouraging. If nothing else were available, I decided to try my luck at the local *gendarmerie* or police barracks. Maybe they'd have an extra bunk.

Before leaving, at my urging, the manager agreed to write a note I could present to the villagers in Dagbeli. It explained in Turkish what I was doing and asked for a place to sleep. That was all he could do.

The following day was destined to be another of giving and grateful receiving. Although the visitor office's manager had assured me the road to Dagbeli would be flat with "no climbing," I began a long, torturous ascent just outside of town. It continued winding for several long hours as I circled Celtikçi, a craggy mountain reminding me of the Grand Tetons. In the shadow of that peak, I paused to eat some of the grapes the lady had given me the day before. Relaxing in the shade of a weathered tree, I was attracted to a colorful parasol where ladies sold fruit farther up the road. It made perfect sense to replenish my food supply there, considering how far the next town might be, so I hurried ahead to check out their apples. As I did, a tiny woman, the dusky shade of the soil and dressed in a *hijab* and poo-pants, rose to greet me.

"This apple, please," I said, pointing at one shining in her crate.

"No, you want this one."

"Okay, if you say so." I reached into my pocket for change.

"No, no charge," she cried, with a wave of her hand.

"Yes! How much?" After all, it was bleak out there and earning a living must have been a grueling task.

But she stood her ground, insisting, "No, no!" as she held up hands stained black from a life feeding charcoal to heat their *çay* water.

I was touched once again, appreciative for her kindness to a passing stranger. Still, as I studied her and the two other women tending their fire, I was surprised at what I saw. It was already eighty degrees on the high desert pass and they were garbed from head-to-toe in scarves, baggy blouses and heavy harem pants, as you or I might be dressed on a cool autumn day. Nevertheless, they clearly looked like they enjoyed life—even if it meant sitting on a carpet by the side of the road and fixing tea—no matter how difficult it might appear to you or me.

So many times on my odyssey, I'd been reminded how much food was a revered part of life elsewhere on our planet. It was a gift, a sharing, and a personal statement. It was a reflection of a people's soul.

Long ago, on my first job out of the university, I'd worked for a recent Greek immigrant in his successful family bakery and restaurant business. Besides having too many warm, freshly baked baguettes and braided challah breads to tempt me every day, Christmas turned out to be a special, if baffling time of the year. Tommy, the owner, led me into his walk-in freezer, handed me a large plastic bag, and then told me to take whatever I wanted to eat for the holidays. That was my bonus, Greek-style. At the time, I was confused and a little disappointed, since I'd expected a small check. But nowadays, looking back, I appreciated that day and his unique kindness even more.

All afternoon, I continued following the endless pass, as it rose and dipped to reveal incredible panoramic vistas. Until finally, I reached Bucak, a tiny village set among flaxen plains beneath an azure sky as vast as the sea.

The next morning in the muted light, I must have had five offers of
"*çay*" from shopkeepers before losing sight of town; yet to make any time,
I could only accept a few. I still had no idea where I'd stay that night, and
was intent on reaching Dagbeli as early as possible.

With the wind at my back, I sailed into "Dag" by the early afternoon
and quickly confirmed there was no *pension* in town. Staying at the mosque,
as a local might do, was out of the question. Things didn't look good.
Although the fellow running the café in the community center offered me
a wooden floor to sleep on, I had to walk at least fifty kilometers to Antalya
and knew I'd feel like camel dung in the morning.

Nursing a cup of tea at his café, I considered catching a bus back to
Bucak, until two local *gendarmes* who spoke a little English joined me. (My
arrival must have been big news in the one-camel town.) When they
demanded to see my "papers," I had the uneasy feeling someone was trying
to get rid of me. In fact, the lieutenant was ready to point out my visa had
expired, until I showed him it was good for three months—not thirty days.
So we sat through a tense cup of tea together. When they finally left, imagine my surprise when the café manager said they'd invited me to stay at the
local police barracks. Where? Behind bars? After their chilly welcome, I
really wasn't looking forward to it, but what choice did I have? It was late
and a long ride back to Bucak.

I thanked him and walked a mile to the *gendarmerie* set on the hillside
behind a chain link fence topped by barbed wire. An armed sentry instantly
stopped me at the gate. He had no idea what I was talking about, but he
had the sense to run inside to fetch his commander, who was curious
enough to allow me inside. For quite some time, we drank tea and chatted
about my journey. I showed him my letter of introduction from the tourism
office and mentioned the lieutenant had promised I could sleep there.
Eventually, satisfied I wasn't leading a one-man revolution, he led me past
their weapons arsenal to a bunkroom and allowed me to take a cold
shower. I thought I was home free—but something was lost in translation.

As soon as I returned to my bunk, the commander insisted I had to
leave immediately. Why? I'd never know, only that I had to throw my gear
back into my backpack before being escorted all the way back to Dagbeli
city hall. Once there, from what I could tell, my guard asked Mr. Mayor if
I could sleep there?

"No!" the bald fellow fumed. "Tell him to go to Antalya!" Easier said
than done. It was early evening and another fifty kilometers to the coast.

As it turned out, at just that moment, an elderly, slightly threadbare character passed by and was drawn into our conflict.

"Hey, can this man sleep at your house?"

The stooped fellow warily looked me over.

"I can pay. Okay?"

After a translation was made, his puffy eyes lit up and I knew I'd found a bed for the night. Savoring another small victory, I tagged behind him like an adopted mutt, out of the building and across the sleepy village to a haggard house that had seen happier days. Once inside, he led me to a shadowy room with little furniture, except for a garish tin-decorated steamer trunk and a stack of multicolored Turkish carpets where I'd sleep.

Later, after kneeling for evening prayers, the lonely gent served me tea, bread, feta cheese and grapes on a dented silver tray. Then, in stilted conversation, the bachelor explained that he had once been a chauffeur for Nazi officers, who dumped him without a pension after their defeat.

As for me, grateful to have a place to lay my head, I hoped a little companionship and lira helped brighten the old soldier's otherwise cheerless night.

Before sunrise, I woke my host to offer him a final thanks and then headed out in the still darkness of the morning, unsure exactly what to expect. It was going to be a long, tough haul over those mountains. But I anticipated the adrenaline to kick in at any moment, since I was finally near the sea and reaching another benchmark on my odyssey.

My daily challenge began almost immediately with a steep ascent over the final mountain pass, where a few stray black goats were my only companions. It was too early for even the truckers. There was no food or water along the mountain trail, and I'm sure Dagheli's café was still closed, as I'd left early to beat the heat. Nevertheless, the mountains were ethereal, dusted in a delicate morning light. The backdrop was stunning with sharp jagged peaks ringing the Antalyan Basin. It was a climber's paradise. At one point, I counted five layers of mountains, one behind the other.

As it turned out, it was surprisingly painless to reach the summit at 1,925 meters, after which I drifted down a twelve-kilometer descent. All too soon, I was back on the plains, yet it was another hour before I finally reached the first restaurant I'd seen all morning.

Ravenous, I ducked inside to where the chef, a fellow originally from Edirne, treated me to a salad and I ordered soup while we talked about peace. When I tried to pay, he refused my money, only wishing me a "safe journey." As always, I was impressed by his humanity, but it was only the first minor miracle of a magical day.

The highway grew wider and better maintained, as I drew nearer to the coast. Although the road's center island was planted with pines and palms, there was absolutely no shade. Temperatures soared to nearly ninety degrees. Imagine my relief when I finally spotted one of those fruit stands with an umbrella. A mound of watermelons waited, as enticing as a stack of gold bars. Seeing my sweaty condition, the kindhearted vendor pulled up a stool, gave me a plastic fork and treated me to half a melon. That simple fruit had never tasted better.

Although the sign back at the base of the pass read "Antalya-50 km.," I figured the distance was only measured to the city limits, and my suspicions were soon confirmed. It took me several more hours to eventually enter the city, and then another to descend past pines and manmade waterfalls adorned with colossal Turkish flags and a three-story high profile of President Ataturk. Yet all in all, I'd seldom set my eyes on such an exquisite setting. The Taurus Mountains, a choker of radiant jewels, circled the seaside siren.

I'd made it. No trumpets blared—except in my own mind—plus the occasional welcoming blasts from passing trucks. I'd always imagined Turkey would be the most difficult physical part of the journey, and it was; yet I'd arrived with body and soul intact.

Our greatest obstacles are created in our own minds.

All the same, there was no time or place to savor the victory—not yet. I continued in a heat daze, walking through the suburbs for several more kilometers, as I searched for a place to celebrate my arrival and relax for the next day or so. Eventually, I spotted a lone hotel—one more luxurious than usual. Determined to see if my luck still held, I entered The Çevik Palace and approached the desk clerk.

"Do you have a room for thirty lira?" I asked. Then I noticed their posted price was fifty, but I knew that was always open to negotiation.

The fellow hemmed and hawed a second, while I tried not to appear too desperate. Finally he answered, "I can let you have it for thirty-five."

"All right, that's fair. You know this is a celebration. I've just walked all the way from France for peace."

"You *walked* from France?"

"Yea, it's been quite a trip, but people have been very kind."

Without a moment's hesitation, he declared, "We believe in peace, too. So you can have the room for twenty-five lira."

With that, he presented me with the key and I headed into the elevator to the sixth floor. Opening the door, I found my room still unmade and made a quick call downstairs to let him know. I still don't believe what happened next. The manager apologized and insisted on upgrading me—to the penthouse. I couldn't believe my luck. Its air-conditioning was an incredible treat, especially after the day's sweltering trek of more than fifty kilometers. All told, I'd been blessed three times that day by the unlikeliest of "angels."

Besides celebrating, I'd scheduled two full days for Antalya. I planned to catch up on sleep, do laundry, call Cheryl, confirm the ferry schedule to northern Cyprus, and meet Kate Clow. She'd developed two of southern Turkey's newest long-distance walking paths: the Lyceum Trail and St. Paul's Way.

The end of my journey was near. I planned on taking just four days to walk across Cyprus, spending maybe an extra day in Limassol. Afterward, I'd hop a short ferry to Haifa and trek four or five days to Jerusalem. With thousands of kilometers behind me, my destination was so close I could practically taste the *matzo*.

Shortly after daybreak, I was light and carefree as I left the hotel for the visitor information office to check on departure times for the Cyprus ferry. Weaving through the high-density condo living that passed for life on the "Turkish Riviera," I soon arrived at the waterfront. After broaching my plans to the fellow who worked at the newspaper stand-sized office, he politely uttered the words I'd dreaded: "There is no ferry from Antalya to northern Cyprus. It has been discontinued. You must go Alanya to catch the ferry to Girne."

I was shocked, disappointed and irritated at my own carelessness. Whether it was because of the recent war in Lebanon and evacuation of civilians to Cyprus, a seasonal schedule, or a change made long ago—I'd never know. Only one thing was for certain. I'd have to leave town the next morning in order to meet the boat in Alanya, east of Antalya. I could catch a bus, he assured me, or I figured it would take four days to walk. Of course, it would have been a little more direct to head there from Istanbul, if only I'd known. Then again, their visitor office had assured me that the ferry was operating again and still left from Antalya.

I should have known. I should have followed my own "Ask three times" rule.

With that in mind, I tried to phone the shipping company in Crete that operated the ferry from Limassol, Cyprus to Haifa. No success. It was another of those variables. Although Cheryl had contacted their Cyprus office, the departure time was still a big unknown. I hated to risk trekking all the way across Cyprus—just to discover I'd missed the only ship—and would have to wait another week.

Along the way to rendezvous with Kate Clow, I wended my way through the most Westernized Turkish city I'd seen. It was wall-to-wall with condos, upscale boutiques and street vendors. Their tiny harbor teemed with deep-sea fishing vessels, day-cruisers and remarkable Turkish *gulets,* those miniature, wooden pirate ships that visitors could charter for exclusive holidays along the turquoise coast.

Tracing the city walls past the Old Clock Tower, I soon arrived at Hadrian's Gate where I was to meet Kate. Legend had it that Belkis, the Queen of Saba, once passed through those gateways with trunks full of diamonds when she came to pay her respects to King Solomon. Nowadays, couples sipped tea and gossiped in the shade of olive trees. One weathered gent shined shoes from an elegant brass and ivory shoeshine box, while another weary pilgrim mustered his courage to face an unexpected four-day trek across the Turkish desert.

'I could always catch a bus to Alanya. Who could blame me? I'd arrive in a few hours. But it hardly seems right, after I've been so diligent about making this pilgrimage on foot.'

Kate, an intense Brit expat, soon arrived and we ducked back to her place to enjoy a cold drink on her vine-draped terrace. After I shared my plan to continue walking across Israel, the first words out of her mouth were, "You're going to walk the Israel National Trail, aren't you?"

In all my travels, I'd never heard or read anything about it. So I was surprised to learn it crossed the length of the country. It had been too long since I'd heard such a welcome idea. I was tired of competing with trucks for space. Besides, a country trail would put me more into contact with ordinary Israelis and maybe even Palestinians. Kate promised to contact her friend Dany, who might be willing to provide me with more information once I arrived.

At dawn, I awoke with the realization I *had* to walk to Alanya, no matter how painful it might be. It wasn't so much the physical challenge. It was the mental setback. I'd only planned another eight days to Jerusalem, so now I had to ration my diminishing energy to last an additional four days. On long-distance treks, your mind and body work together in concert, establishing a goal and then commanding the body to "make it so." Since you never knew what challenge waited just ahead, you could never afford to give 110% at any one time. You always needed to keep something in reserve for the unknown.

So with resolve, I went down to the hotel's front desk where the clerks and I spent the next hour trying to confirm the sailing schedule from Alanya to Cyprus, but no one was working on Sunday morning. All we knew was that the shipping company's website stated there was a Wednesday 3 p.m. crossing. I'd shoot for that. Although I'd have to average thirty-five kilometers a day, that shouldn't be a problem. I just didn't want to arrive an hour late and be delayed another week.

After breakfast, I took advantage of overcast skies and began trekking toward Alanya. Traffic was already heavy on the major west-east thoroughfare, but a wide shoulder kept me from dancing my usual dodgy salsa with semis. Before long, I found myself back in the tranquil countryside amid cornfields and sunflowers. Every hour or so, I paused for water, chugging it down in great gulps, until I reached Serik at sundown.

As thirty-five mile an hour winds and rains wracked the village, I ducked into a local inn and only braved going outside long enough to head to the quick-mart next door for Turkish cheese or *peynir* to eat with my leftover crackers. While savoring the simple dinner, I couldn't help but worry about the logistics of making it to Haifa on Israel's northwest coast. But as much as it ran counter to my character, I decided to do the only thing I could—face one hurdle, one day at a time.

Dawn rose, as did I, thanks to the roosters' "doodle-doing" that'd kept me on edge all night. Between their racket and the relentless eighty-degree heat, I was far from cheery or rested, but there was no time to sit around and feel sorry for myself.

All day, the parched landscape varied little from the past week. There were few villages, matched in number by places offering water. I could just barely discern the sea far off to my right, although I was more tempted to visit ancient settlements like Side and Perge, where the Apostle Paul had once roamed. Then again, I was walking, so even that was out of the question. An eight-kilometer diversion would amount to walking two extra hours in each direction.

On the other hand, the bleak landscape allowed my mind plenty of time to wander on its own. I traveled outside, while traveling within.

Walking allowed me to free my mind, or "clean my hard-drive" as it were. Many times in today's frantic world, where people are constantly bombarded with messages, who has time to fully process all the information? All those unresolved ideas, issues and emotions are pent up, until folks feel overwhelmed. Some seek counseling to process or "download" these emotions. Yet some of those same results can be achieved by walking. Alone on a trail, you have time to deal with your thoughts, to listen to them, and then to accept, validate, reject, or re-think your reasoning objectively from a distance. So walking becomes "a trampoline for the mind," allowing it to bounce unfettered from thought to feeling. It also enables a psychological cleansing and healing—and promotes an inner peace.

By early afternoon, I arrived on the outskirts of Manavgat and made my way to the center of the popular resort town set on a turquoise river of the same name. I could immediately tell it was a favorite European hangout. Prices were inflated and posted in euros. So I was especially pleased to find a room in the center of town, thanks to some advice from fellows roasting corn over a wood-fed box across the street.

After checking in and showering, I immediately set off in search of an Internet café where I was relieved to receive news from Cheryl, who'd sent me the names of hostels in Nicosia, Limassol and Jerusalem. Also, Kate had been in touch with her friend Dany, who looked forward to providing information for hiking the Israel National Trail. So my plan was coming together. I was even successful in convincing the hotel manager, a gruff guy hanging out in a dirty singlet and a haze of cigarette smoke, to call the shipping company in Alanya and confirm the ferry's departure time and date. It was a good thing, too, since they'd already changed schedules. They'd leave Thursday morning at 11:00, instead of Wednesday at 3:00. After all, it was Turkey. Timetables, like prices, were never set in stone.

That evening, in search of a much-needed drink, I wandered the banks of the serene river. A Van Gogh-like tableau of multi-hued boats lined its shores. Dropping into a riverside pub, I was thrilled to find Western food. I'd eaten enough *kabobs* and *böreks* to last a lifetime. In the tranquility of the river, I also had a chance to speak with villagers about my journey, and how much we had in common—no matter what flag we flew.

As one younger fellow translated, his well-educated friend assured me, "Yes, Christians and Muslims are "brothers." We worship the same God, share many of the same prophets, and want many of the same things out of life." He added with a wink, "It is time to bury the hatchet...just not in each other."

Out of curiosity, I just had to ask that one question, one last time: "Do you think it would be safe for me to walk across Syria to Jerusalem?"

The gentleman stroked his beard for only an instant. "No, not now. You should avoid Syria."

Later that evening, I learned why. There'd been a foiled car bomb attack by terrorists on the American Embassy in Damascus, Syria's capital. Four were killed, another injured.

The next day, the road to Avsallar was backbreaking and blistering. For the life of me, I just couldn't get my body to rise to the occasion. As I slogged in the searing heat without shade for hours, the old line, "Water, water everywhere, but not a drop to drink," kept running through my mind, as I fantasized about diving naked into a freezing pool. To my right, the sun-drenched coast mocked me with posh beach resorts catering to bikini-clad Russians. In contrast, the local villages were miniscule. Thatched-roof stands where shriveled fellows hawked bananas were rare oases.

Near collapse, and still twenty-five kilometers from Alanya, I wandered into a *pension* across the street from the beach. The manager with his white t-shirt rolled above his belly, (the universal redneck summer uniform), sat spellbound by a Muslim televangelist. My simple request for a room began the usual awkward dance of the bazaar. He immediately asked fifty liras, I countered with thirty, he asked forty, and I finally offered twenty dollars (equal to thirty liras) that he eagerly accepted. For that price, I settled into a two-room suite with a kitchen, plus a balcony looking out to the sea—far better than I'd ever expected.

Then, still worried about my sea connection from Limassol to Haifa, I emailed Cyprus Tourism and Salamis Shipping Lines, hoping one of them might help. I only needed to confirm the boat's existence and schedule before leaving for the remote hills of Cyprus. The Lebanese/Israeli border was still closed. If stuck in Limassol, my only option at that point was to fly to Amman, Jordan and walk to Jerusalem—definitely a last resort.

Leaving the snug apartment at sunrise, I reveled in the beauty of nature. The air was infused with the heady aroma of laurel and resin, stirring deep memories of the Med. Earthy and soothing, it was the essence of retsina; the incense of a forest Mass. Yet I didn't dare to slow down. I hoped the latest schedule for Kyrenia (Girne) was correct—and the ferry didn't sail that same day.

After all the busy highways, it was a relief to walk on sidewalks all twenty-five kilometers into town, past so-called resorts of varying 5-star quality. There must have been a hundred hotels, timeshares, and condos lining the beach, filled with package tourists from Russia and Scandinavia. For once, locals assumed I was Norwegian instead of German, and I was tempted to reply, "Yea, sure, ya bettcha."

As I drew nearer the city, the road entered three tunnels, one of which was close to two kilometers long. As I cleared the last, a beach resort rose into view, nestled by mountains flowing to the sea. I could hardly believe it was Alanya. At first, it looked too small for a city of nearly half a million.

With the help of locals, I found the visitor information office and quickly confirmed the ferry's sailing time for the following morning. Hürriyet, an attractive lady who worked there, invited me to relax in their lobby while she treated me to a glass of sweet tea.

As I shared details about my peace walk, she excitedly asked, "Would you consider doing an interview with the Alanya newspaper and television?"

Regrettably, I hadn't done any others in Turkey. With Émile's departure, our time in Istanbul had been so frantic. Plus, I was a little hesitant at that point, not knowing how Muslims would react, or if I'd draw unwanted attention to myself. But since then, I knew my concerns were unfounded, so I jumped at the chance.

With that, my Alanya angel phoned her media contacts, and then arranged a substantial discount for me at the nearby Hotel Divan. After showering, I returned with my walking stick and pack for an impromptu interview held right on the busy sidewalk. Although one persistent interviewer repeatedly tried to steer his questions to political issues and especially our government leadership, I remained focused on the need for waging peace, particularly in critical times.

"If I have one message," I explained, "it is to stop fighting and treat each other like brothers…while there is still time."

Afterward, the television production crew took me for a scenic drive along the beach, until they stopped and conducted another interview and shot "b-roll," as we walked again and again along one lonely stretch of road until it was a "wrap."

That evening, I had the chance to watch our segment on *Kanal A Television*. Of course, they'd dubbed over my voice with a translation or narrative, so I had no idea what they had me saying. Only that I concluded with a "*Salaam malakim!*" as I walked away from the camera and headed down the highway.

What better way to end than with, "Peace be with you"?

My final night in Turkey was spent in air-conditioned bliss. I was especially contented. I'd finally confirmed there was, in fact, still a cargo ship sailing from Limassol to Haifa on Wednesdays and Saturdays. So it was all systems go.

After picking up my ferry tickets in the morning, I wandered down to the harbor where *gulets* moored, waiting to cruise the picturesque, bay-dotted coast. They were magnificent vessels, reminiscent of earlier times. I'd have loved to hop one myself and sail those turquoise waters. But another, faster vessel awaited. The passenger ferry to northern Cyprus was soon boarded and we pushed off for blue water.

Alanya occupies a dramatic setting, best appreciated from offshore. Atop the peninsula's promontory sits an early Seljuk castle with crenellated walls winding down the mountainside. Not so long ago, the entire town was sequestered within those fortified walls, but it did little good. The town changed flags nearly fifteen times throughout its long history.

As we sped past Turkey's craggy coast at thirty-five knots, I spotted villages tucked into rugged coves, still mercifully underdeveloped. Trees dotted umber cliffs. Amethyst mountains shrouded in a bluish haze cascaded to the sea. The heat, brutal even in September, made me happy to spend an afternoon on the water, just as pilgrims of old had once done. A thousand years earlier, there had been many routes to Jerusalem. Northern Europeans and British often came by sea, while Brindisi, Italy was another popular embarkation port for pilgrims living farther south. Others had come overland, as I had done. But then, as now, it was always fraught with danger and dependent on the state of unrest along the path.

After only four hours, we docked in the ancient port city of Kyrenia, whose history dates back to the Neolithic period. Now called Girne, since the Turkish invasion in 1974, I made certain to ask the customs officer to place my visa and entry stamp on a separate piece of paper. Cypriots in the south were still understandably livid by the occupation of the north. In fact, until recently, it had been impossible to cross between the two regions. But with the pending entry of both Cyprus and Turkey into the European Union, regulations were relaxed. You could finally walk across Nicosia's Green Line—although relations were still far from cordial. The Cypriot embassy in Washington even went so far as to say they couldn't "guarantee my safety." Considering the rest of the trip, I had to laugh.

Leaving the port, I found my way into *centrum* a few kilometers away and checked into the Sidelya Hostel, where the manager welcomed me with open arms. I wasn't the first traveler for peace to cross his doorstep. A fellow pilgrim, bicycling from Geneva to Jerusalem, had passed through in 1999. They still proudly displayed his calling card at the front desk.

After sunset, I ambled down toward the magically illuminated Kyrenia castle. Twinkling restaurant lights framed the harbor walkway, while the garlicky perfume of freshly broiled seafood enticed all but hardcore vegetarians to sit and linger awhile. There, while nursing a Guinness, I reflected on my final impressions of Turkey.

I had to ask myself, "What is the typical Turk? Is there such a thing?" I'd seen so many "types." Some women still dressed traditionally and wore a black *chador* covering everything but their coal-black eyes. However, those were relatively few. Many simply wore attractive scarves and a topcoat over their dress, even though it was nearly ninety degrees. In the villages, I spotted some ladies wearing scarves or *hijabs* and more practical harem pants or long skirts. Then again, many of the young were dressed in modest t-shirts and jeans, much like you might see in a Middle American mall.

The men ranged from the stereotypical swarthy, dark, mustachioed and muscular fellow with short-cropped hair to light and fair-skinned guys with thin features. These, I was told, had immigrated long ago from Croatia and Eastern Europe. Perhaps Crusader blood still ran through their veins. Some of the older fellows wore formal shirts with suits and embroidered vests with *kufis*, those small, round Muslim hats. In contrast, the younger guys, even bus station attendants, were well-groomed, wearing cologne and t-shirts or white shirts and ties. Many wore short pointed boots, "cockroach stompers," that made their feet appear three sizes larger.

Turkey was jumping into the 21st century and the European Union with both feet. For me, a Western stranger, I felt completely at ease and welcome. All in all, there was a politeness and respect on the streets and in the shops and restaurants. I'd seen no screaming or public fits of anger. People smiled easily and kissed friends on both cheeks in European-style when they met. Everyone under forty had a cell phone, and the Internet cafés and pizza parlors were the most popular places in town.

Forty days had passed all too quickly. They had been so unexpectedly filled with kindness, generosity and warmth. I'd seen so much—still, just a tiny portion of the vast country. Along the way, any preconceptions I had about Muslim cultures had vanished. Our ways of life might be different, but underneath the surface we were not so dissimilar after all— more alike than politicians dare to admit. To a person, we all desire (and deserve) peace in our lives.

FROM ALANYA, TURKEY

CYPRUS

KYREN

UN BUFFER ZONE (GREEN LINE)

N

LYTHRODONTAS

TOCHNI

LIMASSOL

MEDITERRANEA

CHAPTER TWELVE
Cyprus

Crossing The Line

*"Yet the Lord pleads with you still: Ask where the good road is,
the godly paths you used to walk in, in the days of long ago.
Travel there, and you will find rest for your souls."*
~ Jeremiah 6:16

A t first light, I began a long scramble up the Kyrenian marble and limestone mountain range through Nicosia Pass, skirting ancient St. Hilarion castle and monastery. Reaching the top, I paused to admire the sweeping panoramic views of the northern coast below, before scampering down the other side to the Mesaoria Plains. The terrain was arid and the air was dust-laden, yet I pressed on and reached the outskirts of Nicosia (Lefkosia), the divided capital, by noon. In my search for the infamous Green Line, I soon found a restaurant by the same name and figured I must be pretty close. Wandering past tables already set for diners, I stopped a waiter and asked if there was something I could buy for ten Turkish liras.

"What do you want?" He looked confused by my unusual way of ordering.

"It doesn't matter. It's just that I only have ten liras left, and I'm crossing the border after lunch."

At first, there was some discussion among the workers, since they expected the press corps to arrive soon, but the cook must have relented because a sizeable meal soon arrived at my table. Just as I began to eat, the chef himself joined me, eager to know what brought me there. Between bites, I talked to him about peace, especially for Cyprus, an island that had suffered for the last thirty years. Not surprisingly, his sentiments were like most of the Turks with whom I'd already spoken.

"The Turkish Cypriots want peace and a united island again," he assured me, with great passion. "Now, if only our politicians will listen and get out of the way."

In light of their checkered history, I suggested, "Maybe it's time for two of the world's great cultures, Greece and Turkey, to sit down like people of wisdom, reason and honor. Let Cyprus be Cyprus—one sovereign, united nation."

The good-natured fellow nodded, adding, "Besides, it will set a good example for other countries that have been unable to solve their problems for so long."

Thinking of the Israelis and Palestinians, I couldn't agree more.

At last, standing to leave, I handed the chef my ten-lira bill in payment. "No," he insisted. "Lunch is my treat. Use the money to further peace."

While walking the short distance to the frontier, once again I was touched by a stranger's heartfelt generosity and unshakable faith in the possibility for peace. One chef and a pilgrim had just solved another crisis over *kabobs*. If only world leaders could find a solution so pragmatically.

As promised, the border crossing was now wide open, although Nicosia's two halves were still separated by barbed wire, sentry posts and mine fields. Once you were stamped out of the country, there was just one lone policeman to briefly glance at your passport on the "Greek" side. I walked past deserted, sandbagged buildings for a hundred yards through an eerie "no man's land," then I was suddenly in southern Cyprus: same dirt, same sun, same air, different flag.

Downtown Nicosia was as faded and worn as the first time I'd seen her, more than twenty years earlier. She was still awaiting an influx of euros, even though the Russians did their best to buy her wholesale in the 1990s. Wandering through her narrow alleyways, I let muscle memory be my guide, until I found myself back at a "falling-star" hotel where we'd stayed in more foolish times. After crossing Africa, it had been a sight for weary, bush-wracked eyes—and surprisingly affordable. By 2:00 a.m., we realized why. The Filipino staff was kept humping, er, hopping all night.

This visit, my hotel was right next-door and I recognized the same hairless, fossilized man, who looked like he hadn't moved from his chair in the years since. He was quick to point out that the air-conditioning didn't work, even though it was still close to ninety degrees, and then begrudgingly slipped me the key to a disappointing eight by ten foot cell that opened onto the porch where I could run around in a cold shower.

In order to iron out the details of my trek south to Limassol, I ambled over to the visitor information office. Most Cypriots speak English, a welcome change. Although the pleasant lady who worked there showed me several different routes on her map, I was attracted to a less traveled path that would take me through tiny villages, including Lefkara. With any luck, I'd arrive in the port of Limassol by Monday night, in time to catch the Wednesday cargo ship to Haifa. Before leaving the bureau, I was curious to hear what a professional woman felt about the recent border opening to northern Cyprus.

"Until recently, I know Cypriots have been unable to go north to visit towns and family remaining there. It's been thirty years now, right?"

"More," she nodded, sadly brushing the hair away from her dark eyes. "But most of our families left after the occupation."

"With the border recently opening, have you gone back?"

"Absolutely not," she hissed.

"Why? After all this time, I'd have thought everyone would welcome the chance to visit—and at least see how it's changed."

"Why? Because they demand us to show identification papers."

"So? We have to as well, just traveling from Hawaii to mainland America."

"Well, I refuse to carry identification papers to enter my own country!" she huffed, shaking her glasses for emphasis.

In principle, I understood what she meant. However, it was so unlike some countries that could napalm a nation back to the Stone Age one decade and establish factories there the next. Or spend billions of dollars waging a Cold War against communism for fifty years—and then sell the communist Chinese their country—one Treasury note at a time. No, that part of the world had a very long memory.

At dawn, since breakfast wasn't served until 8:00 a.m., I used the sun as my compass and headed south out of town. The street kept changing its name every hundred meters or so as I made my way past the Presidential Palace, and finally, an hour later, into the countryside. By mid-morning, it was ninety degrees. I trudged across the desert landscape like a snail across a block of salt. Villages were hours apart and I forced myself to re-hydrate as often as I could manage. Fortunately, I discovered a coffee frappé drink created in one of those quickie-mart chopped ice machines. What a godsend. One of those frozen concoctions cooled me down much faster and longer than an ordinary soda, plus the caffeine added a little speed to my otherwise lackluster pace.

The barren landscape undulated all morning, as I wended past two remote military bases with sentries looking bored and equally seared. A few farms grew figs, pomegranates or olives, but I saw no other sign of mad dogs or Hawaiians out in the noonday sun.

Not a moment too soon, I reached Lythrodontas, one of two possible villages in which to spend the night. As I staggered into the village square, one elderly, well-dressed fellow wearing dark glasses waved me over and insisted on buying me a strong Greek coffee, while the bartender called the local guesthouse. I'd had the foresight to pick up their name and telephone number the day before at the visitor information office.

"Yes," he soon announced, "they have a room, but they want twenty-nine Cyprus pounds." Even he looked shocked. That was nearly sixty U.S. dollars for a single—more than I'd paid in five months—and in one tiny village? How strange. Cyprus used to be a bargain. Still, I only had one other option. I could trek the remaining fourteen kilometers to Lefkara, but I ran the risk their rooms might already be filled with day tripping lace aficionados. It also meant hiking another three hours in brutal heat. So I figured it couldn't hurt to at least meet the innkeeper. Maybe he had a more "flexible" rate.

The man's stately stone, wood and white plaster house lay concealed behind a sturdy wooden gate that opened onto a grape arbor-draped courtyard. His house and its five rental units were part of Cyprus' "Agrotourism" program. Recently, the Tourist Authority realized that some visitors expected more from their holiday than just an umbrella drink at a beachside resort, so they'd worked with village folks to open guesthouses and farms. It was a practical way of exposing visitors to a more authentic Cypriot lifestyle, while revitalizing village industries.

It turned out that Andreas, the owner of the house, was a writer/painter, so we hit it right off. He proudly pointed out his handiwork, the beautiful paintings and mosaics decorating his family's hundred-year-old house. After I briefly answered his questions about my odyssey, he was quick to talk politics, echoing the chef from the Green Line Restaurant.

"People on both sides of Cyprus want unification. If left on our own, we can live together in harmony as we have done for centuries. It is only the meddling of others that keeps us apart."

Then, at long last, it came down to business. Such things were never rushed in Mediterranean countries. Knowing the traditional Greek-Turk rivalry, I spoke in glowing detail about all my experiences with Turkish hospitality, and then added that Nicosia's tourist office had told me his rooms were considerably less.

"Their price is several years old. We charge extra for air-conditioning now."

Ultimately, after all our "talk-talk," my situation appeared hopeless. Sensing we'd reached an impasse, I dramatically rose to put on my pack, until he blurted out, "Okay, I'll give it to you for the price the tourism office quoted." Then handing me his keys, he only asked that I lock the gate in the morning when I left.

"Let's hope Cyprus is soon re-united," I said as we parted.

"We can only pray."

Walking the trail from Lythrodontas in the morning was an unexpected pleasure. There was no traffic and I passed just two groups of local walkers that greeted me with a warm *"Kalimera!"* Then the village road began a serpentine climb, as it shed its asphalt and reverted back to a simple dirt path, one more comfortable for pilgrims anyway. There were tire tracks in the dust, so someone obviously drove the mountain pass, but I was blissfully alone. The limestone hills were cool and serene; their silence only shattered for an instant when a hunter fired at sparrows far off in the distance. The continual climb, at times steep, persisted for an hour until it turned asphalt again, winding past a dam and up into the village of Lefkara.

While thankful I hadn't tackled that stretch in yesterday's unforgiving sun, I was even more grateful to duck into a *taverna* where older gents gathered to sip a demitasse of espresso, play backgammon or dominoes, but mostly to gossip. It was the equivalent of the British neighborhood pub and just as clannish. Already by 9:00 there was quite a crowd, yet you could have heard a pin drop when I entered. Offering a polite *"Yassas"* to the group, I strode across the arbor-covered terrace, slid off my pack, planted my stick, and slumped into a chair. I was left alone, as I gulped cold drinks and ate from a silver platter of salted nuts. But I was far from ignored. They discretely scrutinized my every move, wondering why I was up there in the hills and obviously not on the usual tour. I hardly looked like a typical lace fanatic.

Eventually re-hydrated and eager to continue, I asked the owner for directions to Skarinou, the adjacent village. My simple question broke the ice and I was soon up to my neck in questions.

"Why are you doing this? When did you leave? Where have you been? How fast do you walk? Where do you sleep? How old are you?"

I was happy to answer. Yet that being Cyprus, talk soon turned to politics.

"You walked across Turkey?" asked Costas, a robust fellow, as he brushed phyllo crumbs from his salt and pepper mustache with the back of his hand.

"Sure, and I was made to feel welcome."

He looked aghast. "From what I hear, I'd have thought it would be dangerous for you."

"No, not at all," I assured him, relating my story about the trucker who'd stopped his rig to give me lunch that day in the desert. Cutting to the chase, I added, "Actually, I think they want to settle this Cyprus problem as much as you do."

"So tell them to give us back the land they've taken," one fellow snarled.

I knew I was being baited.

"The Turks tell me the ordinary people there want peace," I replied. "It's the politicians who get in the way."

"It's the same here," another slight fellow joked with a gleam in his eye. "The same everywhere."

I had to agree. "Look, we just have to elect officials who believe in peace and who'll keep their promise once they're elected. We need to take back our governments." There were nods all around.

"Then I imagine you're not a big fan of your president?" Costas asked.

I just smiled. Perhaps, it was like Mark Twain once said, "Patriotism is supporting your country all the time, and your government when it deserves it." Since traveling, I'd seen how our leaders had done more to sabotage our credibility than most of my countrymen could imagine. They'd squandered the world's sympathetic outpouring of support after 9/11 with their arrogance and ham-fisted policies like the indefinite detainment of uncharged suspects at Guantanamo Bay detention camp in Cuba.

"Maybe you should move here?" chuckled another bald, owl-eyed fellow in oval glasses.

"Oh, I've thought about it, but my wife tells me that she doesn't look good in black," I joked. Actually, although widows in Cyprus and Greece once dressed that way as a sign of mourning, it wasn't "required" any more. With the recent influx of northern European retirees, Cyprus was more modern with each visit, destined to continue its tradition as a melting pot between two continents.

Finally, eager to leave before it became any hotter, I suggested, "Maybe we should leave Cyprus for the Cypriots to resolve their own problems—and other nations should just stand aside." With that, everyone enthusiastically nodded in agreement, then returned to backgammon, the more civilized game.

By early afternoon, after passing Choirokoitia, an early Neolithic village, I arrived in the silent hill town of Tochni. The lady in Nicosia's tourism office had promised I'd find guesthouses there, but they were well disguised, and there wasn't a person to be seen in the broiling sun. I headed downhill to the church. Closed. I climbed another street to what looked like an old hotel and knocked. The entrance was shuttered tight. It was frustrating. I didn't look forward to trekking any farther in that heat, but options were limited.

Fortunately, at just that moment, a car pulled up in front of the village's closed grocery, and men started unloading cases of Keo beer. Without a moment to lose, I scampered down to ask for help.

"Yes, there's one place to stay here," a skinny fellow told me, with a point of his boney finger. "Top of that hill. Look for an office under the pink bougainvillea."

With his directions, I found the Cyprus Villages Tourism office that rented country homes, and was in luck. They had just one place left—twice my daily budget.

"I'm sorry," I apologized, certain I'd have to continue. "But I can only spend twenty Cyprus pounds."

The slender German looked through her listings again and smiled. "Oh, I *do* have one I can let you have for that price."

I was both astonished and relieved. As I filled out their paperwork, her assistant brought me a cool drink. Then I told them about my journey across two continents.

"Although this trip started out as a peace pilgrimage, it's become more of a lesson about the kindness of strangers."

Nodding in appreciation, the lady reached into her desk drawer and pulled out a yellow slip of paper. "Here, for peace, for your journey," she said, proudly handing me a coupon for a free dinner that night in their *taverna*.

I grinned from ear-to-ear. "You know, I've met so many "angels" along the way like you. I'm convinced the good people in this world still outnumber the bad." Sometimes we only have to give them a chance to shine.

My apartment was nicer than expected. It was set behind another large wooden gate on a second story, overlooking a courtyard draped in magenta bougainvillea. With its thick plaster and limestone walls, it was naturally cool inside. I would have been happy spending a week, but still needed to leave for Limassol in the morning to meet my lift to Haifa.

It was hard to believe I'd walked across Cyprus so quickly. I'd like to go back in the winter sometime and join those fellows in their country village. But first, I'd have to brush-up on my backgammon skills—and politics.

After a restful night, I set off toward Limassol along the "old" road. It had been the main highway not so long ago between Nicosia, Limassol and Larnaca, and it showed its pits and ruts. There was little shoulder to walk on for fifteen kilometers, and even less to eat or drink. All the mom and pop *tavernas* were shuttered, since most of the traffic sped along the faster A1. By mid-morning, it was already ninety degrees when I passed Governor's Beach. Then I traversed a long stretch of high-rise condos and shops along the Bay of Akrotiri for another three hours before reaching Limassol's center. All that time, there wasn't a soul to be seen, except for one seared Russian waif in search of tanning lotion.

Limassol, an ancient port city dating back to 2000 B.C., had played a rich role in three Crusades. Richard the Lionheart, King of England, captured it from the Byzantines in 1191, and then sold it to the Knights Templar. It'd changed hands countless times because of its strategic location. Templars controlled the port city until it was handed over to the Frankish Dynasty. Then the Germans, Egyptian Mamluks, Venetians, Ottomans and British held it, before Cyprus gained independence in 1960.

Nowadays, it teemed with hotels, English-style pubs, nightspots and tourists—but where to stay? Figuring it had been far too long since I'd slept in a monastery, it was the perfect time to check out that option again. It didn't take long for me to find the Franciscan church, but a Brother screamed from an upstairs window, "No room for pilgrims. Try the Sisters a few blocks from here."

I found their convent easily enough, and then gently explained to them about the nature of my journey. I even showed them my letter of introduction from the Vatican. Although sympathetic, one cherubic Sister explained, "Sorry. This is a school. We have no room for you here."

"Fair enough. Is there another place you can suggest? I only need a place for two nights. Maybe you can recommend an inexpensive *pension*, or

I could stay with one of your parishioners. I'm certainly willing to pay them for their trouble."

With that, the kind Sister disappeared into her office. I figured she was making some phone calls, but she returned a moment later holding a fistful of Cypriot pounds.

"Here, you take these. And come back later for dinner."

"No. Thanks, Sister. It's not a matter of money. I just thought, since I'm on a pilgrimage and these are my last days before reaching Jerusalem, it would be fitting to rest with an order, as my friend and I did in Beuron, Vienna, Weltenburg, Melk and Dillingen."

She nodded sympathetically and disappeared again, only to return with an older, more persistent nun. She flowed across the marble floor with an air of authority. All of a sudden, I was thrust into a tag-team match.

"Here, take this money, now!" the Mother Superior demanded in a no-nonsense tone. It reminded me of my own lovable, curly-haired grandmother. When I'd visited as a child, she could be relentless when it came to slipping me a few dollars before I headed home.

"No, it's really not necessary. I have money. I'm not destitute, just a pilgrim." I fought accepting the money because it was against my own personal code of conduct: to harm no one on my journey. If I took the pounds, it would mean less for the school kids, the Sisters or the truly needy—and I couldn't live with that. So I parried off the Mother Superior's wily attempts to slide the cash into my pockets for as long as I could. Eventually, she dodged my block, stuck a still larger wad of Cypriot notes into my camera case, and swiftly skirted away.

"Mother, I truly appreciate your generosity, but I just can't accept these. I'll only leave them here with the girl at the front desk after you go."

They were persistent, yet our interaction was a melodramatic play. We each had our respective roles. The Cypriots, much like their Greek cousins, were dukes of drama. Finally, convinced she had won, the Mother turned to go back to her work. But before joining her, the younger Sister sidled over and whispered, "Pray for us in Jerusalem."

"I certainly will."

With the kind nuns out of sight, I quietly left the money with the secretary at their reception desk. Then I slipped away before she could summon the Mother Superior to run after me, robes flapping in the breeze. I was pretty sure I could outrun her, but I'm not in the habit.

That afternoon, I found Salamis Shipping Company and purchased my one-way ticket to Haifa on a cargo ship sailing in two days. After all, I certainly couldn't swim there—or walk. At $160, it included a shared room and food, and they even helped me find a comfortable place to sleep nearby.

If all went according to plan, I'd reach Jerusalem within a week. Of course, given the region, who knew? Only the week before, Pope Benedict XVI, quoting Manuel II Paleologos, a 14th century Byzantine emperor, made disparaging comments about the Prophet Muhammad and Islam. There was a furor. Muslims were outraged and burning him in effigy. Then again, Ramadan, a month of fasting when everyone was one edge anyway, began in just five days. Meanwhile, Iraq simmered on the verge of a civil war. Timing, as they say, is everything.

After a day's rest, I made it a point to arrive early at the port, since there was little reason to hang around the hotel. It was a fortunate decision, too. As I ran the gauntlet, everything went smoothly until I faced the final hurdle at customs. At first, the ex-military immigration officer was cordial, admiring my journey—and walking stick, of course. Then he innocently asked if it was my first time to Cyprus.

"No, I've visited here several times by plane."

"How did you get to Cyprus this time?"

"I left Alanya by boat to Kyrenia, crossed the Green Line, and walked here."

I'd accidentally lit a fuse. All of a sudden, there was an unexpected tension.

"You entered through an unauthorized port!"

"I entered through Kyrenia, Cyprus," I explained, careful not to call it Girne, its Turkish name.

"But that is in Turkish-occupied Cyprus."

"I had no choice. I was in southern Turkey and following the ancient path to Jerusalem."

He remained unimpressed. He grabbed his phone to call his superior.

I was quick to point out, "Your embassy assured me there'd be no problem." But that was Washington—and this was Limassol.

The officer shouted in rapid, staccato bursts of Greek into his phone, before slamming down his receiver. He ranted and wildly shook his fist at the two indifferent immigration officers standing nearby. Then he thumbed through my passport again.

"Why don't you have a Turkish stamp for leaving the occupied territory?"

"Oh, I have one," I explained. "I just asked them to put it onto a separate piece of paper, as I didn't want it in my passport." I'd learned that trick after visiting Israel and South Africa. Once their stamp was in your passport, you couldn't enter many other countries.

I handed him the crumpled slip of official-looking paper and he examined it carefully, before making a copy of both it and my passport. As he did so, one of the other officials shot me a knowing wink and mischievous grin to tell me it would be all right. It was just another drama played out for my benefit. All that was missing was the Greek Chorus refrain. Finally, he produced a large stamp and smacked it with a thud of finality in my passport before waving me through.

After all that nonsense, I eagerly went outside and followed the long dock to the *Salamis Trader I*, the plainest vessel in the harbor. It was primarily a freighter that occasionally carried folks to Haifa, or Piraeus, Greece. In fact, on my voyage, there were only four passengers: an Israeli fishing boat operator, his two young North Vietnamese crewmembers, and me. The kids had worked for him in the past and were returning for another long stint at sea. It was a hard way to earn a living, but they made a fortune compared to what they'd earn back home.

The Israeli and I spent hours chatting as we watched ships loading in the port. Even though we had to check in at 11:00 in the morning, it was 6:00 before we weighed anchor and finally cast off. It was certainly a no-frills voyage, but the international Muslim crew did their best to make us feel welcome, including feeding us fried calamari and chips. It wasn't long before we turned into our stateroom—the infirmary retrofitted with bunk beds.

At ten knots, we weren't breaking any speed records, but we were at least moving in the right direction.

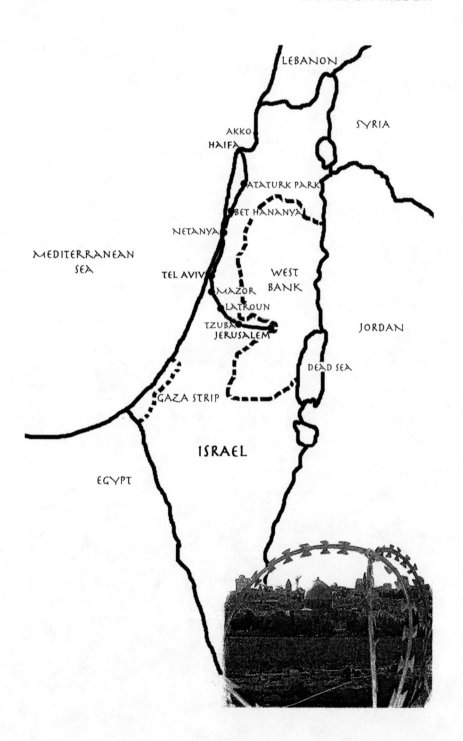

CHAPTER THIRTEEN
Israel

Life in a "Sea of Sharks"

"When you walk across the fields with your mind pure, then from all the stones and all growing things, and all animals, the sparks of their soul come out and cling to you and become a holy fire in you."
~ Ancient Hasidic saying

We dropped anchor at 6:00 a.m., right on schedule, and the port security team was aboard for our grilling before I even had time to finish a second cup of coffee. The crew and passengers were summoned to the captain's quarters, where the officers were thorough in their questioning.

"What are you doing here? When were you last in Israel? How did you get here? What do you do for a living? How can you support yourself here?"

Just when I thought I'd passed their pop-quiz, I was ushered to a waiting car and chauffeured to the Port Police station, where I alone was interrogated by six female police officers. However, their questions were less demanding and I was soon on my way.

The seaside town was barely awake. I wandered until my feet led me to the Port Inn hostel, a clean, cozy and affordable place. At that early hour, the fellows in my room were just checking out, and there'd be only two of us sharing a room for nine. Hezbollah's recent Katyusha rocket attacks had recently killed eight and wounded seventeen. They'd also done a good job of keeping all but the most determined travelers out of northern Israel.

After dropping off my pack, I began a long trek up Ben-Gurion Street, searching for the local tourism office. I hoped to find a detailed map of the

Israel National Trail. Of course, they didn't have one, but at least I had the chance to walk through the German Colony and catch a glimpse of the stunning terraced gardens ascending Mt. Carmel to the Shrine of the Báb, the holiest of Bahá'í sites that held the remains of Bahá'u'lláh, the faith's founder.

As much as I was relieved to finally land in Haifa, I was especially eager to head to the fabled city of Acre (Akko), and wasted no time in catching a train for the short trip north to the famed Crusader fortress on the sea. One of the oldest continuously inhabited cities in the world, its origin could be traced all the way back to the rule of Pharaoh Thutmose III in 1504 B.C. Later, it played a major role in the Crusades as their chief port in Palestine. Captured by King Richard, it became capital of the Kingdom of Jerusalem, and then the Knights Templar headquarters in 1191. In 1229, it was placed under the control of The Knights Hospitaller, or The Knights of the Order of St. John. They were founded in 1080 after the First Crusade to care for pilgrims to the Holy Land. It seemed only fitting that I pay my respects.

All afternoon I wandered through the underground fortress that today lay partially covered beneath a later city constructed by the Ottomans. Although still undergoing renovation after suffering attacks by the Mamluks, Turks, Napoleon's troops, the Genovese and others, I marveled at the ingenuity of its massive Knights' Halls, Gothic arches, courtyard, dungeon, and dining room with its tunnel leading to the lighthouse and waterfront. For a brief time, in the late 1940s, the same castle held Zionist Independence fighters, until their daring escape from the British in 1947.

Nowadays, most of Acre's old city is Arabic in flavor and it boasts several fine mosques, including the El Jazzar, along with a Turkish bazaar, a *hamman* and a city market that reminded me of Marrakech's bustling *souk*. Everyone was hospitable, even though I was one of few Westerners to be seen. A pomegranate seller was especially friendly and gave me a more intimate look into local life.

Giuseppe and I became fast friends. We met beside his cart as I waited to meet Dany, the fellow who'd helped establish the Israel National Trail. I'd called him earlier from a payphone booth, but how do you describe your surroundings when there are few street signs—and when he has no idea what you look like?

However, the pomegranate man was unmistakable: forty-eight years old, dark, and shaped like his fruit with a juice-spattered white jacket barely

buttoning over his ample belly. To pass the time, Giuseppe and I played
twenty questions with each other. He was curious about my journey and
confessed he had a hard time believing me. On the other hand, he told me
about his difficult life, his wife and their four small children with another
on the way, life in his village where the neighbors were buying big homes,
and his losing battle to stop smoking.

"I smoke because I am nervous about supporting my children."

"But don't cigarettes take money away from what you'd normally spend
on food for your family?"

"No," he laughed, "I roll my own."

He resembled other Arabs, so I wondered, "How'd you end up with a
name like Giuseppe?"

"I'm a Catholic," he began, singing me a blessing in Latin. "My father
was Italian." Carefully sprinkling cut tobacco onto a thin rolling paper, he
continued, "After Mussolini fell, my father escaped to Libya, then fled here
where he was put into jail by the British. Eventually, he was released and
fell in love with an Arab girl. Funny, she didn't speak Italian and he didn't
speak Arabic, but they were married anyway. As you might guess, it turned
out to be horrible." Then he paused to ask, "Do you have any children?"

"No. We decided not to, since there are already plenty of kids in the
world who need good homes."

"Well, if you like, I can introduce you to a nice village girl that can take
care of you," he offered with a sly aside.

"Thanks, but that's not necessary."

Matchmaking aside, Giuseppe had a heart of gold. He not only kept me
company, but also fixed me a fresh juice and even offered to let me use his
cell phone to call Dany, who finally arrived and had no trouble picking me
out of the crowd. I was hesitant to leave my new buddy, but Dany seemed
anxious to leave. We walked along the waterfront past a girl taking her
horse for a swim just outside the castle walls, and then we loaded into his
pickup truck.

On the ride back to Haifa, the tall, gregarious man with curly white hair
and beard told me about the trail extending all the way south to Eilat. Then
like nomads everywhere, we shared stories of the road, discovering our
paths had nearly crossed twice: once in the Himalayas and again on the
Camino de Santiago.

By car, it didn't take us long to return to the port city and we continued
to the outskirts. He wanted to show me where I'd actually start walking the

next morning. Parking beside the trailhead in Yagur, Dany pulled out three detailed 1:50,000 topographic trail maps, far better than I'd been able to find in town. Then he briefly went over the two hundred kilometer section I'd trek to the fringes of Jerusalem. He was especially familiar with the signage, as he'd set up most of the national trail.

"It's marked with tan, blue and white tri-color stripes painted on rocks, trees or the infrequent post. At times, it'll share the trail with red, green or black markings. Often you'll see the two of them combined," he warned. "Remember, if the tan stripe is on top, you're headed south toward the desert. If the white's on top, you're going north."

Where? Toward the North Pole?

That sounded easy. Then he pulled out something even handier: a list of "angels" on the route to contact for lodging and assistance along the way. I was content. What better way to get to know a country and its people? I looked forward to meeting them and shedding light on the somewhat mysterious Israeli life. Plus, it'd be a welcome relief to walk rugged dirt trails again, especially for the final approach to Jerusalem.

Before sunrise, Yonatan and Hila pulled up to the hostel in their live-aboard van. He was a friendly, impish teddy bear of a fellow in his early twenties with a great bushy beard and twinkle in his eye. His girlfriend Hila, a cute intellectual, did most of the talking, since she spoke much better English. Dany had phoned them the night before and they'd generously agreed to take me back to the trailhead. That would save me from walking through a disgusting industrial area in the dark. Consequently, we arrived back in Yagur at daybreak. After agreeing to meet later that evening along the trail, they wished me luck and I was off.

When I first began walking, I wasn't too concerned to see both the national and red trail markings together, as Dany had warned. The red ones appeared more frequently, but I figured the national markings would eventually surface again, if I kept following the path. Not far out of the gate, I slid down into a "red" river gulley, and then began climbing, huffing, puffing, and scrambling with a full pack up over boulders, as I attempted to climb out again. At times, I climbed six or eight feet straight up, hanging on by narrow handholds. Something was terribly wrong. Dany had told me it was a "family trail." A family of what? Goats? One false move and I'd tumble backward onto the rocks below.

Shimmying down the other side of each massive boulder was even more precarious. Still, I continued to climb for two hours, breaking out into a heavy sweat as my muscles strained. Every ten meters, to free up both hands, I threw my walking stick ahead and then slowly pulled myself up—or lowered myself gently down the other side—again and again. My shoes, clothes and pack were all wrong for that type of hard scramble. If the entire trail was going to be like that, I vowed to head back down to the roads. It'd take me a month to walk two hundred kilometers at that rate—if I didn't break something first.

By the time I'd finally left the gulch and was on the top in a clearing, I was scratched, drenched, bruised and panting. Worst of all, after all that, I discovered I'd walked two and a half kilometers on the wrong path. I'd missed the tri-color sign back at the first junction. As a small consolation, however, I was soon able to reconnect with the right trail in the village of Mt. Carmel, the highest point in the region and a Druze community.

Although considered Arabs, 100,000 Druze had split with Arab nationalism in 1948, and had since served honorably with both the Israeli army and police. Their religion was a unique blend of Judaism, Christianity and Islam with Greek philosophy and Hindu influences. Mentors and prophets from all three great religions lived together side-by-side in harmony, including John the Baptist, Jesus, Muhammad, Moses, and Salman the Persian.

Setting off again, I resolved to become even more aware of the trail markings, since I couldn't afford another tiring diversion. As the terrain rose and fell dramatically, I was forced to climb and then make wobbly descents all morning. Worse still, after my first exhausting two hours, I was alone and nearly out of water, without a drop or anyone in sight. Finally, as the trail swerved to cut across dry grassland, I spotted a man and his son in a white pickup truck heading up the road toward me. They stopped twenty-five meters away. As I began a steep climb, I noticed they moved as well. I stopped. They stopped. I climbed again, as did they, always keeping their distance. Our tense tango continued until I reached Mt. Carmel's crest and gazed down at the jaw-dropping vista below. When the driver finally neared, I walked over to meet him, curious to find out why he'd been trailing me.

As an icebreaker, I casually asked, pointing, "Do you know if the trail goes this way—or that?" I was already well aware of the answer.

The military-looking man stepped out of his truck. He awkwardly hemmed and hawed.

'How odd. Wouldn't a local know where the ocean was from the area's highest peak?'

Then I asked the more pressing question, "Where I can find water?"

He immediately offered to give me his liter, but I was content just to split it and get on my way. I never did find out why he was following me.

By early afternoon, as I scrambled up and down hillsides to the sea, I found myself in a park along with ten Muslim high school kids playing drums, drinking sodas and fooling around like teenagers anywhere. As usual, I searched again for trail markers, until one chunky fellow with spiky hair volunteered his help and acted like a bloodhound, sniffing his way up and down the road to everyone's delight. Then they insisted I join them, sharing chuckles, drinks and taking photos of one another. From the looks of things, you never would have known there was a perpetual war going on.

On my way out of that same park, I ran into Yonatan and Hila, lounging around their van in their underwear, talking on their cell phones, and fixing drinks in their blender. I was shocked to see them. They'd waited to make sure I was getting along all right. We talked for as long as I could afford, before agreeing to meet later by the forest lookout tower in Ataturk Park.

The afternoon's hike proved to be just as demanding. Steep climbs were followed by equally sharp drops to narrow ledges just wide enough for your feet. There was no room for error. It was several hundred meters to the valley floor. All the same, I finally did reach the bottom, as picnickers wrapped up their day and loaded their cars. By then, I looking for water again, so I wandered over to an attractive Middle Eastern woman washing dishes at a concrete basin.

"Is this water drinkable?" I asked.

She shrugged and continued packing her car.

Her husband who'd overheard us, replied, "Here, you can take this," as he offered me a bottle of mineral water.

"Thanks. That was quite a climb," I said, wiping the sweat from my face. "Glad I made it down in one piece. I had my doubts."

"You must be hungry," he said, with a sympathetic smile.

"A little." That was an understatement. I hadn't eaten all day.

Hearing that, the dark, well-dressed man reached into his open trunk and offered me an entire barbecued fish and salad, but I was content to polish off some sesame *tahini* spread on pita bread while talking about my peace pilgrimage.

After listening intently for quite some time, he finally whispered, "I am a Palestinian," as if revealing a closely held secret. Then he shook my hand. I was surprised, since I'd never met one before. Frankly, he wasn't at all what I'd imagined. He had no bomb (that I could see). No bubbling rage. No burning flag. With his appearance, manners and hospitality, he could have just as easily been a Christian or a Jew—or, with his brown skin and dark hair, Hispanic for that matter.

For a few moments, we spoke as two men sharing water from the same bottle—without any flag-waving nationalism or dogma. In the small park, on just another typically sunny afternoon, we reached rapid agreement on the brotherhood of man, the similar peaceful teachings of all major religions, and the need for an end to war before it was too late. Then just as suddenly, we parted company with a *"Salaam malakim"* and *"Malakim a salaam,"* and I was back on the lonesome trail.

The path carried me up over more jagged rocks where one false move could break an ankle in the failing light. Markings would disappear, and then reappear a hundred meters off in another direction. Bushes with inch-long thorns cropped up in all directions. My legs soon sported bloody cuts on top of scratches. Finally, I'd had enough. Since it was dusk and I'd soon be unable to see either trail markings or the lookout tower, I scrambled and slid down the hillside to a dirt trail beside a banana farm. Figuring I still had another three kilometers to go, I sailed down the road at top speed, not wanting to be stuck out there in the dark and unable to spot Yonatan and Hila's van.

As night swiftly fell, I reached Ataturk Park, named after the Father of Turkey. Then, not bothering with switchbacks, I began one final three hundred-meter ascent straight to the top. I was walking blind. I'd hoped to eventually spot the massive lookout tower, but no, I was only able to find trail markings and followed those to the van. At last, after twelve long hours, I trudged into camp.

"Guess you were ready to send out the St. Bernards, huh?"

All in all, it turned into a night to remember. I had no idea it was Rosh Hashanah, the Jewish New Year. Yonatan's mother and aunt were joining us for a forest celebration. The drinks were already cold and I took a hot shower inside their van using one of Yonatan's amazing inventions. As I dried off, our guests arrived with a banquet of food: *gefilte* fish with beets and horseradish, potato salad, chicken soup, wine-marinated beef, and chocolate mousse ice cream for dessert. We feasted and toasted each other for hours with red wine and shouts of *"L'chaim!"* Then Hila, in an angelic voice, led us in a rendition of traditional Jewish songs under a canopy of brilliant stars.

"To life!" indeed.

I spent the night sleeping atop a picnic table under the heavenly awning. After a quick breakfast with the sociable couple, Hila and I headed south on the rolling trail, walking together for an hour. Before leaving to visit a friend, she called one of Dany's "angels" in Bet Hananya, who offered me a mattress in their community center.

Hours later, I borrowed a cell phone to call him again from Zikhron Ya'aqov Park to confirm my arrival time. Then I scrambled down the mountainside, carefully picking my way through the "tumults" or ancient burial sites for shepherds that'd once inhabited the craggy, sienna slopes.

It was mid-afternoon when I arrived at the center, but no one was there. I asked around the village, until I found my host at home. The friendly, middle-aged Jewish policeman welcomed me into his kitchen. Sensing I was hungry, he brought me a late lunch, as we talked about peace and trekking, two subjects close to his own heart. Then he and his young son took me back to the community center where he provided a sleeping bag and pad before they left to visit his aunt on that holiday weekend.

I was grateful for his hospitality—even though I soon discovered their water, unknown to him, had been shut off at the main. Nonetheless, I eventually found enough water in the bottom of a coffee percolator to wash off, and a water tap at a nearby soccer field where I could fill my bottle. I'd survive.

Dawn came slowly and I was eager to find something to eat, yet the market was still closed because of the holiday. So I began my trek on an empty stomach. Ben Hananya was nearly on the coast, and as I slipped out of the sleepy village, I soon spotted the sea on the horizon. Although the National Trail proceeded to Caesarea, distracted, I missed the marker and ended up wandering through Jisr az-Zarqa, Israel's only seaside Arab village. It bristled with tension.

Figuring their fight wasn't with me, I put on my best face while meandering down its derelict main street, as I searched for an open café. Mostly children were out at that early hour and hustling off to school, yet I eventually spotted an older fellow leaning back in a chair against the wall of his porch.

"Can you please tell me where I can get a cup of coffee and something to eat?" I asked with all the friendliness of a golden retriever.

"I will give you a cup of tea right here," the massive dark man replied, motioning for me to join him on his deck.

'So far, so good,' I thought. 'They're as gracious as their Turkish neighbors.'

Then again, after ordering an older woman shuffling about to bring us tea, the fellow's demeanor dramatically shifted to one of confrontation.

"You know, we have real problems with the British here."

"I'm sorry to hear that, but I'm not British. I'm from Hawaii."

"Americans, too!" he growled. His eyes glazed over and grew visibly red. A Kilauea-like fury simmered just below the surface. For once, my residence didn't make a difference.

Perhaps too innocently, I began to tell him about my walk. I was convinced he'd calm down once he heard about our mission of peace. Yet the more he listened, the more agitated he grew. He looked as if he'd explode at any moment—or pounce from his chair. Sensing I was getting nowhere, and nervous about his mounting rage, I stood to excuse myself. It wasn't worth causing an international incident for the sake of a cup of tea.

"Sit!" the burly man ordered. "Lady fixes tea! Five minutes, five minutes."

Well, the lady was nowhere to be seen—certainly not in the kitchen. Still, I wanted to believe I could reach him; at least show him we could share a cup of tea—peacefully. So I told him of my plans to tell others about the kindness shown by people from all countries, but that did nothing to ease his rage. I'd never seen such anger flood someone's eyes like that before. They grew more crimson with each passing minute.

At last, he screamed at the top of his lungs, "Where's the tea?" Rising, he stormed into the kitchen where the teapot still sat on the countertop. Picking it up, he swore at the heavyset woman, and then flung the pot into the sink. That definitely was my cue to leave.

As I headed south down the vacant beach, I was shaken by the experience, so contrary to all the rest. Who knew what caused it? He had a story waiting to be told—only not to me.

Herod the Great had founded the village's neighbor, Caesarea Palaestina, on a seaside promontory in 25 B.C. For as poor and decrepit as Jisr az-Zarqa appeared, Caesarea, after 2,000 years, was still awash with opulence. Once the largest Roman port in the eastern Mediterranean, it boasted an amphitheatre, a hippodrome for chariot races, decorative pools, stunning villas and aqueducts. In ancient times, it had been the center of Christianity in Palestine and it was there the Apostle Paul was imprisoned for two years before he was sent to Rome. Like most cities in that region, it had changed hands over the ages, invaded by Persians, Crusaders, Mamluks, and Ottomans. Nowadays, it was assaulted by hordes of package tourists.

The next five hours provided a calming change, as I trod the sandy shore north of Tel Aviv. On that last day of a long holiday weekend, the beaches were packed with throngs of Israelis in all shapes and sizes, soaking up the sun and summer-like weather. Many had pitched house-sized wall tents on the sand and looked like they'd moved in for the duration. I'm sure I must have puzzled many as well, as I strolled the beach with my backpack and walking stick. Even in my bare feet, I was certainly over-dressed.

After a short while, the path carried me inland over red cliffs where I ran into my first fellow trekkers, two young Israelis on their way to Mount Eilat in the far south. He was lanky and might have been mistaken for a Santa Cruz granola-head, while his girlfriend was a tiny blonde weighing all of ninety pounds. Lisa carried a pack weighing at least fifty, along with another incredible twenty-five pounds of water. After comparing notes on the early portion of the trail, we spoke of our mutual interest in peace. Honestly, I was surprised to hear their sentiments, since they'd both been recently discharged from the army.

Sam, the ex-commander, explained, "Every kid in Israel has to serve two years in the military. You really don't have much choice. But it has altered the way I think. When we first joined, like many, we were very supportive of our government's policies. Yet all that changed when we were assigned to patrolling within the Palestinian territory, especially when it came to controlling the people's everyday movements."

"It was a totally new experience to see our country like that—alone and on foot," Lisa chimed in. "One day we had the chance to visit a village in the north. At first, the Arabs were sweet and curious about us. I felt like we were accepted for whom we were. All that changed when two or three boys started taunting us and throwing rocks. In my uniform, I really felt their resentment toward us—and considering how we treat them, I guess it's understandable."

"How's this new wall going to change their lives?" I asked, referring to the barrier Israel was building on the West Bank for separation, security or containment, depending on your political point of view. At completion, it would be longer than the Berlin Wall; multi-strands of barbed wire and sensors surrounded by a swath of no man's land. Other sections would be built of more permanent concrete, twenty-four feet high and manned with guard towers.

"It'll only add to the tension," Sam confided, shaking his fuzzy head. "It's dividing towns, even family properties, and making it nearly impossible for Palestinians to cross into Israel for work, medical care, schools and water. Plus, they're losing a major amount of land in the process."

How could that ever create better relations between two nations? Could a country build a wall high enough to keep out its problems, without fixing the root causes? It struck me as a cruel irony that such a barrier would be even considered by those very people who had historically suffered such unspeakable sorrow behind walls of inhumanity.

For an hour, the three of us wound through olive groves, and then down dusty Jeep tracks and dirt trails, until we parted ways when they left to meet Lisa's father for lunch. I was sad to see them go. Walking together and sharing our mutual experiences had eased my loneliness of trekking solo for a month, over more than a thousand kilometers. Yet, oddly enough, even though I'd been on my own since Istanbul, I seldom felt "alone." It was as if the memories of all those Templars, pilgrims and "angels" walked beside me every step of the way.

Before long, after passing through the fragrant, low-lying brush of the sea scrub, I descended back to the beach for the final few kilometers into Netanya. I had no idea where I'd stay, since there were no contacts on my list. But life, as always, had a way of working out. I soon met a very "mellow" Jewish Rastafarian with dreadlocks piled up into his tri-colored cap. He led me the short distance into town, where another fellow took me to a nearby hostel. Finally, I could shower, wash clothes, catch up on the latest news—and count scores of mosquito bites stealthily earned back in Ataturk Park.

The next morning, by the time I left the hostel, it was already muggy. So I was relieved to be able to spend all day walking along the beach or its seaside cliffs. Compared to the day before, the seashore was empty, except for a few white-haired, hunch-shouldered men alongside equally stooped white herons, both fishing for breakfast.

Right up the beach, I skirted past a few crazed fellows racing sleek Arabian mares along the windswept shore. That was the way races were meant to be held; men riding bareback on magnificent creatures, exhilarated, eyes ablaze with the terror of possible defeat, nostrils flaring, black manes whipping like pendants in the salty breeze.

I was somewhat less agile. While rounding a bend in the beach where waves pummeled soaring red cliff walls, I came across ancient ruins blocking my path. While scrambling over the blocks, all was going well until I climbed onto a sandstone boulder—only to have it crumble underneath my weight. My leg became wedged in a tight crevasse and I fell backward. In the process, I managed to remove the skin from my shin and scrape both arms. But all in all, the crimson bloodstains down my leg helped add a more authentic touch to my gritty *peregrino* "look."

It wasn't long before Tel Aviv rose on the horizon and I reached its outskirts by mid-afternoon. For a sprawling beach city of nearly 400,000, its planning and design instantly impressed me. It struck me as an extremely livable place, melding the culture of New York with Honolulu's tropical ambiance.

Within ninety minutes, I'd maneuvered its clean (or "*propre*," as Émile might say) streets, past high-rise condos and Bauhaus buildings to Mugraby Hostel where I was met with a hearty traveler's welcome. I could always tell the places run by real travelers, as they knew exactly what you needed. It's not a pillow mint or a shower cap. Besides the basic comforts, it's a coziness and interest in where you've been and where you're going—without being intrusive. It's as simple as a warm cup of tea, friendly local advice and camaraderie. That makes all the difference.

After showering, I wandered down the street to the beach promenade to feast on a brilliant sunset and Tel Aviv *shawarma*: chicken braised on a rotisserie grill, then thinly sliced and stuffed into pita bread, all topped with a spicy sauce, cabbage, tomatoes and French fries.

Finally satiated, I waddled back to the hostel where I contacted another Danny, whom I called Danny #2, an "angel" in Mazor who was interested in having company the following night.

'Was it only three more days of hiking east now to Jerusalem?' After nearly five months, I found that difficult to believe.

At dawn, I backtracked up Allenby Street and then east to catch the National Trail. As I traced the river through manicured parks of fragrant eucalyptus, bamboo, banana, exotic fruit trees, and psychedelic pink bougainvillea, I had to remind myself I wasn't at home, since it could've passed for the tropics. All morning long, I felt a little homesick, but was far from alone. Besides joggers, bicyclists and lovers out walking their dogs, I spotted herons and other waterfowl feeding at the river's edge. I even surprised a fox trotting down the middle of the pathway.

Eventually, the trail led away from the water, heading inland past verdant groves of oranges, lemons, limes, persimmons, grapefruit, guava and figs, all fed by irrigation ditches and tended by Thai guest workers. For a walker, those groves provided a movable feast. No sooner did I sense I was hungry, than there was fruit for the taking. I never plucked any from the trees, but easily managed to find ripe produce that had fallen and would only spoil if left on the ground.

With sweet fruit and cool water from the farms to sustain me, I reached Mazor, a country village, by mid-afternoon. Danny dropped everything to come and cart me back to his chicken farm, where he and his wife Ronit lived. My host, an exuberant fellow with a military physique and close-cropped hair, was far from your typical chicken farmer (if there was such a thing). Although they lived in the peaceful countryside, they were well-traveled, gregarious entrepreneurs, who also owned a 4 x 4 touring company and aerobics studio. Not surprisingly, they were also the perfect hosts, unable to do too much for the weary pilgrim. After relaxing over an early dinner of pasta, we were joined by Ofra and Avner, their equally footloose and fascinating friends bound for Central America.

Spending the evening with Danny and his family and friends once again reminded me how much we're alike once we break bread together and share a good bottle of wine—no matter what our nationality, religion or cultural background.

As you might expect, we were "up with Danny's chickens," and after a quick breakfast he drove me back to the trailhead. My last visual memory of the kind fellow was of him standing beside his beat-up "farm pickup" as he called it, waving from atop a bridge that overlooked a freeway of commuters. He continued until I was out of sight.

It was a warm send-off and well appreciated, since it was already brutally hot. I quickly managed to misplace the trail twice because of road construction, and once more within a park because of too many conflicting signs in Hebrew (that I couldn't read). Then again, for as many parks as I passed, I was discouraged that few had drinking water. In the heat, I soon ran out. Of course, I could have been like the Israeli soldier couple and carried five liters of water at all times, as they recommended. But that was contrary to my ultra-light mode of hiking. It would have added nine pounds to my backpack, designed to comfortably carry no more than two liters. Besides, running low always gave me an excuse to meet the locals.

The first appeared to be a "juppie," or Jewish yuppie that lived at a house where I randomly asked, "Could you please fill my water bottle?" Without skipping a beat, the young bearded professional, dressed in his *yar-*

mulke and talking non-stop on his cell phone, grabbed a cold bottle of mineral water from his fridge and sent me on my way. Shortly after, three Arab linemen working in the sun-baked hills shared the freezing water from their ice chest, as they shared their dream of peace. Down the same hill, I ran into their boss, a Jewish fellow, who gave me an apple for the road, encouragement and directions out of the dusty park. Then once again at a road construction site, another Muslim shared a freezing grape soda, violet ambrosia in that heat.

Generosity was universal, unfettered by nationality or religion. That selflessness shocked me when I first began to travel. At first, I didn't know what to say? Or I awkwardly offered to pay each time some kindness was shown—but that was either met with laughter—or it offended my hosts. Gradually, I learned to accept their hospitality and embrace it, perhaps a difficult task for an individualistic American. But I grew to learn that in many cultures, one gains merit by giving. In my experience traveling through nearly a hundred countries, I found that hospitality toward travelers is a tenet of all major religions. Cheryl and I experienced it day after day while crossing Tibet and staying with poor local Buddhists. I also found it daily on the Christian Via Francigena through Italy and France. I felt it first-hand through Muslim Turkey—and now I'd seen it in Jewish Israel.

All day, the trail rippled over parched and desolate hills dotted with pine, palms, cypress, and fragrant herbs. I spotted no other hikers on the trail, which was just as well. I'd rushed to link up with Benyamin and his wife Ruth, who lived near Latroun, between the Plains of Sharon and Esdreion. I'd done my best to rendezvous before 3:30, as I knew he had an important meeting, but with the signage delays it was a lost cause. I was already an hour late by the time I entered the gates and solitude of the Trappist monastery at Latroun, once a Templar stronghold. Surprised to find a refuge out in the middle of nowhere, I felt compelled to stop into their chapel for reflection, and meanwhile called my hosts.

While waiting for Ruth, I had the chance to briefly talk with one of the Brothers garbed in ivory robes, as he served fresh lemonade to me on their shaded terrace. As I caught my breath, he briefly broke their traditional silence to ask about my peace pilgrimage, and then promised, "I will pray for your continued safe journey."

It wasn't long before Ruth arrived and drove me the short distance to their beautiful suburban home. After showering, I joined her and her girlfriend in their backyard for drinks and appetizers until Benyamin returned.

An army officer, he was poles apart from the Dannys. Pragmatic and battle-hardened, he'd fought Palestinians most of his life and would shed a different light on Israeli survival.

As we philosophized about the Israeli-Palestinian tribulations over dinner, Benyamin solemnly explained, "I don't know if the problem here will ever be solved. You see, Israel has enemies all around it; an "island" in a sea of sharks."

"Will the new wall solve the problem?" I asked.

"Wall? You mean the fence?" he snapped back.

I'd hit a nerve. There was a national debate whether to call it a "fence," "wall," or "barrier." Evidently, he was part of the camp insisting a concrete wall with watchtowers was a fence, but I was still interested in hearing his opinion.

"Well, it'll be finished in two years and some people hope it'll create a permanent boundary between Israel and Palestine. Then again, we'll have a major logistical problem: moving all the Israelis from the Palestinian Territories in Judea and other areas."

"Palestine suffers from crushing poverty. How will the wall affect that?"

"After so many years of aid from Arab nations and more affluent Western countries, it still lacks infrastructure and commerce."

"Why?"

"Corruption, I think," he said, laying a finger to his temple.

"With the "fence," will Palestinians still be able to enter Israel for work?"

"No. They can barely do that now. It takes hours to cross in each direction."

"I guess it's not the easiest place to form a Jewish state," I kidded.

Benyamin laughed. "You know, we have a joke here. It goes like this: "Moses stuttered. When God asked him where he wanted his Promised Land, Moses said, "Ca-ca-ca-ca," and God at last answered, "Canaan? Okay, Canaan it is!" But Moses was trying to say 'Canada.'"

"I hear that Saskatchewan is lovely."

"So what do *you* think of Israel?" Ruth finally asked, as she served us small, strong cups of coffee.

Now, in any country, that can be a loaded question, but I tried to answer honestly, given what little I knew—without getting into politics.

"I'm very impressed with your National Trail. It's nice to finally get off the roads and out into the countryside where I can meet folks. I've also been impressed with how this barren land has been farmed to produce such beautiful fruits and vegetables. And the planning and design of Tel Aviv is incredible."

"Have you been here before?" she asked, visibly relieved.

"Yes, my wife and I were here about ten years ago. The heightened security shocked us. It seemed like every seventeen-year-old kid on the street carried an automatic weapon. We'd never experienced such scrutiny as when we tried to board the ferryboat to Cyprus. First, they patted us down and then they x-rayed our shoes and thoroughly searched our bags."

'Then again, look at travel in America these days.'

"Yes, that was a difficult period in our country," Benyamin explained, stirring his coffee.

"If you want my opinion, there will always be war in Israel," Ruth lamented. "It is written in the Scriptures."

Fortunately, I couldn't share her pessimism, although it seemed wide-spread in that land of milk and honey.

"The oddest part," I confided, "was when we were visiting Jerusalem. One day, we were looking for the site of the Last Supper. We knew we were close, but we just couldn't see any sign of it. Finally, we asked a fellow who said, "Sure, I'll take you there—for five shekels." We were surprised someone would actually charge us, but figuring it was farther than we thought, we paid the fellow anyway. Imagine my surprise when he pocketed our money, and then pointed at the building behind us, saying, 'There it is!' We really felt like fools."

"He must have been an Arab. A Jew would have charged you fifty shekels!" Ruth guffawed, throwing her head back.

"So," Benyamin interrupted, "where are you headed tomorrow?"

"I'd planned to reach Jerusalem and find a place to rest for a few days."

"Why don't you take another half day to reach the city?" he suggested, with concern. "It's another day of climbing for you and we're expecting record temperatures."

"That makes sense, but I have no place to stay in between. I've been working off Dany's "angel" list and you're the last in this direction."

The National Trail continued south through the Negev Desert to Mt. Eilat, while I had to divert east to Jerusalem over the hills, finding my own way.

"I know a lady in a *kibbutz* about twenty-five kilometers from here. Let me call her," he suggested. "Maybe she can put you up."

Although Bina, a transplanted American, had only met Benyamin once years ago, she readily agreed to let me camp in her yard. Even though it wasn't a real bed, I was excited. At last I could see what life was like on a *kibbutz*, if only for a night. Then again, I was grateful for the can-do attitude I'd found in Israel so far. There was still a pioneer spirit; something necessary, I guess, when you think you live on an "island in a sea of sharks."

Late that night after turning into bed, I decided to open my barred bedroom window to let in some cool night air. Earsplitting sirens erupted as soon as I slid it open just a crack. So I quickly closed it, only to listen to the barking dogs, phone calls from the security company, and frantic padding up and down the stairs for the next fifteen minutes. Walls, indeed.

After breakfast, I was handed a supply of fruit, nuts and energy bars for the journey ahead, as well as three liters of water to strap to my pack. It was an all-time record amount of fluid for me, but it was predicted to be a sizzler—and they were right. Dry Sharav winds were already blowing when Benyamin dropped me off at the trailhead in Latroun and wished me luck. Weather aside though, the distance would be shorter, so I decided to take my time and "smell the cedar" along the way. Although I saw no other backpackers, I did surprise another fox, and in turn was shocked when a group of twenty teenaged soldiers toting automatic weapons passed, heading in the opposite direction.

Did that really make anyone feel more secure?

Nevertheless, it was remarkable to see what the Israelis had done with the otherwise arid strip of land in the parched Judean Hills. It was a land of "milk and granola" with every type of fruit imaginable.

For some time, I followed what was called the "Burma Road." Back in 1948, during the Arab-Israeli War, the Jordanians had blockaded Jerusalem. That makeshift, secret highway through the hills broke their siege and allowed supplies, food and weapons to enter the city. It ultimately saved the fledgling Jewish state from surrender.

By mid-afternoon, I needed supplies of my own and spotted a fellow dripping wet, heading down the trail toward me.

"Is there water nearby?" I asked.

Offering me a fresh pomegranate, he replied, "Yes, there is an old cistern right above us," so I scampered up to the cool, spring-fed oasis. Five young Israeli backpackers already cooled their heels. Stripping off my shirt and shoes, I slid into their icy pool up to my shoulders. Ah... In that dry furnace, it was invigorating, as was the company. Spotting my small lightweight pack, they were curious about my trek, since I must have looked wild and odd to them. Yet after I explained I'd walked more than 4,200 kilometers for peace, one curly-haired girl gushed, "I couldn't imagine walking forty kilometers—let alone four thousand. You're an inspiration to us all."

I was a little embarrassed by all the attention, yet their unbridled enthusiasm made me realize my trip and all its challenges had been worthwhile. I felt especially pleased when I could influence the young, brash and still optimistic to never settle for "impossible," never listen to naysayers, or hesitate to try and create a better, more peaceful world. What better legacy could I leave?

It turned out that Bina's apartment was just over the hill and her rowdy boxer growled then slobbered all over me. At first glance, their family seemed so typically American, constantly on the go, connected by cell phones; complete with a dreadlocked, teenaged son who was stoked by the NBA, and a self-assured daughter whose room was an explosion of works in progress. Bina arrived immediately after I'd cleaned up. A native New Yorker, she was a slender "live wire" full of frenetic energy. As we talked about peace, I was surprised to learn she had attended Quaker schools and we shared many of the same beliefs. So, before long, I was adopted into their family. Her son graciously offered his room and I didn't have to camp outside after all.

For dinner, we headed over to the *kibbutz* dining hall where I was eager to hear Bina and her son tell me all about their life on the collective. Currently, she was caring for wayward animals at their zoo, while her son cared for the fruit in their fields. Everyone from the age of twelve-and-a-half contributed work in exchange for a free apartment with utilities, subsidized dinners at the restaurant (mine was less than a dollar), a mechanic-maintained community car when needed, and an extended family to help take care of the kids, the sick, and the elderly, without shipping them off to some assisted living farm. Plus everyone received a cash stipend each month depending on the number of children in their family. From what I understood, the government even provided free healthcare and a free education. Imagine that.

Perhaps their system runs counter to our strictly capitalist "sink or swim" approach to life. However, if we truly longed for a "kinder, gentler America," maybe we could learn a lesson or two from the Israeli *kibbutz* system? Consider it a worthwhile return on the billions of dollars in foreign aid we've invested in their country.

After we finished eating, Pierre, a French journalist who lived there, joined us to conduct an interview for their local newspaper. Before leaving, he promised to show me a wonderful archaeological discovery in the morning, prior to my setting off on the final fifteen kilometers into Jerusalem.

At first light, Pierre and I borrowed a *kibbutz* car and drove just a minute down a simple dirt road. Across from the orchard, they'd recently finished an excavation and discovered ritual cleansing baths dating back to the time of the First Temple.

"Then, while digging out tons of mud, we uncovered something even more amazing," Pierre explained. "Come see."

My interest was definitely piqued. After parking, we climbed down a short passage whose entryway was etched with a Byzantine cross. Ducking our heads, we descended another twenty-eight carved steps into a small, dimly lit cave. As Pierre pointed out the sedimentary layers of dirt on the cave's walls, he traced its history thru Hellenistic, Roman, Byzantine, Ottoman and Modern Eras.

"Through carbon dating, it's theorized that this cave was a reservoir as early 800 B.C. Then it was used as a ritual immersion bath. Look, you can still see the foot-anointing stone," he said, pointing to a foot-shaped indentation in a rock. "And the hundreds of thousands of pottery shards found here attest to its early use. Why, even today, it still functions as a working cistern."

It was all quite amazing, but that was just the beginning.

Shining his light with excitement, Pierre pointed out deep etchings dating from the time of Jesus scratched into the wall. One depicted a long-haired man holding a cross. He wore a traditional tunic, possibly made of spotted animal hide, and had one breast exposed, as was traditional in Biblical times. I could just barely detect the three crosses of the Crucifixion.

"We believe this etching portrays John the Baptist. It's similar to depictions found at other sites around the world," he reverently whispered, presenting a paper with other verified St. John carvings. Then he solemnly read a few passages from the Bible that spoke of hiding the baby John in a cave.

"Perhaps this is the very cave, since we know John was born in Ein Karem, just a few kilometers from here. Furthermore, we believe this may have been the place where John the Baptist took refuge in the "wilderness" and where he first practiced the baptism ritual."

If true, it was an incredible discovery.

Finally, having to get back to his real job, Pierre dropped me at the trail-head, but not before pointing out a path leading to the crumbling remains of Belmont castle, once a Knights Hospitaller fortress—until Saladin cap-tured it in 1187.

Leaving the ruins behind, I followed the red route and then green markings down the mountainside, until I was forced to take a small road over a few last, steep mountains into town. Not a moment too soon, I spotted a sign I'd dreamed about for five months, and it brought a tear to my eye: JERUSALEM.

After having walked more than 2,620 miles (4,223 kilometers) through eleven countries, and with the help of countless "angels," I had finally, miraculously arrived. The date was September 29, 2006. It had taken me just over five months. From past odysseys, I knew there'd be no marching bands, no welcoming committees, and no fireworks. No, it was still the journey that mattered and not the destination. I was just an anonymous pil-grim finally stepping foot in the city of Jesus, the prophets, the Templars and pious to come before me—one simple *peregrino* realizing his dream.

I was hardly alone. That day I was one of thousands flooding through Jerusalem's Old City walls and Jaffa Gate during the month of Ramadan and the beginning of Yom Kippur. Because of the holy days, security was especially intense. Soldiers cradled automatic rifles, profiling people from atop the wall's ramparts. I found it far from reassuring. It was just another sad reminder that Israel was a country in a continual state of war.

Eager to authenticate the end of my journey, if there ever was an "end," I headed to the Franciscan-run visitor office just off David Street. At first, it seemed reward enough just to relax in their air-conditioning. But after I told a sweet Swiss lady about my long walk for peace, she presented me with a certificate. It was identical to one you'd receive if you'd arrived by bus or airplane.

"I hate to ask, but do you have one for pilgrims on foot, similar to what they're given after walking the Camino de Santiago in Spain?"

She smiled and apologized. "No, we only receive a few foot pilgrims each year. Maybe the Latin Patriarch's office has something more appropriate."

Thanking her, I set off to find a room one last time. The Patriarch could wait. It was a quick stroll down the smooth, timeworn steps of vibrant David Street to the New Sweden Hostel. They flew a bright blue and yellow Swedish flag outside their door. Although several of my Jewish hosts had cautioned me against staying in the Old City during Ramadan because of supposed dangers, I felt more at home there surrounded by thousands of years of history. Besides, I had a hankering for fresh herring with the Swedes.

Imagine my surprise when Arab Muslims greeted me at the front desk. Talk about false advertising. Even though they were far-removed from the Norseland, they were just as accommodating with free tea and a U.N. of world traveling guests. At first, they showed me an inexpensive dorm room. However, I opted for an upgrade to celebrate, choosing a tiny, private room with a low, rounded ceiling nestled above the stairway. Cool and cave-like, it felt appropriate. I was home.

CHAPTER FOURTEEN
Jerusalem

One Step, One Seed

"The love of one's country is a splendid thing.
But why should love stop at the border?" ~ *Pablo Casals*

L eaving my personal grotto at sunrise, while even the *souk* was
still shuttered tight, I wandered over to the Church of the Holy
Sepulchre nearby. Stepping through the open door in its south
transept, I was struck with awe. It was hard to believe I was actually inside
the holiest of Christian shrines, supposedly the site of Christ's crucifixion
and burial. I'd visited it on an earlier trip, as well as the Church of the
Nativity in Bethlehem. But now having walked there, I experienced it in an
all-new light. It became a physical manifestation of that ethereal spiritual
notion of faith.

After attending a Franciscan Mass in front of the *Edicule*, the Tomb of
Christ, I was enraptured for several hours exploring the cathedral that had
been fought over for centuries by Christians and non-Christians alike. Its
original construction began by order of Emperor Constantine I in 325
A.D. on top of what was thought to be the excavated hill of the Crucifixion. At that time, it consisted of three separate churches built over three
holy sites. But Jerusalem, then as now, was in the center of a never-ending
maelstrom. The church suffered partial destruction by the Persians, was
restored, and then destroyed by the Egyptian Fatimid Caliph Al-Hakim in
1009. His action may have partially led to the First Crusade. Then Godfrey
de Bouillon's soldiers, including those who were to become the original
nine Knights Templar, reclaimed the church and city after bloody battles
on July 15, 1099. Renovations and additions were made until 1187, when

the Muslim general Saladin retook Jerusalem. Frederick II negotiated for the return of the Holy City in the thirteenth century, only to have it recaptured by the Egyptian Ayyubids, the Mamluks and Ottoman Turks.

Although the Franciscans and Orthodox Christians had restored and cared for the church throughout centuries, they also fought for its control. Until finally, an edict was issued dividing the holy site between the Greek Orthodox, Roman Catholic and Armenian Apostolic churches. Later in the nineteenth century, the Coptic, Ethiopian and Syriac Orthodox churches were also allowed shrines, chapels and services. So today, the church, as well as the city, remained divided.

After the service was over, I couldn't wait to explore the cathedral, wandering from its subterranean levels to its heavenly reaches. The sanctuary was a many-faceted jewel, from its *Edicule* to the golden-chandeliered *Kouvoulkion*, once considered "the center of the world" with golden icons glistening under a magnificent rotunda of the *Catholicon*. Next I placed my hands upon the rose marble Stone of the Anointing or Unction where Christ was laid in preparation for his burial. Then ducking my head, I entered a rough-hewn chapel into what was said to be the tomb of Joseph of Arimathea, where a New Age group chanted in Aramaic under the direction of their guru.

Afterward, I found a set of stairs leading deep beneath the church to the mystical Chapel of St. Helena, Empress Mother of Constantine the Great. She'd supposedly discovered the Holy Cross on the site in 331 A.D. In the faint light, I was particularly touched to discover an otherwise ordinary wall covered by hundreds of tiny etched Byzantine crosses made by devoted medieval pilgrims.

Up on the second floor, I paid my respects at Golgotha with its rich golden mosaics depicting the Crucifixion. As one Orthodox priest pointed out, you could still see where the Holy Cross was anchored and where an earthquake caused the ground to split. Next door at the Stabat Mater (Sorrowful Mother), I took a reflective moment in the luminescent glow to light a candle for my aged father.

Finally, on the way out, I paused at the small Coptic chapel on the other side of Christ's tomb, as well as the Ethiopian Monastery built around the column where Jesus fell for the third time. It was the ninth of fourteen stations on the Via Dolorosa or "Way of Sorrows" which I later trod, retracing Christ's tortuous journey as he carried his cross from the Lion's Gate through the narrow alleyways of Jerusalem to his crucifixion.

The morning's experience was intensely personal and emotionally exhausting. Since it was so evocative, I vowed to visit the cathedral again before leaving. In its place that afternoon, I continued my walk through history, returning to the site of the Last Supper or *Coenaculum* atop Mt. Zion. This time I had more luck finding it than we did before—and no shekels changed hands. Nowadays, it looks far from biblical. Crusaders rebuilt the site of the first Eucharist a thousand years ago, complete with Gothic arches and vaulted ceilings. Then Muslims seized control in the fifteenth century, preventing others from visiting for five hundred years.

The next stop on my sacred journey was a 4th century church holding the Tomb of King David. A cloth decorated with crowns covered his simple stone sarcophagus set atop Torah scrolls.

Then finally, I was anxious to attend a service at the Armenian Orthodox Cathedral of St. James, the apostle and brother of Jesus. The interior of the muted and musty church was mystical, aglow with oil lamps or *ganteghs* suspended from its vaulted dome. Candlelight sparkled from its altar. The air was heady with rich incense. Its walls were ablaze with golden reflections from gilded icons. Ornate cobalt and ivory Kütahyan tiles bejeweled its pillars. One chapel even held the head of the apostle. As black-robed, cone-hooded monks began singing ancient chants, mantras predating those of the Gregorian or Byzantine eras, a moment of pure enchantment transported us back in time. We in the small congregation grew intoxicated. I felt a warm communion once again with all those pilgrims who'd come before; who'd walked those same pathways throughout two millennia. Our souls had intertwined. Humbled, I gave thanks to God and all those "angels" who had aided us along the winding path.

The following day was more "interdenominational," as I visited some of the holiest sites of Christianity, Judaism and Islam. I felt I'd only scratched the surface of the Church of the Sepulchre. My return visit was more to "feel" the holy, rather than to merely "see." For all the opulence of the Church of the Holy Sepulchre, I felt drawn back to the simple rustic chapel hewn in the rocks, the Tomb of Joseph of Arimathea. One chanting replaced another. I found myself in the middle of an Ethiopian Coptic Mass led by a dark, bearded priest garbed in deep purple, Kelly green and golden vestments. With its heady incense, brass rattles shaking, bells rattling, and chanting in ancient tongues, it was all mystifying to me, yet primeval and pure.

Satiated, I decided to visit Haram Es Sharif, or "The Noble Sanctuary." It was the third most holy place of pilgrimage in Islam after Mecca and Medina. With a gold-leaf roof and ornately tiled interior, its Mosque of Omar or Dome of the Rock had a fascinating history.

It was built on the original site of the Temple of Solomon, that had once housed the Ark of the Covenant and Ten Commandments before Nebuchadnezzar destroyed the temple in 587 B.C. Herod the Great built the Second Temple in 20 B.C. which was ruined by the Romans is 70 A.D. After the Muslims arrived in 638 A.D., they transformed the temple into a thirty-acre pilgrimage shrine, believing it to be the site where the Prophet Muhammad made his Night Journey to heaven upon his horse. Inside today, you could still supposedly see his horse's hoof-print set into the rock. Muslims also believe it to be the spot where an angel will appear to announce the Last Judgment at the end of the world.

It is interesting that Judaism holds this rock sacred as well. According to some, it was the site where Abraham prepared to sacrifice Isaac. Some also claimed it was the spot where Jacob dreamed of the ladder to heaven. It is also associated with the "Holy of Holies."

In 1118, shortly after the recapture of Jerusalem in the First Crusades, that holy shrine became headquarters for the newly founded Knights of the Temple, or Poor Knights of Christ of the Temple of Solomon—the Knights Templar. Those formidable warrior-monks, originally dedicated to protecting pilgrims to Jerusalem and defending the Holy City, have since become "an enigma, wrapped in a riddle, shrouded by mystery."

Nevertheless, their legacy was legendary. As far back as 1135, Bernard de Clairvaux in *In Praise of the New Knighthood* wrote:

> "[A Templar Knight] is truly a fearless knight, and
> secure on every side, for his soul is protected by
> the armor of faith, just as his body is protected by
> the armor of steel. He is thus doubly-armed, and
> need fear neither demons nor men."

I wandered a maze of shaded passageways, past hundreds of small clothing, jewelry and food shops, amid a flood of Muslim pilgrims on their personal *hajj*. Finally arriving at its courtyard gate, I was gently turned away. It was Ramadan. Only Muslims were permitted to enter. Of course, I was disappointed, but I understood. Besides, I'd been inside when I had explored Jerusalem ten years earlier.

Undeterred, I opted to visit the nearby Western Wall (Hakotel Hama'aravi). The "Wailing" Wall was a remnant of the western retaining wall of Herod's Temple Mount and the holiest accessible sacred Jewish site. Historically, during their long exile, Jews could only return once a year to mourn its destruction—hence the "wailing." For nearly 2,000 years, it remained a symbol of hope for reunification of the Jewish state. Nowadays, after the creation of Israel in 1948, you only needed to pass through metal detectors and a cadre of armed soldiers and police to approach.

Once through the tunnel and barriers, I was caught up in the fervor on that day before Yom Kippur—the Day of Atonement—the holiest of days for the Jews. Hundreds of worshippers stood before the wall, men to one side and women to the other. Some read scripture. Others prayed, rhythmically rocking back and forth, or with foreheads pressed against the roughhewn wall. A few wedged written prayers into cracks between the stones. I was especially intrigued to watch the faithful parade past in the searing afternoon sun in their unique garments from around the world.

There were the Hasidic with their black *Shtreimel* hats, long black coats, wild beards and ringlets by their ears. Others looked eastern European, garbed in round, sable fur hats or brown fur *Kolpiks* and white coats in the ninety-degree heat. Some might have passed for well-dressed Baptists coming out of Sunday service. Others, like me, took advantage of their paper *yarmulke* bin to respectfully approach the wall with prayers of our own.

Timing is everything. The following day was my birthday, but oddly enough I didn't feel like celebrating. I was alone and exhausted. Jerusalem was a ghost town. Everything was closed in the Jewish quarter because of Yom Kippur, including post offices, travel agencies, and restaurants. Even broadcast stations were off the air. Then again with Ramadan, the Arab quarter was on reduced hours, since Muslims weren't allowed to eat or drink from sun-up to sundown.

Since they'd assured me earlier that the Latin Patriarchal office would be open, I headed over to meet the Chancellor, Father Humam Khzouz. I shared my impressions from the trail with him for quite some time. Then intrigued by my journey, he prepared a small certificate to commemorate my foot pilgrimage, saying it was a "first," since they didn't offer one similar to Santiago's *Peregrino Compostellae*.

Afterward, although tired from playing "tourist" the past few days, I visited the nearby Garden Tomb outside the walled Old City. An English Protestant association offered an interesting theory suggesting that theirs' was the actual site of the Crucifixion and burial of Christ. First they showed me a nearby hillside with a rock formation discovered in 1882 by Major-General Charles Gordon. I had to admit, it still uncannily resembled a skull, the original translation of "Golgotha." Then they led me to a tomb dating to Jesus' time with a symbolic anchor, a sign of Christ, etched into its outer wall and roof beam holes suggesting services might once have been held there. Plus there was a track for the tomb entryway's stone to be rolled into place, as well as an interior closely matching Biblical descriptions. Ironically, the site where the cross might once have stood was not atop "The Skull," but in what was now a parking lot. All in all, it was a dramatic contrast to the pomp and splendor of the Church of the Holy Sepulchre where millions worshiped. What if the serene garden and parking lot were the actual sites?

Returning to the walled Old City via the Damascus Gate, I passed hundreds of Muslim pilgrims mingling and chatting like shoppers anywhere. One man played hide and seek with his daughter, and then grinned when he saw me watching. At no time, even with the massive crowds, did I sense danger, even though I was one of the only Westerners in their midst. On the other hand, before long, I arrived back on David Street near the Citadel, where eight young soldiers with automatic rifles watched and waited. The difference was chilling.

How long could people live in such a perpetual state of fear?

Early the next morning, I decided to catch a bus to the Dead Sea near the Jordanian border. Its terminal was easy enough to find, but I couldn't believe the security. First you had to pass through a metal detector, just to enter the building. Then the gate looked like Fort Bragg. Close to a hundred teenaged warriors milled about. Boys and girls with automatic rifles slung over their shoulders waited for buses out of town. By the time we were loaded and ready to pull out of the station, mine looked like a troop carrier with soldiers even crowded in the aisles.

One civilian (or "soldier on an eleven-month furlough," as they liked to joke) sat beside me. He was a twenty-something Israeli Jew, who taught disadvantaged kids in one of the villages. In between nuzzling his girlfriend, he was happy to point out some of the more disturbing landmarks on our ninety-minute journey across the parched wasteland.

"Over there," he explained, not far outside of town, "is where they're building the wall."

"You mean "fence," don't you?" I asked with a grin.

"No, it's a wall."

"Funny thing about walls...you have to wonder whether they're built to keep others out—or you in."

"And those," he explained, as we passed tin-roofed shanties, "those are Palestinian settlements on the West Bank." They were reminiscent of Soweto, South Africa when I'd first visited, and a stark reminder of the desperate living conditions in the Palestinian community where unemployment topped fifty percent.

"I hear it can take a Palestinian up to three hours each way to clear the checkpoint, just to go to work or to a doctor in the Jewish area," I said.

"*If* they can still work there. This wall could change all that. No one knows for sure right now."

"One fellow I talked to suggested it might create a permanent border. Is that true?"

"If it's any indication, the resettlement of folks from the Gaza Strip has been a nightmare. Wait until the time comes to convince 260,000 Jewish settlers to move from the West Bank. Some will refuse—then we'll have a real problem."

Looking out the bus window at those poorest settlements in the scorched, bleak terrain, it was easy to see how hopelessness, resentment, fears and loathing were all spawned in that inhumane Petri dish. What happens when people have no work, no food, no home, no participation in their government, no freedom, no passport to even leave, and no future? Can violence be far behind? Would conflict only be resolved by the means one Arab businessman suggested to me just the day before—when a "A nation who lives by the sword, dies by the sword?"

I hoped it would never come to pass. As Gandhi once said, "An eye for an eye only makes the whole world blind."

If negotiations didn't succeed, the predictions of those pessimists might prove to be right. There would always be war in Israel. That self-fulfilling prophecy could easily become the fuse to set off a global powder keg of apocalyptic proportions. History might prove them wrong. Politics might change. Cooler heads might ultimately prevail. But based on the draconian changes I'd witnessed over the past decade, and more importantly the increase in fatalism, time was running out.

The Dead Sea and Ein Gedi Spa were a welcome diversion. Before long, we passed craggy red cliffs flowing down to the sixty-seven kilometer long lake and lowest spot on the planet, 418 meters below sea level.

Compared to glamorous Palm Springs resorts, Ein Gedi Spa was unassuming and run by the local *kibbutz*. Nevertheless, their history was regal, stretching all the way back to the time of King Herod. As for me, I was pleased to discover the perfect tonic for aching *peregrino* muscles, both in the inside whirlpools and the outdoor lake. With its high salt content, it was impossible to sink in the sea, although I gave it my best try. The spa was also renowned for its therapeutic baths. I had to giggle at mud-slathered guests in their swimsuits traipsing down the road from the spa to the sea, looking like they'd escaped from some Serengeti pond.

Arriving back in town at twilight, I meandered from the bus terminal back down Jaffa Road toward the Old City walls. Along the way, I spotted an American pizza chain and dropped inside. A slice of gooey goodness had been at the top of my fantasy list for weeks. After ordering, imagine my surprise when the cashier asked, "Can I add a shekel to your bill for security?"

Yes, even they had an armed guard at their entrance.

"Security in a pizza shop? Why? To keep out mozzarella addicts? Oregano abusers?"

With an imposing "fence," most every teenager toting an automatic weapon, police vans, Jeeps or troops posted every few blocks, and metal detectors at most public places, I wondered how much more secure they could feel? It looked like there were close to as many active troops in Jerusalem as America had in Baghdad. (Plus, I wasn't convinced that passing out M16 assault rifles to hormone-perplexed teenagers was always the best idea.)

Unless peace, tolerance, and negotiation prevailed, I was afraid they'd never be able to build a wall high enough, or long enough, to keep the lion from the gate.

My final two days in Jerusalem ran together, combining last-minute sightseeing with rest for the long flight home. Nevertheless, I did make it a point to visit the Israel Museum where I had a chance to view the famous Dead Sea Scrolls. They were discovered in caves not far from Ein Gedi Spa. Nowadays, they were impressively housed in their own jar-like building, designed to resemble the original clay vessels. My other interest, Templar relics, was surprisingly absent. Then again, the First Crusades had been deadly for all the inhabitants of Jerusalem: Muslim, Jew and many Christians alike.

Before leaving, I had a chance to wander the Gardens of Gethsemane with their ancient olive grove where Jesus endured his agony before he was arrested. Its Church of the Nations was perhaps the most simplistically beautiful I'd ever seen, with a mosaic façade and floors, amethyst-colored stained glass, and altar surrounded by a strand of metal thorns. Afterward, I hiked up the Mount of Olives to the Franciscan Church of Dominus Flevit where Jesus wept over the coming destruction of Jerusalem. While there, I photographed the Temple Mount from an interesting perspective.

Checking out of the hostel early, I caught the bus back to Tel Aviv to meet Dany and his two female friends for dinner. I had the chance to give Dany a recap of my experiences on the trail, as well as share my confusion with him about the widespread Israeli pessimism I'd discovered. His clever Parisian girlfriend expressed her own and agreed all too quickly. I was especially discouraged by her reaction when I mentioned I'd retraced a Templar trail from France for peace.

"You're not a Crusader, are you?" the otherwise modern, twenty-first century Frenchwoman asked in total sincerity. Her look of scorn was barely disguised.

"Me, a Crusader?" I enigmatically smiled. "Where *is* my sword?"

My humor was lost on her. But Dany remained the genial host, and after one last plate of *hummus*, he drove me to Ben-Gurion Airport on the outskirts of town.

Security was tight, but not nearly as bad as I'd expected. After standing in a long check-in line, I approached several policemen examining passports and tickets, as they asked routine questions. A petite airport security officer naively asked, "Where have you been?" and "What have you been doing?" as she'd done thousands of times before—but she could little imagine my answer.

After I briefly explained, "I've just completed a walk from France to Jerusalem for peace," she excused herself to confer with others standing nearby. She soon returned, beaming. "We all really admire you for what you've done."

I grinned in gratitude, yet it was a humble beginning, one small step. Maybe there was still hope. Perhaps Samir's prophetic "river of blood" would never run.

CHAPTER FIFTEEN

Reflections

"This is the way of peace–overcome evil with good,
and falsehood with truth, and hatred with love." ~ Peace Pilgrim

Cruising home at thirty thousand feet, in between the tiny bags of pretzels and constant interruptions, I had time to reflect on my wanderings. My introspection would continue long after my feet returned to their normal size. Although my journey of self-exploration felt gratifying, I hoped I'd accomplished more than finding personal peace and a communion with spirit. If anything, I hoped I was successful in sowing seeds of peace along a trail long used for war. Like a Johnny Appleseed, perhaps I'd planted a vision, while reminding folks they had non-violent options—one village, one person at a time.

Along the trail, I often imagined the possibilities if this same route were to become a pathway open to people of all cultures, faiths and nationalities to walk together; an international trail of peace. The simple act of walking together would nourish tolerance while dispelling fear, prejudice and hatred. Once people share a similar experience as intense as this one, they realize how much our hopes and fears are alike. Then again, everyday pilgrims would discover a tranquil sanctuary within, once they disconnect from an ever-more chaotic world. Returning home, more at peace and enlightened, it was only natural they would share this serenity and inspiration with families, friends and co-workers, as other *peregrinos* I know had done.

On the other hand, immersing yourself in other countries can be the best way to re-discover your own. I had five months of quiet, sometimes painful, sometimes inspired contemplation. Many days, I reflected on the root causes of our never-ending wars; a global imperative as we stand hip-deep in another quagmire.

Remembering back to those horrendous events of September 11th, 2001, with everyone seeking answers or revenge, we were promised the illusion of safety and freedom. All it took was war—and a pre-emptive one at that. Congress willingly complied, with few dissenting voices. The government would try not to disrupt our lives too much. As citizens, we were only asked to "keep shopping" and sacrifice a few liberties via the Orwellian-named Patriot Act—for our own security, of course.

However, war is never freedom; no more than black is ever white. The absence of war, peace, is freedom.

It's one thing to protect our homeland against aggressors, and I'd never advocate abandoning self-defense. But our invasion of Iraq was clearly not a case of self-preservation. Saddam Hussein had no links to Al-Qaeda, as we all know by now. Instead, we were sold a polished, pre-planned confrontation for "freedom" (and oil). It was a costly fabrication whose consequences will eat away at the fabric of our nation for generations to come, just as the debacle in Vietnam has done.

In today's world, it's far too easy to declare war, invade, and fire missiles at faceless targets below. In one sense, we can blame the media that present us with a sanitized view of death and destruction. Once the celebratory fireworks of "shock and awe" have passed, we see nothing of its aftermath and huge civilian casualties. After the devastation is complete, we leave our children and the rest of the world an even more precarious and pernicious legacy.

America deserves better.

Why is it the "Mission Accomplished" leaders of the world are often those who have never smelled the stench of gunpowder, gone deaf from the mortars' roar, or held a bloodied buddy in their arms? Let them first taste the grotesque horror of war, the sheer repulsion, and gut-wrenching fear—before sending another mother's naïve child to a needless, futile death on any foreign shore.

America deserves better.

I feel deeply sorry for the latest brave men and women who volunteered for our country, misled into believing they were protecting our homes. I mourn with my country for those thousands who will never see their sons and daughters again. I grieve over those tens of thousands whose scarred lives, and those of their loved ones, will never be the same because of the latest grand deception.

America deserves better.

If one thing, after this journey, I am certain most people of the world truly want and crave peace. If only their leaders will listen.

We can no longer continue on these paths of recklessness. The wanton destruction of nations' infrastructures—let alone their honor—only creates poverty, despair and more people left with nothing to lose. In the name of fighting "terrorism," we douse flames of poverty and resentment with oil. We create new generations of terrorists through our invasions, economic sanctions and wide-reaching actions. We bankrupt our own society by devoting the bulk of our national budget to the military industrial complex. At the same time, we dismantle freedoms and destroy the guiding principles on which our nation was founded.

If we are to eliminate the root cause of war and suffering, we need to assure the basic needs of our citizens at home are met, and in proxy, those of the world. As American president, general and military hero Dwight D. Eisenhower once said, "Every gun that is made, every warship launched, every rocket fired, signifies in the final sense a theft from those who hunger and are not fed, those who are cold and are not clothed." Today, our country feels that loss.

As someone traveling with his home upon his back for five months, I often thought of the less fortunate in our land of plenty. In my nightly search for a place to sleep, I remembered those thirty-six million Americans living in poverty. As I worried where my next meal would come from, I was reminded of the thirty-eight million of my countrymen who have trouble finding the money to keep food on their table—and the eighteen percent of American children who live in poverty. On my worst days, limping in pain, I sympathized with forty-five million Americans suffering because they have no health insurance to buy medicine. At those times when trucks zoomed past, throwing me into the ditch, I knew the fleeting transient nature of life and empathized with those who live day-to-day with violence. While nearly 4,000 soldiers have died in Iraq since our invasion, more than 65,000 people have been killed in America during the same four year period. While walking cold and battered in the rain, I thought of those more than 3.5 million who would experience homelessness in America this year—25% of them employed—40% of them military veterans.

This is an American tragedy.

Fortunately the brave are among us, awaiting a finer destiny, waiting to feel part of a greater, more noble cause. It's part of our nature and human heritage. It's one altruistic reason that some enlist in the military; to make life better, I believe—not to kill in the name of democracy.

As still free, conscious citizens of the world and true patriots, let us be the first to say, "Enough!" in one voice.

It is time to channel those same selfless citizen efforts into social action, instead of destruction. Devote our abundance of resources to creating better lives. Eliminate poverty. House the homeless. Protect human rights. Care for the elderly. Protect our planet. Educate and teach our children tolerance. Rebuild our highways and infrastructure. Develop energy independence. Revitalize our cities and protect them from natural disasters. And wage war against devastating diseases.

It is time to win support for democracy through our generous deeds and social progress, instead of through aggression and violence.

It is time to never allow another politician to claim that improving the welfare of our citizenry and the state of the world is beyond our budget. For when it comes to war, America's wallet is always full—and always open.

These are national values that transcend bi-partisan politics. They are the ideals that helped our forefathers build a nation from wilderness. Once we set our mind to it, surely we can wage peace just as effectively as we've waged war. When there is hope and progress, when people can live their dreams, the need for international confrontation will wither on the vine. War profiteers, those peddlers of death, will disappear. Peace will prevail.

After seven million small steps, in my heart I know we can each make a difference. What progressive world movement has not begun small, even if by just one person with truth and determination; pilgrims committed to walking "roads less traveled."

We are all pilgrims, each on their own path, each with their own story to tell. Walking is only a first step, but one we each can take to discover the peace within. In that way, eventually, war will become unconscionable. Darkness will be dispelled with light—one person, one step at a time.

Lessons of the Trail *

Be trusting. Have faith that the trail knows where it's going—even if you don't.

Be generous. Travel lightly. All in life is a gift. What you don't need, give away.

Be kind. Even the smallest word of encouragement makes a difference.

Be humble. Walking on dirt is easier on the feet than walking on pavement.

Be human. There is no harm in getting lost—only in staying lost.

Be a friend. Folks on the trail impact your life, if just for a moment.
All too soon they leave to follow their own path. Bid them good journey.
Thank them for their gift.

Be content. Savor the small victories now, along the way.

Be grateful. Even the smallest things on the trail are either a gift or lesson.

Be flexible. Sometimes trails just vanish. That doesn't mean
you were on the wrong path—there's just a better one now.

Be focused. Never look back. Sempre diretto!

Be courageous. A mountain is always highest when you're climbing it.

Be hopeful. Tomorrow is another day awaiting with the possibility of success.

Be happy. Laughter and song are nature's tonic for adversity.

Be aware. It is the journey that ultimately matters, not the destination.

Above all else, love all living things on the trail.
Love God, your fellow travelers, yourself.

* originally appeared in
Yak Butter Blues: A Tibetan Trek of Faith
by Brandon Wilson

Date	Stage	Approx. Distance
April 23	St. Jean de Losne, **France**	30 km.
April 24	Dole, France	23 km.
April 25	Dampierre, France	25 km.
April 26	Besançon, France	40 km.
April 27	Baume les Dames, France	34 km.
April 28	Isle sur le Doubs, France	34 km.
April 29	Exincourt, France	27 km.
April 30	Dannemarie, France	27 km.
May 1	Hegenheim, France	35 km.
May 2	Hegenheim	Rest
May 3	Schopfheim, **Germany**	25 km.
May 4	Brandenberg, Germany	28 km.
May 5	Titisee, Germany	28 km.
May 6	Donaueschingen, Germany	40 km.
May 7	Möhringen, Germany	31 km.
May 8	Beuron, Germany	30 km.
May 9	Sigmaringen, Germany	32 km.
May 10	Riedlingen, Germany	35 km.
May 11	Ehingen, Germany	37 km.
May 12	Ülm, Germany	30 km.
May 13	Ülm	Rest
May 14	Günzburg, Germany	27 km.
May 15	Dillingen, Germany	28 km.
May 16	Donauwörth, Germany	36 km.
May 17	Rennertshofen, Germany	34 km.
May 18	Weichering, Germany	30 km.
May 19	Vohburg, Germany	26 km.
May 20	Weltenburg, Germany	26 km.
May 21	Matting, Germany	31 km.
May 22	Worth, Germany	38 km.
May 23	Bogen, Germany	31 km.
May 24	Deggendorf, Germany	27 km.
May 25	Regensburg, Germany	Rest
May 26	Hofkirchen, Germany	27 km.
May 27	Passau, Germany	34 km.
May 28	Engelhartszell, **Austria**	26 km.
May 29	Aschach, Austria	40 km.
May 30	Linz, Austria	26 km.
May 31	Au on der Donau, Austria	28 km.
June 1	Grein, Austria	28 km.
June 2	Ybbs, Austria	22 km.
June 3	Melk, Austria	28 km.
June 4	Oberloiben, Austria	36 km.
June 5	Zwentendorf, Austria	32 km.
June 6	Greifenstein, Austria	25 km.
June 7	Vienna, Austria	25 km.
June 8-10	Vienna	Rest
June 11	Schönau, Austria	35 km.
June 12	Hainburg, Austria,	26 km.
June 13	Bratislava, **Slovakia**	17 km.
June 14	Bratislava	Rest

Date	Location	Distance
June 15	Dunakiliti, **Hungary**	31 km.
June 16	Lipót, Hungary	27 km.
June 17	Györ, Hungary	29 km.
June 18	Bábolna, Hungary	28 km.
June 19	Tata, Hungary	33 km.
June 20	Tarján, Hungary	20 km.
June 21	Zsámbek, Hungary	22 km.
June 22	Budakeszi, Hungary	19 km.
June 23	Budapest, Hungary	26 km.
June 24-27	Budapest, Hungary	Rest
June 28	Szigetszentmarton, Hungary	35 km.
June 29	Szalkszentmárton, Hungary	33 km.
June 30	Dunaföldvár, Hungary	25 km.
July 1	Paks, Hungary	22 km.
July 2	Kaloçsa, Hungary	18 km.
July 3	Baja, Hungary	42 km.
July 4	Baja	Rest
July 5	Bezdan, **Serbia**	42 km.
July 6	Sombor, Serbia	18 km.
July 7	Odzaci, Serbia	35 km.
July 8	Backi Petrovac, Serbia	36 km.
July 9	Novi Sad, Serbia	25 km.
July 10	Beska, Serbia	28 km.
July 11	Batajnica, Serbia	30 km.
July 12	Belgrade, Serbia	18 km.
July 13	Belgrade	Rest
July 14	Grocka, Serbia	32 km.
July 15	Lozovik, Serbia	48 km.
July 16	Markovac, Serbia	27 km.
July 17	Jagodina, Serbia	34 km.
July 18	Pojate, Serbia	35 km.
July 19	Aleksinac, Serbia	39 km.
July 20	Nis, Serbia	36 km.
July 21	Nis	Rest
July 22	Bela Palanka, Serbia	44 km.
July 23	Pirot, Serbia	26 km.
July 24	Dimitrovgrad, Serbia	25 km.
July 25	Slivnitsa, **Bulgaria**	28 km.
July 26-27	Sofia, Bulgaria	20 km.
July 28	Intiman, Bulgaria	50 km.
July 29	Kostenets, Bulgaria	18 km.
July 30	Pazardzhik, Bulgaria	46 km.
July 31	Plovdiv, Bulgaria	38 km.
August 1	Plovdiv	Rest
August 2	Parvomaj, Bulgaria	40 km.
August 3	Dimitrovgrad, Bulgaria	38 km.
August 4	Simeonovgrad, Bulgaria	25 km.
August 5	Ljubimec, Bulgaria	34 km.
August 6	Kapitan Andreevo, Bulgatia	22 km.
August 7	Edirne, **Turkey**	28 km.
August 8	Havsa, Turkey	27 km.
August 9	Babaeski, Turkey	27 km.

Date	Location	Distance
August 10	Lüleburgaz, Turkey	17 km.
August 11	Çorlu, Turkey	47 km.
August 12	Silivri, Turkey	30 km.
August 13	Kumburgaz, Turkey	40 km.
August 14	Küçukcekmece, Turkey	30 km.
August 15	Istanbul, Turkey	20 km.
August 16-18	Istanbul	Rest
August 19	Tuzla, Turkey	35 km.
August 20	Hereke, Turkey	30 km.
August 21	Izmit, Turkey	30 km.
August 22	Sapanca, Turkey	35 km.
August 23	Geyve, Turkey	35 km.
August 24	Osmaneli, Turkey	41 km.
August 25	Bilecik, Turkey	38 km.
August 26	Böröyuk, Turkey	38 km.
August 27	Ilica, Turkey	57 km.
August 28	Kütahya, Turkey	26 km.
August 29	Kütahya	Rest
August 30	Altintas, Turkey	40 km.
August 31	Afyon, Turkey	47 km.
September 1	Sandikli, Turkey	59 km.
September 2	Sandikli	Rest
September 3	Dinar, Turkey	52 km.
September 4	Keçiborlu, Turkey	27 km.
September 5	Burdur, Turkey	35 km.
September 6	Bucak, Turkey	45 km.
September 7	Dagbeli, Turkey	35 km.
September 8	Antalya, Turkey	52 km.
September 9	Antalya	Rest
September 10	Serik, Turkey	42 km.
September 11	Manavgat, Turkey	35 km.
September 12	Avsallar, Turkey	32 km.
September 13	Alanya, Turkey	25 km.
September 14	Kyrenia, **Cyprus** (boat)	764 km.
September 15	Nicosia, Cyprus	27 km.
September 16	Lythrodontas, Cyprus	32 km.
September 17	Tochni, Cyprus	32 km.
September 18	Limassol, Cyprus	35 km.
September 19	Limassol	Rest
September 20	Limassol-Haifa, IS (boat)	272 km.
September 21	Haifa, **Israel**	Rest
September 22	Ataturk Park, Israel	24 Km.
September 23	Bet Hananya, Israel	24 Km.
September 24	Netanya, Israel	32 Km.
September 25	Tel Aviv, Israel	33 Km.
September 26	Mazor, Israel	32 Km.
September 27	Latroun, Israel	32 Km.
September 28	Kibbutz Tzuba, Israel	21 Km.
September 29	Jerusalem, Israel	15 Km.
Total days:	**Time:** 137 walking days / 160 trip days	
Total distances:	**Distance:** 4223 km. walking (2620 miles)/	
31 km. av./ day	5259 km. (3264 miles) including sea	

Equipment List

packing cube with:
  convertible pants
  nylon shorts
  2 wicking t-shirts
  2 pr. GoLite air-eator socks
  2 pr. wool socks
  cotton kerchief
  cotton cap
  synthetic camp towel
  undershorts
  synthetic vest*
  Patagonia Capilene shirt*
wool felt hat*
Teva sandals*
GoLite Reed waterproof pants
GoLite pack cover
Goretex rain jacket*
nylon pouch with:
  MagLite (small)
  plastic foldable cup
  10 yds. nylon cord
  compass

small roll duct tape
small lock and key
toilet paper
re-hydration concentrate
waterproof matches*
cotton sleep sack*
Olympus U700 digital camera
LEKI Super Makalu Air Thermo Nordic sticks*
Kelty Redwing backpack*
GoLite Vision backpack**
Montrail Susitna shoes (1 pr.)
Montrail Continental Divide shoes (3 pr.)**
watch
Swiss Army knife
GoLite chest pouch
bottle holster
Cicerone Guide to *Danube Cycle Way**
French dictionary*
journals & pen***
address book
German/Slovak phrase sheets*
water bottle

nylon pouch with passport, debit card, Youth Hostel card
leaflet of papers: letters, itinerary, ticket
nylon sack with:

analgesic cream	antibiotic cream
small mirror	nitrate cream
muscle cream	petroleum jelly
100 naproxin	small sewing kit
200 aspirin	hairbrush
btl. New Skin	toothbrush
deodorant	earplugs
shaving cream	athletic bandage
plastic scissors	soap
sunscreen	nail clippers
detergent	athletic tape
30 blister wraps	

pack weight approx.
15 pounds total (7 kilos)
* sent back after Budapest
** brought or replaced in Budapest

For Further Information:

Camino de Santiago (Spain)
Confraternity of St. James
First Floor, 27 Blackfriars Road, London SE1 8NY UK
phone: (+44) (0)20 7928 9988
email: info@csj.org.uk
www.csj.org.uk

Via Francigena (Canterbury to Rome)
Association Via Francigena
email: info@francigena-international.org
www.francigena.ch

St. Olav's Way (Norway)
Eivind Luthen, Pilegrimsfellesskapet St. Jakob, Norge
Kirkegaten 34A, 0153 Oslo, NORWAY
phone: 22.33.03.11
email: pilegrim@pilegrim.no
www.pilegrim.no
(or) Eiler Prytz, Pilgrim Roads to Nidaros
email: eiler@pilegrim.info
www.pilegrim.info/en/

Israel National Trail
Dany Gaspar
Israel Trail Committee for the Society for the Protection of Nature
2 Ha'Nagev Street, Tel Aviv 66186 ISRAEL
email: dany@spni.org.il

Lyceum Trail/St. Paul's Way (Turkey)
Kate Clow
Hasim Iscan Mahallesi, 1297 Sokak, No 14, Antalya, TURKEY
phone: (+90) 242 243 1148
email: kateclow@lycianway.com
www.trekkinginturkey.com

Friends of Peace Pilgrim
PO Box 2207, Shelton, CT, USA 06484-2207
phone: (203) 926-1581
email: friends@peacepilgrim.org
www.peacepilgrim.net

Special Thanks:

Adelaide Trezzini, Association Via Francigena
Father Jim Dallen, Gonzaga University, Spokane, Washington
Monsignor Angelo Comastri, Vatican
P. Adalberto Guiseppe Piovano,
Abbazia di San Giovanni Battista, Vertemate, Italy
Giorgio Costanzo, Iubilantes, Como, Italy
Ellie Booher, formerly of Montrail
Montrail/Columbia
LEKI USA, especially Lindy Spiezer
GoLite
Dany Gaspar
Kate Clow
Émile & Sophie
Zsuzsana and her mother for Hungarian translations
Lin for insight into the Qur'an
Teri Kahn for her sage advice and aloha
Friends of Peace Pilgrim and Bruce Nichols
Dr. Bob Rich, my editor
Nexus Design + Marketing
Nancy, my final proof-meister
My late father for his encouragement
Cheryl for her logistical support, love and understanding
And all the "angels" along the way.
May their kindness be returned
a hundred-fold.

About the Author

BRANDON WILSON is an award-winning author and photographer, explorer and adventure travel writer.

He is author of two other true travel adventure books, *Yak Butter Blues: A Tibetan Trek of Faith*, an IPPY award-winner, and *Dead Men Don't Leave Tips: Adventures X Africa*. His story about a year spent living in the Arctic, "Life When Hell Freezes Over," appeared in *They Lived to Tell the Tale: True Stories of Adventure from the Legendary Explorers Club* (The Lyons Press/Globe Pequot), while his photographs have won awards from *National Geographic Traveler* and *Islands* magazines.

When not writing, he enjoys inspiring others to discover life's possibilities through long-distance walking. A voracious explorer of nearly one hundred countries, he is an expert long-distance, light trekker. He has walked many of the world's major pilgrimage trails: the 2620-mile Templar trail from France to Jerusalem, the famed Camino de Santiago across Spain (twice), the Via de la Plata, and the St. Olav's Way across Norway.

He and his wife Cheryl were the first Western couple to complete the 650-mile Buddhist pilgrim's trail from Lhasa, Tibet to Kathmandu, and he was the first American to traverse the 1150-mile Via Francigena trail from England to Rome.

Wilson, a member of the prestigious Explorers Club, is a graduate of the University of North Carolina at Chapel Hill.

Other Books by Brandon Wilson:

Yak Butter Blues:
A Tibetan Trek of Faith

What does it take to survive? *Yak Butter Blues* exposes the raw challenge of traveling deliberately, one-step-at-a-time on an incredible 1000-kilometer (650-mile) trek across the unforgiving Himalayan plains. Join a daring and somewhat crazed man and woman with Sadhu, their Tibetan horse, as they set off to attempt to become the first Western couple to trek this ancient trail across the earth's most remote corner.

Their true story is a riveting tale of human endurance. It also provides a candid first-hand look at the lives of the Tibetan families who secreted them into their homes—and at a culture teetering on the edge of extinction. Nothing could prepare the couple for what would become the ultimate test of their resolve, love, faith…and very survival.

An Independent Publisher IPPY award winner.

"Recommended for adventure travel and Tibetan culture collections."
~ *Library Journal*

"A moving and emotional testimony, and a travelogue that is the next most vivid experience to hiking upon the trail oneself." ~ *Midwest Book Review*

"A high-altitude tale of synchronicity, divine providence, begging monks, trigger-happy Chinese soldiers and dehydration." ~ *Pittsburgh Post-Gazette*

"A soaring travel diary. It places the reader in the thick of the action every bit as well as Marco Polo transported Italians to China and, as it seems to me, better than Lowell Thomas led readers in the dust of Lawrence of Arabia." ~ *Maui Weekly*

"Told with humour and insight, this vivid narrative allows you to vicariously experience life at true Tibetan pace, one step at a time: so close, you can smell the yak butter." ~ Michael Buckley, author of *TIBET: the Bradt Travel Guide*

"I came under the spell of Brandon Wilson's lively and vivid prose. He is a fine writer – perceptive, funny, a great way with words – making the book a whopping good read." ~ Royal Robbins, renowned mountaineer/author

"A wonderful and wild read…alive, and a little threatening" ~ Richard Bangs, Producer, Richard Bangs ADVENTURES/co-founder, MountainTravel/Sobek

Dead Men Don't Leave Tips:
Adventures X Africa

What does it take to follow your dream? Quite a bit, if it involves crossing Africa. That's what a couple discovers when they set off on a seven-month, 10,000-mile overland journey from Morocco to Cape Town. They'd traveled around the world—but was a trans-African odyssey too much for even them?

Against their better judgment, they join a do-it-yourself safari with a bizarre band of companions. As their dream turns into a nightmare, they set off across the continent alone. And that makes all the difference.

Join their adventure. Meet mountain gorillas face to face. Melt down during a Saharan breakdown. Hunt dik-dik with Pygmies. Climb Africa's highest mountain. Hop the "gun-run" through a civil war. Rush down thundering Zambezi rapids and dive into South Africa's cauldron of turmoil.

Wilson, in a style one reviewer described as "a hybrid of Paul Theroux and Tom Robbins," takes you onto the crazed roads of Africa and into the hearts and lives of its people.

"Journeys of body and soul in every sense of the word. The author writes with honesty and a sharp eye for detail...for readers of adventure travel or anybody who is considering "do-it-yourself" safaris or simply visiting Africa. Interlaced with this honesty and detail are Wilson's beautiful prose, obvious passion for adventure and a deep inquisitiveness about other cultures, making this book a pleasure to read. Highly recommended." ~ Mayra Calvani, *Midwest Book Review*

"A masterful crossroads of characters, exotic places, history and human drama in a rig that never stalls." ~ Richard Bangs, author of *The Lost River*

"Honest, gritty and insightful. Best of all, it makes the world's most exciting continent read just like that."
~ John Heminway, author of *No Man's Land: A Personal Journey into Africa*

"Travel writing at its most sublime, a paean to Africa in all her contradictory beauty, and a tribute to the resiliency of those who travel beyond boundaries not only in search of meaning, but also of understanding."
~ C.W. Gortner, author of *The Secret Lion* and *The Last Queen*

"A monument to those who would take on the challenge of land travel across one of the most dangerous, unhealthy continents in the world." ~ *Heartland Reviews*

Give the Gift of Adventure to Your Friends, Schools, Libraries and Colleagues.

Visit your Favorite Bookstore, Internet Bookseller

~ Or Order Here Today. ~

_Yes, I want _____ perfect paperback copies of *Along the Templar Trail* : *Seven Million Steps for Peace* signed by the author for only $17.95 each.

_Yes, I want _____ perfect paperback copies of *Dead Men Don't Leave Tips: Adventures X Africa* signed by the author for only $16.95 each.

_ Yes, I want _____ perfect paperback copies of *Yak Butter Blues: A Tibetan Trek of Faith* signed by the author for only $16.95 each.

Include $5.75 shipping and handling for one book, and $1.95 for each additional book. Hawaii residents must include sales tax. International orders must include payment in U.S. funds. Contact us for int'l. shipping options. Payment must accompany all orders. Allow 2-3 weeks for delivery.

My check or money order for $ _____ is enclosed.

Name_____

Address_____

City/State/Zip_____

Email (in case there's any problem with your order)

_____

Special signing instructions_____

Make your check payable and mail to:
Pilgrim's Tales, Inc.
P.O. Box 791613
Paia, HI 96779 USA

Photo books for all expeditions will be published in the future. Contact us for details. Meanwhile, for more photos, previews, stories, or to book speakers, please visit:
www.pilgrimstales.com

CPSIA information can be obtained at www.ICGtesting.com
Printed in the USA
LVOW041222120212

268302LV00001B/339/A